# Idaho

# Real Estate Handbook

## 1st Edition

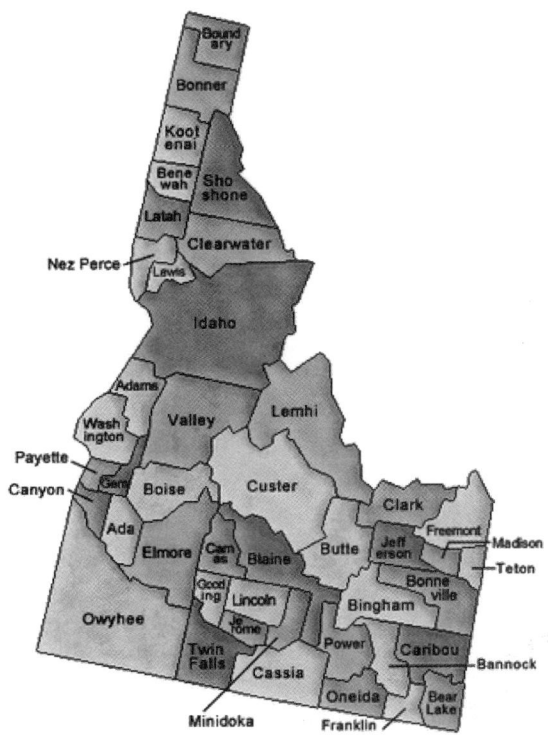

## Chuck Byers
### GRI, CRB, e-PRO

Professional Marketing Concepts, LLC, Nampa, Idaho

**Idaho Real Estate Handbook, 1ˢᵗ Edition**

Published by:
Professional Marketing Concepts, LLC
Nampa, Idaho 83687

Copyright © 2010 by Professional Marketing Concepts, LLC

The publisher and author make no representations or warranties in respect to the accuracy or completeness of this work. Advice or strategies contained herein may not address all situations and is rendered with the understanding that the publisher is not engaged in rendering legal, accounting, or other professional service. Neither the publisher or author shall be liable damages arising from any inaccurate, incomplete, or error contained herein.

Library of Congress Cataloging-in-Publication Data Control Number available from publisher

ISBN: 978-1-930910-50-9

Printed by:
The Caxton Printers, Ltd
Caldwell, Idaho 83605

# Contents

# PREFACE

This book is intended to help students to prepare for a real estate career or as a reference manual for the general public to acquire a basic knowledge of Idaho real estate.

It is highly recommended to have a general real estate book to accompany this book to further explain the basics of real estate and real estate terms. Such books are usually available at most Idaho real estate schools. General real estate text books may also be available at local book stores and public libraries.

Although the information contained in this book is intended to be current and up-to-date, newly legislated laws may be passed that supersede the information contained in this book.

The information in this book follows the general sequence of topics taught in pre-license courses in Idaho and cites numerous laws with code identification for further reference by the readers.

At the end of each chapter, there are multiple choice questions to test comprehension and knowledge as well as prepare for the state exam which is also a multiple choice exam. The answer key at the end of the text has the answers as well as detailed explanations including specific Idaho code for additional reference.

# ACKNOWLEDGMENTS

Permission to reprint forms was given by the Idaho Association of REALTORS® and Pioneer Title Company of Ada County. The reproduced forms throughout the text are for illustrative purposes only and may not be reproduced in any manner without written permission from the organization holding the copyright.

A special thanks to Dave Ewy, Tim Bundgard, R. Gail Heist, Jill Randall, Mike Gamblin, and the Idaho Real Estate Commission for their wonderful support and encouragement to create a handbook that can be used in everyday life. A very special thanks to my wife of 46 years who constantly reminds me, 'the impossible only takes a little more time than the difficult'.

# ABOUT THE AUTHOR

Chuck Byers has been actively engaged in the real estate industry since the early 70's. During his career, Chuck has been an owner/broker of several real estate companies in Oregon and Idaho. He is a certified real estate instructor and past director of a real estate school and has authored several books and articles on various real estate topics.

Chuck holds a Bachelor of Science degree from the University of Oregon and has earned the Certified Residential Brokerage Manager (CRB), Graduate Realtors® Institute (GRI) and Internet Professional (e-PRO) designations from the National Association of REALTORS®.

Accomplishments include REALTOR® of the Year, Instructor Of The Year, and past Board Director of the Real Estate Educators Association.

# Chapter 1

# Real Estate Business & Idaho License Law

**National Statistics**

## Real Estate Is Big Business

The real estate industry is big, big business involving millions and millions of people. In 2005, the National Association of Real Estate License Law Officials, or ARELLO, stated that there were more than 2.6 million real estate licensees in the United States. Given a population of around 300 million, that is one licensee for every 115 persons. In the same year, the National Association of Realtors® reported nearly 1.3 million or 50% of the total licensees were members of this trade organization. Around 5,000,000 existing home sales occurred in 2009 for the United States

Real estate industry isn't only selling homes. It involves all kinds of services and specializations including but not limited to: building and construction, property management, brokerage, appraisal, financing, property development, education, financing, code enforcement, just to name a few activities.

Add all the different classifications such as residential, commercial, industrial, agricultural, and special purpose projects and one can see just how much the real estate industry impacts the local, regional, and national economy.

The National Association of Realtors®, one of the largest trade organizations in the U.S., was founded in 1908 to promote and preserve the real estate industry. The Code of Ethics greatly assists all members to work with and cooperate with each other to help buyers and sellers with the upmost professionalism.

To assist in the acquisition and sale of real estate there are many federal, state, and local laws to make sure the consumers are treated with good business, safety, and equality. Various regulations include: fair housing, environmental issues, financing regulations via the Real Estate Settlement Procedures Act.

**Idaho Statistics**

## Idaho Information

The real estate industry touches virtually every living person regardless of whether they own or rent property. Based on the United States Census Bureau, Idaho has a population of 1.5+ million people living in 600,000+ households.

In the first quarter of 2010, the Idaho Real Estate Commission reported around 1,200 active brokerages and over 7,500 active salespersons and brokers.

# Idaho Real Estate Commission

## Idaho Real Estate Commission

In 1947, the Real Estate License Law was enacted to be enforced by an agency known as the Idaho Real Estate Commission. This regulatory entity is totally financed by mandatory fees paid by all active and inactive estate licensees.

Charged with *protecting the public* and real estate industry alike, the Commission enforces laws and rules to regulate the industry. The Commission also requires minimum education requirements to secure and maintain a real estate license.

**Idaho Real Estate Commission**

## Who Regulates Real Estate Activities?

The regulatory agency that oversees the practice of real estate is the Idaho Real Estate Commission. The Commission consist of 4 members. All members are active Idaho real estate brokers with a minimum of 5 years experience. Each Commissioner is appointed by the Governor of Idaho and serves a 4 year term. The Commission is charged with administrating and enforcing all the provisions of Title 54 of the Idaho code.

The Commission in turn may hire an Executive Director and other support personnel to manage the various activities within the real estate commission.

An advisory group to the Commission is known as the Idaho Real Estate Education Council. It is compromised of 4 members appointed by the Commission plus 1 Commissioner and the Executive Director, for a total of 6 members.

| | |
|---|---|
| **Commission Meetings** | **When Does The Idaho Real Estate Commission Meet?** |

The IREC meets monthly in Boise with occasional meetings held elsewhere in Idaho. These meetings usually last from a half to a full day. A real estate licensee can attend the full meeting and not only better understand the workings of the Commission but receive elective Continuing Education credit.

| | |
|---|---|
| **Education Council** | **What's The Function Of The Education Council?** |

The Education Council recommends education policy and course content quality for all education courses approved by the Commission. In addition, the Council prepares any additional recommended procedures or guidelines for certifying educational courses, instructors, and course providers for Commission approval.

| | |
|---|---|
| **IREC Departments** | **Idaho Real Estate Commission Departments** |

The Commission consists of 5 different departments: Administration, Education, Enforcement, Licensing, and Legal Counsel.

*Administration* - oversees and coordinates all departments and reports directly to the real estate commissioners.

*Education* - coordinates IREC's educational programs, and is the contact for issues relating to the Idaho real estate license exam.

*Enforcement* - supervises, investigates complaints, manages IREC's disciplinary actions program, and oversees the Subdivided Lands/Timeshare Registration program.

*Licensing* - processes new salesperson and broker applications, broker firms, branch office applications, license renewals and office changes. Oversees fingerprints and exception reviews. This department is also the contact for Idaho's Errors & Omissions insurance program.

*Legal Counsel* - represents the Commissioners and assists with legal issues involving the Real Estate Commission including legislative changes.

# Complaint & Investigative Process

Consumer complaints must be submitted to the Commission in writing to initiate an investigation by Commission Staff or information received by the Executive Director of the Commission.

The Staff will pursue disciplinary action only if the facts warrant such action. However, the final say remains with the Commission members to determine if the facts are sufficient.

If the gathered facts turn out to be insufficient, the Staff will issue a letter of 'no action' and the matter will be closed.

**Investigation Process**

## Initiating The Investigation Process

If the written complaint warrants investigation, the Commission investigator will inform the licensee in writing of the alleged allegations and request a written response. The licensee may also be requested to provide documents or other information in the licensee's response.

In addition, the investigator may request a personal meeting and maybe more documentation from the licensee to clarify various issues.

**1 of 3 Decisions**

## Completion Of Initial Investigation

Once the investigation is completed, the results and recommendations are forwarded to the Executive Director on how to proceed. The Executive Director will make 1 of 3 decisions.

1. Close the case and issue a 'no action' letter
2. Request additional information
3. Pursue disciplinary action

**Disciplinary Process**

## Disciplinary Action Process

Before disciplinary action is pursued, the Executive Director will submit a written summary report with the relevant facts (excluding names, location or other identifying information) to the Commission members. If the Commission determines the facts are insufficient, the responding licensee will receive a written notification indicating a 'no action' determination.

If, on the other hand, there are enough facts to proceed the Commission will advise the staff to pursue formal disciplinary proceedings.

**Licensee Notification**

## Licensee Notification For Disciplinary Action

The licensee will receive written notice from the Staff outlining the facts revealed by the investigation and violations the Staff believes occurred and can be proven.

The Commission strongly recommends that a licensee consult with an attorney upon receipt of any notice, who can advise the licensee what to do. The licensee may seek legal advice from an attorney anytime during the investigation or hearing process.

Staff will provide the licensee, in writing, the option to informally resolve the matter through stipulation, or the licensees right to a formal hearing. The licensee will have a set period of time to advise the Staff on how to proceed.

**Penalties**
**IC 54-2059**

## Penalties For disciplinary action

The Commission may:
- Temporarily suspend license
- Permanently revoke license
- Impose a fine not to exceed $5,000 plus costs and attorneys' fees.

# Grounds For Disciplinary Action

**Disciplinary Action**
**IC 54-2060**

A licensee should be familiar with areas of misconduct which can result in severe disciplinary action. Some examples:

**Fraud**

- *Making fraudulent misrepresentation*

Fraudulent misrepresentation is when a licensee knowingly makes a representation with intent to deceive and with the knowledge that it is false.

**Misrepresentation**

- *Continued course of misrepresentation*

A licensee continues to make false promises, whether done personally or through agents or salespersons, such as zoning uses or a prospective buyer being able to use a property for a specific use.

| **Fail To Remit** | ● *Failure to remit or account for money or property*<br>A licensee receives earnest money and retains it instead of promptly turning the earnest money over to the broker. |
| --- | --- |
| **Failure to Keep Records** | ● *Failure to keep adequate records*<br>All property transactions, while acting in the capacity of a real estate broker or salesperson, must be complete with all paperwork and supporting documents intact. |
| **Failure to Disclose Information** | ● *Failure or refusal to disclose information to the Commission*<br>The Commission may request documents, books, or records for inspection within the persons knowledge. Refusal to cooperate would be considered misconduct. |
| **Acting Under Assumed Name** | ● *Acting as a broker or salesperson under an assumed name*<br>An example could be a licensed salesperson who gives the illusion through advertising they are the broker instead of being the salesperson of a broker. |
| **Unlawful Application** | ● *Unlawful means in applying for a real estate license*<br>Application for a real estate license is intentionally missing information through fraud, deception, misrepresentation or misstatement. |
| **'Double Contract'** | ● *Using or proposing to use a 'double contract'*<br>Intentionally advising parties to a transaction with a side agreement not known to the underwriter is prohibited. |
| **Kickbacks** | ● *Seeking or receiving a 'kickback' or rebate*<br>A conditional agreement in which the licensee will receive something of value that would violate IC 54-2054 (6). |
| **Any Violations** | ● *Violation of any provisions of the Idaho Real Estate License Law and Rules*<br>This could include any aspect of IC 54-2001 through 54-2097; or better put, the whole booklet! |
| **Dishonest Conduct** | ● *Any other conduct which constitutes dishonest or dishonorable dealings.*<br>Conduct not specifically identified in sections 54-2001 through 54-2097 that would allow, and be subject to, disciplinary action. |

**Gross Negligence**

- ***Gross negligence or reckless conduct***
  If conduct substantially fails to meet the generally accepted standard of care in the practice of real estate in Idaho, such conduct would be inappropriate and subject to discipline.

**Additional**
**Discipline**
**IC 54-2061**

## Additional Grounds for Disciplinary Action

The Commission may also take action where a court of competent jurisdiction found the licensee:

Convicted of a felony demonstrating a lack of trustworthiness by the licensee in the real estate business;
Declared incompetent;
Civil action against the licensee with reference to a real estate related transaction.

If any of the above actions have been entered against the licensee or a judgment rendered, the licensee shall within 20 days of conviction forward to the Commission a copy of the evidencing legal document.

**Recovery Fund**
**IC 54-2070**

## Real Estate Recovery Fund

The real estate recovery fund is created to satisfy claims against licensees where a licensee is not able to satisfy such claims. The balance of the recovery fund shall not exceed $20,000. A court order can direct payment out of the recovery fund for actual damages but not more than $10,000 per licensee per calendar year.

If, based on a court order, the Commission pays from the recovery fund any amount to satisfy a claim, the licensee's real estate license shall be automatically suspended.

Reinstatement of the license will not be granted until the licensee has repaid, in full, the amount paid from the recovery fund plus interest.

# Questions

1. The National Association of REALTORS®
   is what type of organization?

   A. Regulatory
   B. Trade
   C. Public
   D. Federal

2. Idaho has approximately how many active
   real estate licensees?

   A. 1,200
   B. 5,500
   C. 7,500
   D. 10,500

3. Where does the money come from to operate
   the Idaho Real Estate Commission?

   A. State of Idaho
   B. All active licensees
   C. All licensees
   D. All brokerage companies

4. The Idaho Real Estate Commission consists
   of how many member commissioners?

   A. 3
   B. 4
   C. 5
   D. 6

5. The Idaho Real Estate Education Council is
   made up of how many members?

   A. 3
   B. 4
   C. 5
   D. 6

6. How often does the Idaho Real Estate
   Commission meet?

   A. Monthly
   B. Quarterly
   C. Semi-annually
   D. Annually

7. How must complaints be submitted?

   A. In person with verbal testimony
   B. In writing
   C. By phone
   D. Through legal counsel

8. Who has the final say to invoke
   disciplinary action from a complaint?

   A. Department of Investigation
   B. Chief Investigator
   C. Executive Director
   D. Commission Members

9. If a judgment surrounding a real estate
   related transaction has been brought
   against a real estate agent, how long does
   the agent have to notify the Idaho Real
   Estate Commission?

   A. 10 days
   B. 20 days
   C. 30 days
   D. Not necessary, since civil action is
      outside the jurisdiction of the Idaho
      Real Estate Commission

# Chapter 2

# Preparing For Real Estate Practice

**Idaho Real Estate License Law and Rules**

## Chapter 20, Title 54, Idaho Code

The primary reference source for the practice of real estate in Idaho is contained in a booklet, Idaho Real Estate License Law and Rules. It is based on Chapter 20, Title 54, Idaho Code and may be amended annually based on legislative action. It's important you have the most current edition to address current laws and rules. This booklet is an excellent resource to reaffirm the course instruction based around Idaho laws.

**Activities requiring a real estate license**
IC 54-2003

## How are license requirements determined?

Any person, who, directly or indirectly, while acting for another, for compensation, a promise of or *expectation of compensation* will be required to have an active real estate license.

This includes any person engaging in the activities of:
- Lists or offers to list for another;
- Sells or offers to sell for another;
- Buys or offers to buy for another;
- Negotiates or offers to negotiate for another:
    Purchase
    Sale
    Option
    Exchange
    Business opportunity
    Interest therein for others

**License Exceptions**
IC 54-2003

## Are there exceptions to licensing?

Yes, there are some exceptions to licensure. Exceptions to licensure shall not be used in any way to evade Idaho laws and shall be considered as an unlicensed and unlawful practice of real estate. Examples of a license not being required are:
- Any person purchasing for his/her own account;
- An employee of an owner acting within scope of his or her employment;

- Acting as a duly authorized attorney in fact granted power of attorney for purpose of consummation of a single transaction;
- Administrator, executor, or personal representative of an estate;
- Attorney not regularly engaged in conduct of business of real estate broker or salesperson;
- Any person selling pursuant to the default provisions of a deed of trust;
- Any property management, rental, or leasing agent.

**License Requirements**

IC 54-2012

## What's required to secure a license?

In order to secure a Idaho real estate license, what are the individual requirements? Each person seeking a real estate license shall meet *all* of the following minimum qualifications.

Be an individual

Be 18 years of age or older

High school graduate or equivalent

No previous revoked, suspended, surrendered, or refused license renewal within 5 years

No misdemeanor convictions involving fraud, misrepresentation, dishonest or dishonorable dealing within 5 years prior to license application

No felony conviction after a period of 5 years from date of conviction or term of probation, sentence confinement or period of parole, whichever is later. However, the Commission may consider an Exemption Review.

**License Requirements**
IC 54-2022

## Education requirements for salesperson license

For a salesperson's license, the applicant shall complete a total of 90 classroom hours or the equivalent in available correspondence hours.

**Course Requirements**

## Courses requirements To secure a license

Applicants seeking a broker's or associate broker's license shall in addition to meeting the requirements for a salesperson's license, successfully complete 4 specified courses in advanced real estate study, for a minimum of 90 additional classroom hours or the equivalent in available correspondence hours.

All prelicense courses must be completed no later than 3 years prior to the date of the license application.

To receive credit for prelicense courses, the student must regularly attend the complete course and such course must meet all requirements for course certification. However, no credit will be given for courses taken for audit.

This option allows the general public to take real estate courses but not for license requirements. Those seeking a license must meet the minimum hours as well as receive not less than a 'C' or better as a final grade for each course.

**Continuing Education**
IC 54-2023

## What type of Continuing Education is required?

Prior to renewing a real estate license to an active status, the licensee shall complete a Core course (developed by the Idaho Real Estate Commission) plus 16 hours of elective courses approved by the Commission. No duplicate credit will be allowed and excess hours are not carried over to subsequent license renewals. Also, courses and course hours mandated by the Commission for disciplinary action shall not be counted for continuing education credit.

In the event of a Commission audit, the licensee should retain proof of all courses taken including Course Completion Certificates identifying:

1. Name of licensee
2. Title of course
3. Completion date of course
4. Course certification number

When required, proof must be provided and received by the Commission in not less than 10 business days from date of notification.

To assure the sales associates affiliated with the brokerage are in compliance, the designated broker will have access to review the continuing education record of any licensee currently licensed with the broker. This helps both the broker and licensee to plan in advance to have all the necessary continuing education requirements completed prior to relicensing.

| | |
|---|---|
| **Application &** | # License application and renewal |
| **Renewal** | The initial signed license application for a salesperson or broker, shall |
| IC 54-2018 | be for a period of 1 year plus the months up to and including the next |
| | birth month date of the licensee. The license shall not exceed 2 years |
| Figure 1 | and shall expire on the last day of month of the birth date of the licensee. |

Or put another way, when you get licensed, go to the last day of you next birth month and add one year. That is when your license expires. Your initial license period will be less than the 2 years you receive upon renewal. You need to pay extra attention to the expiration of your initial license period and make sure you have met your continuing education requirements for renewal.

License renewals shall be for 2 years and applications must be received at the Commission office no later than 5 p.m. of the expiration date.

Should a licensee fail to renew an active license by the due date, the licensee shall be placed on an inactive status and shall not engage in any business act requiring a license.

An expired license that is not renewed within 1 year of the expiration date shall be automatically terminated.

**License Exams**
IC 54-2036 (2) (f)

# Course and State License Exams
Prelicense education consists of two 45 hour courses known as Module 1 and Module 2. A course exam will be given at the end of each module which must be successfully passed with a minimum score of 70%.

**PearsonVue**
www.pearsonvue.com

In addition, you will need to pass the state exam administered by Pearson-Vue. One needs to carefully read the *Idaho Real Estate Candidate Handbook* published by Pearson-Vue. The handbook is available either online or at most real estate schools.

The exam is divided into two parts, national and state.

Figure 2

The national portion consists of 80 questions plus 5 pretest questions that are not scored.

The Idaho state portion consists of 40 questions for the salesperson and 50 questions for the broker exam. The state exam also has 5 pretest questions that are not scored. All questions are multiple choice.

| **State Exam scoring** | Each portion must be passed with a minimum score of 70 for a salesperson and 75 for a broker (which is greater than the 70 score for a salesperson course exam). |

The candidate is given 4 hours to complete the exam. If any portion is failed, the candidate has no later than 1 year from the date the first portion was passed to retake the exam. A minimum of 24 hours is required before one can retake an exam. However, there are no limits to the number of times one can retake the exam.

**Fingerprint Requirements**

## Fingerprints
All license applicants must submit fingerprints and have fingerprint approval prior to submitting a license application.
Even if you have been previously fingerprinted, you will have to have new fingerprints made. Why? To make sure nothing adverse shows up that would prevent you from obtaining a real estate license.

It is recommended that you make an appointment with a testing center and get your fingerprints done early. They will be processed and you will be notified by the Idaho Real Estate Commission when your fingerprints have been approved.

Fingerprint results are valid for 6 months from the date of the Commissions approval. So, don't let the 6 month time frame become overdue and require you to do the whole process again.

**E & O Insurance 54-2013 & Rule 117**

## Errors & Omission Insurance
Idaho requires all active licensees to be covered with mandatory errors and omissions insurance and certify such coverage to the Commission.

Most real estate companies have licensees secure their own insurance via an independent Group Plan made available by the Idaho Real Estate Commission. However, some brokerages have their own company required E&O insurance and must make it available to the Commission proof of such coverage.

**Minimum Coverage**
Minimum coverage shall not be less than $100,000 limit liability coverage for each occurrence, not including costs of investigation and defense with a deductible amount of not greater than $3,500 which shall cover costs of investigation and defense.

**Tail coverage**

Should a licensee leave the real estate industry, tail coverage may be purchased to endorse the policy to apply to claims first made and reported up to 3 years after the effective date of cancellation or non-renewal. To be effective, tail coverage must be purchased within 90 days after the effective date of the cancellation or non-renewal.

**Estimated Costs**

## What are the estimated costs to securing a license?

| Cost | Item |
|---|---|
| $ 500+ | **Salesperson courses*** |
| $ 800+ | **Broker courses*** |
| $ 75 | **Initial State Exam and retakes** |
| $ 50 | **Fingerprinting** |
| $ 165 | **E & O Insurance (Idaho Group Plan)** |
| $ 160 | **Real estate license** |

* Courses and ancillary items will vary between different schools and individual needs.

**Application check list**

## License Application Check List
The license application shall be accompanied with:
> License fee payable to the IREC
> Copy of H.S. diploma or equivalency
> Document showing legal presence
> Certification of E&O insurance
> Fingerprints approved by IREC
> Verification of passing license exams

# Broker Requirements

**Broker Requirements IC 54-2012 (2)**

## Real Estate Broker Requirements
In order to obtain a broker's license in Idaho, the individual must complete 4 specified courses in advanced real estate study for a minimum of 90 additional classroom hours or equivalent beyond the salesperson's education requirements.

Additional requirements include providing satisfactory evidence of having been actively engaged, on a full time basis, for 2 years as a licensed real estate salesperson within 5 years immediately prior to the date of application.

**Sales Accomplishments**

A broker or associate broker may be required to furnish a report of sales accomplishments during 2 of the last 5 years to demonstrate activity and ability to know and understand the real estate industry.

The Commission is looking for at least 30 hours per week dedicated to the real estate business for 24 months with around 15-20 closed transactions resulting in over $2 million in total sales volume.

**New Fingerprints**

In addition, the applicant must provide a *new* fingerprint card for processing even if they are already currently licensed. Why? Because the applicant is applying for a 'new' license, which requires fingerprinting.

A 'designated broker' is a broker who is also known as the 'responsible broker' and is responsible for the accounting and transaction files. In addition, the designated broker is responsible to properly supervise the brokerage company and the activities of any associated licensees.

# Real Estate Brokerage

The real estate brokerage is licensed by the Idaho Real Estate Commission to engage in the real estate business in Idaho subject to meeting mandatory requirements.

**Legal Entities**
IC 54-2016 (1)

## Legal business entities

A legal business entity is a corporation, partnership, limited liability company or limited liability partnership, governmental entity, trust or other entity capable of conducting business. The entity shall have an individual designated broker who shall be one of the following:

    A. Officer of a corporation,
    B. General partner in a partnership or limited partnership
    C. Member or manager in a limited liability company

The entity is effective only while the individual designated broker's license is active. If the license becomes inactive, the business entity shall have 10 days in which to designate another qualified individual as designated broker before the entity's license is terminated. If terminated, *all* associated licensees shall be made inactive.

**Sole Proprietorship**
IC 54-2016 (2)

## Sole Proprietorships

A sole proprietorship is an individual designated broker not licensed with a legal business entity. Approximately 30% of all Idaho brokerages are comprised of sole proprietorships.

The designated broker of either a legal business entity or sole proprietorship shall within 3 years immediately prior to the designation, satisfactorily complete a commission approved business conduct and office operations course (BCOO).

**Secretary of State**

A legal business entity or sole proprietorship, doing business under an assumed name (DBA), shall provide proof to the Commission of having legally filed a certificate of assumed name with the Secretary of State.

**Main Office**
IC 54-2040

## Main Office

Each designated broker shall maintain a physical place of business to serve as the main office to do business and is referred to as his principal place of business.

Any change in business name or location without notification to the Commission shall automatically inactivate the license previously issued. Also, the Commission needs to be notified of any change in the main business telephone number.

A broker shall not lend or permit the use of the brokers license if the broker does not actively manage and have full control. In some circles this practice has been known as 'rent a broker' and is clearly in violation of law.

**Branch Offices**
IC 54-2016 (4)

## Branch Offices

Unlicensed branch offices are allowed providing trust funds and original transaction files are not maintained at the branch office. If trust funds and original transaction files are maintained at the branch office, then the branch office must be separately licensed.

The designated broker will designate a branch manager, who shall be an associate broker who has completed a Commission approved business conduct and office operations course (BCOO). The branch manager shall not manage more than one branch office.

# Designated Broker Responsibilities

**Broker Requirements**
IC 54-2038

## Designated broker requirements:

● Be responsible to supervise and control the activities of all licensees and *unlicensed* persons associated with the brokerage.

● Review and approve all real estate agreements including, but not limited to listing, sales, and brokerage representation agreements.

● Be reasonably available to manage and supervise the brokerage during normal working hours.

● May be licensed as a 'limited broker' if unable to manage and supervise and cannot have any sales associates.

● Determine what corrective or remedial action will be taken if a misdeed of a sales associate or unlicensed personnel is discovered.

● Shall not allow any person not properly licensed to represent that broker as a sales associate in any real estate activities requiring a real estate license. It's very important that brokers carefully observe and be aware of how an unlicensed support staff address the public and/or assist sales associates.

**Unlicensed Personal Assistants**
Guideline #17

Unlicensed personal assistants and support staff should be familiar with Guideline #17 to understand what they are able to do in the line of their work. It is an excellent resource should the employing broker not have a written office policy explaining the duties, responsibilities and limitation on the use of personal assistants.

If unlicensed, they can perform clerical duties which may include gathering information. They can provide access (but not show) a property and hand out preprinted material and objective information. They cannot get involved in negotiation.

An unlicensed personal assistant can deliver paperwork to other brokers and deliver paperwork to buyers or sellers that has already been reviewed by a broker.

The penalty for acting as a broker or salesperson without a license is punishable by a fine not to exceed $5,000 or a violator can be punished with imprisonment in a county jail not to exceed 1 year or both.
A limited liability company or corporation could receive a fine not to exceed $10,000.

**New License**
IC 54-2012 (1) (k)

## Licensee Affiliation With A Brokerage

A new licensee cannot affiliate with a brokerage without written approval by the broker on a form and manner approved by the Idaho Real Estate Commission.

**Transactions**
IC 54-2055

Upon affiliation with a real estate brokerage, the licensee must conduct all transactions through the brokerage with whom they are licensed, including personal transactions dealing with their own property.

In addition, a licensee dealing with their own property must advise buyers or sellers, in writing, they hold an active Idaho real estate license. Such written disclosure must be made no later than the presentation of an offer to buy or sell.

This disclosure requirement also includes a licensee who directly or indirectly intends to acquire any interest or option to purchase real property.

**License Termination**
IC 54-2056

## Licensee termination

If the licensee terminates with the broker, the licensee shall provide the broker written notice to terminate no later than 3 business days after the effective date of termination.

If the broker terminates the licensee, the broker has to provide the associate written notice of termination no later than 3 days after the effective date of termination (same as above in reverse).

Written notice to the Commission does not relieve written notice from one licensee to the other.

**Termination for cause**

## Broker Requirements - Termination For Cause

If a broker terminates a licensee for any license law violations, the broker shall notify the Commission within 10 days of termination together with the facts that led to the termination.

**Property of Broker**
IC 54-2056 (5)

## Property belonging to the broker

Regardless of who terminates whom: all listing agreements, buyer broker agreements, purchase and sale agreements, and any other property belonging to the broker shall be turned over to the broker.

The terminated licensee shall not induce or entice any clients of the broker to end their relationship with the broker without written permission from the broker. Remember, those clients legally belong to the broker, not the licensee who acquired the clients on behalf of the broker.

**Absent Broker**
IC 54-2039

## Absentee designated broker

If a designated broker or branch manager is absent for more than 21 consecutive days, the designated broker shall notify the Commission who will be appointed to manage the office. The appointee can be another associate broker associated with the company or a qualified designated broker from another office.

If a broker or branch manager is absent for more than 60 days, another qualified individual shall be designated to act as broker or branch manager. If no new broker is designated, the Commission shall place all licensees on an inactive basis. In addition, all listing agreements and buyer broker agreements shall be terminated.

If the designated broker license of a legal entity becomes inactive, the business entity shall have 10 business days to designate another qualified individual be to designated broker before the entity's license is terminated and all active licensees are made inactive.

Any change in a designated broker must be in writing and received and approved by the Commission. If the office is closed down and ceases to exist, the original designated broker shall remain responsible for trust account funds, pending transactions and other necessary records.

**Record Retention**
IC 54-2049

## Company records to be retained

The records must be kept by a broker for 3 calendar years after the year in which the event occurred, transaction closed, all funds disbursed, or the agreement and any written extension expired. Examples of required records include:

- Original or true copies of all accepted, countered, or rejected offers
- Listing or buyer representation agreements
- Transaction files
- Trust account ledger cards
- All trust account reconciliation records

# Trust Accounts

One of the primary functions of a brokerage is to be responsible for all money or property entrusted to that broker or to any licensee representing the broker.

**Co-mingle
Exception
IC 54-2042 (7)**

Only money relating to a real estate transaction may be deposited into a broker's trust account. It needs to be noted that entrusted moneys cannot be commingled with any money of the brokerage. However, an exception is that a minimum amount (not to exceed $300) is allowed to maintain the account. The maintenance funds can only be used to cover bank charges and shall not be disbursed for any other purpose.

**Creating Trust
Account
IC 54-2042**

## Creating a trust account
A broker may establish one or more real estate trust accounts by meeting minimum requirements.

**Approved
Depositories**

1. A trust account must be established with an approved depository
   - State or federal banks & trust companies
   - State or federal savings & loan associations
   - Licensed title insurance companies
   - Active licensed attorney at law

**Identification
IC 54-2042 (2)**

2. Each account must be identified by the term:
   "real estate trust account"

**Business name**

3. Trust account must be established and maintained under the licensed *business* name of the broker.

**Complete records**

4. Each trust account must have a complete and separate set of records including:
   - Monthly accounting
   - Deposits
   - Charges
   - Withdrawals
   - Checks (even if deposited with approved 3rd party)

**Subject to withdrawal**

5. Funds deposited in a real estate trust account must be subject to withdrawal at all times and the broker is responsible for ensuring that separate account records are provided by the depository. This includes deposits made at title companies

**Notice to IREC**

6. Notice of opening a trust account must be provided to the Commission with a Commission-approved form signed by both the broker and officer of the bank or depository.

**Cannot commingle**

7. Other than account maintenance funds, no deposits shall be made that belong to the broker or real estate firm.

**Depository Exceptions**

8. Any entity not specified as an approved escrow depository may be accepted subject to approval by the Commission. Requirements by an entity for consideration include:
   - Details of financial structure
   - E&O insurance or bonding
   - Copy of last audit and financial statement
   - Copy of license or certificate issued

The broker shall remain fully responsible and accountable for all entrusted moneys and property until a full accounting has been given to the parties involved.

**Interest bearing account**
IC 54-2043

## Interest Bearing Trust Account

Idaho allows for the broker to open a separate interest bearing account for a single transaction. There must be a written agreement between the parties to the transaction stating who is to receive the interest accrued from the deposit.

Money or property not entrusted to a broker or licensees must have written instructions to transfer such money or property to a third party on a later day.

With the written instructions, the broker shall only be responsible for maintaining a record of the time and date the money or property was transferred from the broker to a third party.

| | |
|---|---|
| **Record Keeping**<br>IC 54-2044 | ## Trust Account Record Keeping<br>Each designated broker is required to create and maintain trust account records and reconcile at least once a month. |
| **Ledger Requirements** | Balances of the ledger record shall be kept current at all times. When a broker or any person representing a broker takes physical possession of consideration, an individual ledger shall be immediately created.<br><br>This activity is mandatory even if the earnest money or consideration is transferred to another broker, 3rd party, seller or another party together with a transaction number. |
| **Ledger record categories** | Each individual trust account ledger must contain:<br>1. Chronological transaction number for each transaction<br>2. Names of both parties to the transaction<br>3. Location of the property<br>4. Date of each deposit and disbursement<br>5. Name of payor and payee<br>6. Account and check number of each disbursement<br>7. Amount and nature of the deposit<br>8. Current balance<br>9. Final disposition of transaction and funds<br><br>Ledger records shall be kept in alphabetical order or by transaction number. Records will be maintained in 3 categories<br>1. Closed Transactions<br>2. Terminated or rejected transactions<br>3. Separate file for pending but not closed |
| **Trust account checks** | Trust account checks shall be maintained with consecutive numbering for each account. Each check shall contain the broker's licensed business name, current address, and be imprinted with the words: "real estate trust account". |

**Check Register**
IC 54-2044 (6)

## Check Register or Journal

Even if funds are held at another approved depository such as a title company, they must be posted and be currently maintained.

The check register must clearly show:

1. Date of deposit or disbursement
2. Payee or payor
3. Amount and purpose of deposits or disbursements
4. Check number
5. Transaction number
6. Current cash balance at all times

**Requirements**
IC 54-2044 (7)

A duplicate bank deposit record shall be maintained by the broker and shall contain the name of the person or party placing the money with the broker, date of deposit, and transaction number. Any voided trust account check shall be clearly marked 'VOID' and retained in numerical sequence.

**Deposits**
IC 54-2045

## Trust Account Deposits

Consideration received by a sales associate shall be immediately delivered to the broker or broker's office.

All money received by a broker for another in a real estate transaction is to be deposited on or before the next banking day immediately following the receipt of such funds unless written instructions by the parties to the transaction state otherwise.

Even though checks may be held with written instructions in an uncashed form, a ledger record must be created and maintained.
No consideration is to be returned to any party without the knowledge and consent of the broker, even if an offer has been made and declined before depositing the earnest money.

**Disbursements**
IC 54-2046

## Disbursements from trust account

The broker is responsible for all entrusted funds until such funds have been disbursed and acknowledged by all parties. To ensure the safety of trust funds, compliance includes:

● Written authorization is required by the parties to the transaction including disbursements in advance of closing.

• Any disbursements to others based on the terms of the purchase and sale agreement, must be evidenced by a receipt and retained in the broker's transaction file.

• Any advance in the broker's commission must be evidenced by written authorization by the buyer and seller.

• Provisions for forfeited earnest money must be included in the purchase and sale agreement to address retention by any person.

**Disputed earnest money**
IC 54-2047

## Disputed earnest money
Although the broker can disburse disputed earnest money at the broker's own discretion, it is highly suggested that the broker take great caution before making a discretionary disbursement.

To minimize the risk of any license law violation, the broker should get written approval from all parties to the transaction before disbursement. Or, the broker can hold the funds until a court of competent jurisdiction makes a decision.

**Responsible Broker**
IC 54-2048

## Responsible Broker
In Idaho, the broker who holds entrusted funds shall be deemed the responsible broker, including cooperative sales. As a responsible broker, there are 3 primary responsibilities.

1. Make sure the closing statement is true and correct. A good review prior to actual closing (usually done with an escrow agent) will identify possible errors prior to closing. Remember, the broker is ultimately responsible for the accuracy of the closing statement.

2. Proof of closing statements, with affixed buyer and seller signatures and written certification of delivery to the buyer and seller, shall be retained in the broker's transaction file.

3. Transaction files must be kept and retained by a broker for not less than 3 calendar years *after* the year the event occurred for all transactions closed, rejected or expired, and all funds disbursed. The transaction file needs to include:

- *Rejected offers* - clearly marked and dated as rejected. The law does not specify who is to date and reject but it is suggested that the seller mark and date the rejection. This proves the seller actually saw the offer and personally rejected it.

- *Accepted offers* - and support documents (counter offers, addendums, inspections, etc.)

- *Written representation agreements* - including consent to 'consent to limited dual representation' if applicable. If a broker only represents one party, the broker shall retain the one representation agreement for that broker.

- *Trust account ledger cards* - and reconciliation statements

- *Signed closing statements* - if applicable

## Selecting a Broker

Selecting the right broker is very important. Think of it this way, you are a one person business (independent contractor) who hires a broker to be your partner. By taking this attitude, you will be careful to make sure you have selected a good partner.

Does the broker's philosophy and business ethics agree with your philosophy?

Does the brokerage have a operation and guideline manual to review that addresses all phases of the business including marketing? What are the advertising policies?

What are the written terms and conditions of the independent contractor contract?

What about training? How can the brokerage help you? How can you help the brokerage? Remember this is a 'partnership' and as partners, each partner needs to be in agreement with business concepts. Think if your relationship with a broker as a team effort.

As you progress throughout your real estate career, you may find the need to have a personal assistant or two. If so, be sure you and your broker have a clear understanding regarding the use of personal assistants. Guideline 17 of the Idaho Real Estate License Law and Rules offers good information for the use of unlicensed personal assistants.

**Compensation**
IC 54-2054

## Compensation

In addition to assisting buyers and sellers to realize their dreams of real estate ownership, compensation ranks high on the scale of reasons for entering the real estate industry.

The opportunities are virtually limitless if you are willing to make the effort to create and build your real estate career. Because the industry is primarily compensated with commission and fees based on productivity, it's important you explore all options for earning power.

It's important that you fully understand what the compensation policies are for:

- Listing properties
- Selling companies listings
- Selling another companies listings
- Selling own listings
- Selling own property
- Referral fees
- Bonus compensation

In addition, you should know what the company policies are should compensation be disputed between brokerages, agents, or clients. Upon what circumstances would compensation be re-negotiated or reduced? What are the arrangements or policies for defending a fee in a court and securing legal counsel?

**Fees thru Broker**
IC 54-2054 (9)

First and foremost, it needs to be understood that *all* fees must be paid through the broker. No sales associate shall accept *any* commission, compensation or fee for the performance of any acts requiring a real estate license from any person except the broker with whom the sales associate is licensed.

However, the sales associate may pay a portion of their compensation to another sales associate who is licensed with the same broker.

Also, the broker may directly pay a former sales associate for services performed while the associate was licensed with that broker.

In discussing compensation, a subject that needs to be discussed, is known as anti-trust.

**Anti Trust**

## Anti-Trust

It is important to review and be aware of illegal aspects and applications of anti-trust issues that address real estate including:

- Price fixing
- Group boycotting
- Allocation of customers or markets
- Tie-in agreements
- Penalties

Idaho follows the federal guidelines for anti-trust. Few law suits have been filed against the real estate industry. However, that doesn't mean real estate licensees shouldn't be aware of and make efforts to prevent in any act that could constitute a violation of anti-trust.

Figure 1 - Cover page salesperson license application

# SALESPERSON
## IDAHO REAL ESTATE LICENSE APPLICATION

**IREC use only**
License # _____
Date Approved _____
Receipt # _____

(208) 334-3285       Idaho Real Estate Commission   Toll-free in Idaho
(208) 334-2050 FAX            P.O. Box 83720              (866) 447-5411
                              633 N. 4th Street
**$160**              Boise, ID 83720-0077              **$160**
                  Website: www.irec.idaho.gov

**INSTRUCTIONS:** Complete this application form, provide all attachments as requested on the "Application Checklist" on the last page, and submit it to the Idaho Real Estate Commission (IREC). Please advise IREC of any individuals needing accommodations. Applications that are illegible, incomplete, not accompanied by the proper fee and/or all attachment(s) WILL BE returned. Checks should be made payable to the **IDAHO REAL ESTATE COMMISSION. The application/license fee is $160.**

You are NOT licensed until IREC **approves** your license application. It is unlawful for you to engage in the business or act in the capacity of a real estate licensee in Idaho without first obtaining your license. Please allow 10 business days to process your completed application.

**PLEASE NOTE:** Applications are processed in the order they are received. <u>Updates on the status of license applications will NOT be given over the phone.</u> You will receive a notification by U.S. Mail when your application has been approved. You may also check the "Licensee Search" section of our website at www.irec.idaho.gov for status information. When your name and license number appear on the website, the license has been approved.

1. **PERSONAL INFORMATION**  ___ ___ ___ - ___ ___ - ___ ___ ___ ___ / ___ ___ / ___ ___
      social security number        birth month  day  year   maiden name or other names used-list all others

(full legal name)  last _____  first _____  middle _____  nickname (if used) _____

home telephone _____  cell phone number _____  e-mail address (required) _____

(physical address) number, street, apt. _____

city _____  county _____  state _____  zip code _____

(mailing address, if different from above) number, street, apt. _____

city _____  county _____  state _____  zip code _____

2. **RECORD OF LICENSURE** (List all states or jurisdictions in which you have held any real estate license, including Idaho, beginning with original state of licensure.) (Attach additional sheet if necessary.)

| State or Jurisdiction | Type of License Held | Dates of Licensure From / To |
|---|---|---|
| _____ | _____ | _____ |
| _____ | _____ | _____ |
| _____ | _____ | _____ |

3. **ARE YOU ACTIVELY LICENSED AS A SALESPERSON IN ANOTHER STATE?** ☐ Yes  ☐ No (If you hold an <u>active</u> license in another state, attach a current (less than 6 months old) certified license history from your present state of licensure.)

4. **HIGH SCHOOL EDUCATION** (Provide a copy of your high school diploma, transcript or equivalency certificate.)

name of institution _____  location (city & state) _____  date of graduation _____

5. **REAL ESTATE EDUCATION** Education must have been completed within 3 years prior to application date. (Prelicense courses completed after June 30, 2008 are valid for 3 years. Prelicense courses completed on or before June 30, 2008 are valid for 5 years. If actively licensed as a salesperson in another state, you do not need to complete this section.)

| Required Courses | Provider | Location (city, state) | Completion Date | Hours |
|---|---|---|---|---|
| Module I | _____ | _____ | _____ | _____ |
| Module II | _____ | _____ | _____ | _____ |

Page 1 of 3

Figure 2 - Pearson-Vue Content Outline - page 1

## General Exam Content Outline
## For Salespersons and Brokers
### *Effective January 1, 2009*

The general portion of the real estate exam is made up of eighty (80) scored questions, which are distributed as noted in the following content outline. Approximately ten percent (10%) of the scored questions on the general examinations will involve mathematical computations.

The salesperson and broker examinations also contain five (5) pretest questions that are not counted toward the score. These questions are used to gather statistics on performance and to help assess appropriateness for use on future examinations. Since pretest questions look exactly like questions that are scored, candidates should answer all the questions on the examination.

The following examination content outline is appropriate for real estate salespersons and real estate brokers.

I. Real property characteristics, definitions, ownership, restrictions, and transfer (Salesperson 16, Broker 12)
    A Definitions, descriptions, and ways to hold title
        1. Elements of real and personal property
        2. Property description and area calculations
        3. Estates in real property
        4. Forms of ownership, rights, interests, and obligations
    B. Land use controls and restrictions
        1. Government controls
        2. Private controls – non-monetary
        3. Private controls – mortgage (deed of trust) and liens
    C. Transfer/alienation of title to real property
        1. Voluntary
        2. Involuntary
        3. Protections
        4. Partition/severance (voluntary or involuntary)
        5. Deeds and warranties: validity, types, covenants
        6. Title and title insurance

II. Property valuation and appraisal (Salesperson 6, Broker 6)
    A Principles, types, and estimates of property value
        1. Valuation definition, purpose, and process
        2. Characteristics
        3. Valuation principles
        4. Approaches to value
        5. Depreciation/obsolescence
        6. Value
        7. Appraisals and list price
        8. Math
        9. Influences on property value
    B. Investment analysis
        1. Application of principles
        2. Math calculations

III. Contracts and relationships with buyers and sellers (Salesperson 18, Broker 20)
    A. Contract elements
        1. Validity
        2. Void/voidable
        3. Enforceable/unenforceable (Statute of Frauds)
        4. Unilateral/bilateral
        5. Executory/executed
    B. Listing contracts
        1. General purpose/definition of listing
        2. Types
        3. Required elements
        4. Establishing listing price
        5. Responsibilities
    C. Commission agreements
        1. Negotiation of commission
        2. Who may collect
        3. Other compensation arrangements
        4. Math: licensee compensation/commission
    D. Sales contracts
        1. Terminology
        2. Procedures
        3. Standard parts
        4. Contingencies and misc. provisions
        5. Contractual rights and obligation
        6. Disputes and dispute resolution terms
    E. Option contracts
    F Licensee-client relationships and responsibilities
        1. Types of relationships – terminology
        2. Relationship powers and obligations

IV. Property conditions and disclosures (Salesperson 7, Broker 7)
    A. Federal environmental regulations
        1. Lead-based paint
        2. CERCLA
        3. Asbestos
        4. Wetlands and flood plains

Figure 3 - Pearson-Vue Content Outline page 2 (cont.)

B. Environmental issues
  1. Mold
  2. Radon
  3. Protected species
  4. Other
C. Material and other property disclosures
D. Liability considerations

**V. Federal laws governing real estate activities
(Salesperson 8, Broker 9)**
  A. Civil Rights Acts/Fair Housing Acts
    1. Provisions
    2. Violations
    3. Enforcement/penalties
    4. Exceptions
    5. Advertising
    6. Required poster
  B. Americans with Disabilities Act (ADA)
  C. Antitrust – (Sherman Act, etc.)
  D. Marketing and financial controls
    1. Truth in Lending Act (TILA—Regulation Z)
    2. Real Estate Settlement Procedures Act (RESPA)
    3. Equal Credit Opportunity Act (ECOA)
    4. Equal Employment Opportunity Commission (EEOC)
    5. UCC/Interstate/Securities (Broker only)
    6. Do Not Call/Privacy Act

**VI. Financing the transaction and settlement
(Salesperson 17, Broker 13)**
  A. Financing components
    1. Financing instruments
    2. Financing sources (primary and secondary mortgage markets, seller financing)
    3. Types of loans
    4. Financing clauses, terminology, and cost of money (calculation)
    5. Lending issues
  B. Lender requirements and obligations
    1. Private mortgage insurance (PMI)
    2. FHA requirements
    3. VA requirements
    4. Escrow/impound account
    5. Credit report
    6. Assumption requirements
    7. Appraisal requirements
    8. Hazard and flood insurance
    9. Federal financing and credit regulation
  C. Settlement/Closing
    1. Procedures and forms
    2. Closing costs and calculations
    3. Documents, title, and recording

**VII. Leases, rents, and property management
(Salesperson 5, Broker 6)**
  A. Types and elements of leases
    1. Leasehold estates
    2. Types of leases
    3. Lease clauses and provisions

  B. Lessor and lessee rights, responsibilities, liabilities, and recourse
    1. Owned and leased inclusions
    2. Reversionary rights of owners
    3. Rental related discriminatory laws
    4. Unit-related disclosures
    5. Effect of sale/transfer/foreclosure
    6. Evictions
    7. Tenant improvements
    8. Termination of a lease
    9. Breach
  C. Property management contracts and obligations of parties
    1. Contracts and contractual relationships
    2. Manager's obligations, duties, liabilities
    3. Owner's obligations, duties, liabilities
    4. Management/owner math calculations

**VIII. Brokerage operations
(Salesperson 3, Broker 7)**
  A. Broker management of funds
    1. Earnest money
    2. Commingling
    3. Conversion of funds
  B. Broker-salesperson relationship
  C. Advertising
  D. Ethical and legal business practices
    1. Misrepresentation
    2. Implied duty of good faith
    3. Due diligence
    4. Unauthorized practice of law
    5. Marketing practices
  E. Forms of business ownership
    1. Corporation
    2. Partnership (general and limited)
    3. Limited liability company
    4. Sole proprietorship
  F. Independent contractors vs. employee

# Chapter 2 - Questions

1. Who is required to have a real estate license to practice real estate?

   A. Anyone assisting another to sell their property
   B. Anyone, with expectation of compensation, acting for another to list property for sale
   C. Anyone, with expectation of compensation, offers to sell personal property
   D. Anyone, for compensation, sells a property at foreclosure.

2. An example of an exception to being required to have a real estate license is:

   A. Purchasing real property for another for compensation
   B. Listing real property for another for compensation
   C. Negotiates for another an option for real property for compensation
   D. Offering property management or leasing for another for compensation.

3. What's the minimum age to secure a real estate license in Idaho?

   A. 16
   B. 18
   C. 20
   D. 21

4. Minimum hours of Continuing Education required to renew a real estate license are:

   A. 16 plus Core
   B. 20 including Core
   C. 20 excluding Core
   D. 18 excluding Core

5. When does a real estate license expire?

   A. The last day of the birth month
   B. The first day of the birth month
   C. 2 years from the date of licensing
   D. 2 years from date of completing CE education

6. A student, whose birthday is June 5, passed their state exam on April 8, and applied for and received their license on April 18, 2010. When does their license expire?

   A. April 18, 2011
   B. June 5, 2011
   C. June 30, 2011
   D. April 18, 2012

7. When do initial fingerprints expire prior to receiving a real estate license?

   A. Fingerprints are fingerprints, they don't expire
   B. Fingerprint results are valid for 6 months
   C. Fingerprints are valid for 1 year
   D. Fingerprints aren't required if the license applicant already has them

8. What type of insurance is required for an inactive real estate licensee?

   A. Errors & Omissions Insurance
   B. Automobile liability insurance
   C. Personal liability insurance
   D. None

9. To be effective, tail coverage for E&O Group insurance must be purchased within how many days from cancellation?

   A. Tail coverage is automatically included with E&O insurance.
   B. 60 days from cancellation
   C. 90 days from cancellation
   D. 120 days from cancellation

10. What document needs to accompany an application for a real estate license?

   A. Verification of taking a license exam
   B. Fingerprints taken a year ago
   C. Proof of automobile insurance
   D. Copy of high school diploma

11. What activities can unlicensed personal assistants perform?

   A. Provide access and show home
   B. Create/distribute listing information
   C. Offer and negotiate lending options to buy a home at an open house
   D. Clerical duties for the broker or broker associate

12. What is the maximum fine for an unlicensed person practicing real estate?

   A. $ 5,000
   B. $10,000
   C. $15,000
   D. $20,000

13. A licensee buying or selling their own property must conduct all transactions through:

   A. Cooperating brokerage
   B. Idaho Real Estate Commission
   C. Broker with whom licensed
   D. No requirements; it's their own property and they can do as they wish

14. If a licensee terminates with a broker, what is required?

   A. Nothing, the licensee just leaves
   B. Licensee must tell the broker they are leaving
   C. Licensee must give written notice within 5 calendar days of leaving
   D. Licensee must notify in writing no later than 3 business days of effective date

15. If a broker terminates an agent with cause, the broker must notify the Idaho Real Estate Commission within:

   A. 3 business days from termination
   B. 5 calendar days from termination
   C. 5 business days from termination
   D. 10 business days from termination

16. If a broker is absent for more than 21 days but less than 60 days, who can be appointed to manage/oversee the office?

   A. Office manager
   B. Long time sales associate
   C. Associate broker
   D. Owner/partner

17. Company records must be retained by the broker for what period of time

    A. 3 fiscal years after a transaction closes
    B. 3 calendar years after the year a transaction closes
    C. 3 calendar years after the year a transaction is initiated
    D. 3 fiscal years from the date company was created

18. What is the maximum amount of personal money allowed to maintain a trust account?

    A. $100
    B. $300
    C. $500
    D. $700

19. Trust account maintenance funds can be used for what purpose?

    A. Cover bank charges
    B. Cover NSF earnest money checks
    C. Cover general operating account charges
    D. Cover delivery of deposits to the bank

20. A trust account must be established under what name?

    A. Designated broker's name
    B. Licensed business name
    C. Registered name with State Tax Department
    D. Owner's name of the company

21. Who must be notified of opening a trust account?

    A. Secretary of State
    B. Idaho Tax Commission
    C. Idaho Real Estate Commission
    D. Internal Revenue Service

22. A broker transferred $500 from the general operating account to the trust account.

    A. It's O.K. to replace a missing check
    B. Is an example of commingling
    C. O. K as long as IREC is notified
    D. Used to maintain the trust account

23. How often must a trust account be reconciled at least?

    A. Monthly
    B. Quarterly
    C. Semi-annually
    D. Annually

24. When is consideration received by a sales associate to be delivered to the broker or broker's office?

    A. Within 24 hours
    B. Within 1 day
    C. As soon as convenient
    D. Immediately

25. Trust account checks must be imprinted with the words:

    A. (Name of company) trust account
    B. Business trust account
    C. Real estate trust account
    D. Trust account

26. Unless otherwise stated, when must earnest money be deposited?

    A. Within 5 business days of acceptance
    B. Next banking day
    C. Next calendar day
    D. Next business day

27. Who is authorized to disburse disputed earnest money without written approval from the parties to the transaction?

    A. Cannot disburse without written approval from buyer and seller
    B. Escrow company
    C. The broker holding the earnest money
    D. Idaho Real Estate Commission

28. Who is considered the responsible broker in a cooperative sale?

    A. The listing broker
    B. The selling broker
    C. The broker holding entrusted funds
    D. Both the listing and selling brokers

29. Who is responsible for the accuracy of a closing statement?

    A. Listing agent
    B. Selling agent
    C. Escrow officer
    D. The broker

30. How are rejected offers handled?

    A. Nothing is required
    B. Need to be marked as 'rejected'
    C. Given to seller for their records
    D. Marked and dated as 'rejected'

31. Sales associates can only accept fees, compensation, or commission from whom?

    A. The broker with whom licensed
    B. Directly from the buyer or seller
    C. From the escrow company
    D. Directly from the cooperating broker

32. Two competitive real estate companies were struggling and over lunch they each agreed to increase their fees so they could survive a down market. This would be an example of what?

    A. Cooperation
    B. Price fixing
    C. Good business practice
    D. Friendly competition

# Chapter 3

# Agency

**General Concepts**

The heart of the real estate industry is centered around working relationships between real estate agents and the public. Although the term, 'real estate agent' refers to our occupation, it does not define our duties or obligations in a transaction.

In the early days and even up into the 1980's a lot of confusion surrounded agency and overall representation between real estate agents and the public. To help reduce the confusion, legislation was initiated to clearly identify the duties and obligations of real estate licensees.

Eventually all states throughout America legislated specific disclosure laws regulating disclosure of agency relationships between the public and the real estate industry.

However, because the legislated laws vary from state to state, it's very important that you know exactly how Idaho laws are written.

The basic principles of Agency revolve around representation based on different obligations and duties between the principal and the agent. When one person (principal) delegates to another person (agent) the right to act on behalf of the principal, an agency relationship is created.

**3 levels of agency**

There are three levels of agency: universal, general, and special. Universal agency is very broad and basically gives the agent unlimited power. On the other hand, general agency gives the agent power to bind the principal in a particular trade or business. As an example, a real estate salesperson is an agent for the designated broker. However, one might find that the most practiced form of agency is that of a special agent. The principal authorizes the agent to do a particular act over a specific period of time. A good example would be a listing.

**Idaho Real Estate Representation Act**
IC 54-2082

The Idaho Real Estate Representation Act was created to clearly identify what duties and obligations exist between the consumer and a real estate brokerage. Any real estate transaction in which a real estate license is required will be governed by agency representation.

## Creating a brokerage relationship

**Creating Brokerage Relationship**
IC 54-2084

A buyer or seller is not represented by a brokerage in a regulated real estate transaction unless the buyer or seller and the brokerage agree in a separate *written* document to such representation.

No type of agency representation may be assumed by a brokerage, buyer or seller or created orally or by implication. In other words, the only client relationship that can be created in Idaho is with a separate, signed, written agreement.

In Idaho, there are 4 types of brokerage relationships.
- Nonagency
- Agency representation
- Limited dual agency representation
- Limited dual agency with assigned agents

**Disclosure Brochure**
54-2085 (1)

Figure 1

**Agency Disclosure Brochure**  (aka Blue Brochure)
One of the first duties a licensee has is that a licensee shall give to a prospective buyer or seller at the first substantial business contact the agency disclosure brochure adopted or approved by the Idaho Real Estate Commission. Each brokerage shall keep a signed and dated record of a buyer or seller's receipt of the agency disclosure brochure.

It should be noted that signing the brochure by a buyer or seller *does not* obligate the signor to any contractual relationship with the licensee. It merely provides proof when the prospective buyer or seller received the disclosure brochure.

A licensee also needs to make sure they are using the most recent version (date on cover) of the disclosure brochure. From time to time, the Idaho Real Estate Commission may change the format or contents.

The agency disclosure brochure shall list the various types of representation available to a buyer or seller in a regulated real estate transaction. In addition, the duties and obligations owed to a buyer and seller will be explained.

The disclosure brochure also contains a conspicuous notice that states *no* representation will exist without a written agreement between the buyer or seller and the brokerage.

A brokerage must disclose its relationship to both buyer and seller in a transaction no later than the preparation or presentation of a purchase and sale agreement.

Many agents take extra time to go through the information contained in the brochure to make sure the consumer understands the terminology before actually deciding what type of agency will be selected.

Failure of a licensee to timely give a buyer or seller the agency disclosure brochure shall be a violation and subject to disciplinary action.

**Agency Confirmation**
4-2085 (4)

## Purchase & Sale Agreement Agency Confirmation

In addition, a purchase and sale agreement, and any additional attachments will contain specific language and confirmation of the agency relationship regardless of whether the transaction involved representation or not.

**Mandatory language**

The confirmation and acknowledgment will also contain a very important disclosure all in capital letters.

> EACH PARTY UNDERSTANDS THAT HE IS A "CUSTOMER" AND IS NOT REPRESENTED BY A BROKERAGE UNLESS THERE IS A SIGNED WRITTEN AGREEMENT FOR AGENCY REPRESENTATION

The confirmation states that the brokerage's agency office policy was made available for inspection and review. Thus, all agents must know exactly what is contained in the 'office policy' and where a copy is located.

Failure of a licensee to properly and timely obtain any written agreement or confirmation shall be a violation and subject to discipline.

**Office policy**
IC 54-2090

## Written Office Policy Required

Each designated broker shall be responsible to adopt and maintain in each office, including branch offices, a written policy which identifies and describes the types of representation in which that brokerage and its associated licensees may engage with any buyer or seller, or both, as a part of that office's real estate brokerage services.

Agency

## Duties To A Customer (nonagency)

A customer is a buyer or seller who is *not* represented in a real estate transaction and the licensee is known as a nonagent. However, there are still duties and obligations that have to be followed:

- Assist buyer and seller in sale or purchase

- Perform acts with honesty, good faith, reasonable skill & care

- Properly account for moneys placed in care of the brokerage

- Disclose to the buyer customer or seller customer, any adverse material fact actually known or reasonably should have been known

The above duties are mandatory and cannot be waived or nullified

A nonagent has no duty to conduct an independent inspection or verify the accuracy or completeness of any statement or representation made by the seller or source reasonably believed by the licensee to be reliable.

A nonagent is not required to conduct an independent investigation of the buyers financial condition or verify any statements made by the buyer.

If a buyer or seller elects to be a customer, the licensee should advise the customer that anything confidential in nature should not be disclosed to the licensee. Why? Because if the licensee does in fact represent the other party to a transaction, the agent owes their duties to their client and may have to disclose such confidential information to their client.

## Duties To A Client

If a buyer or seller enters into a written contract for representation, that buyer or seller becomes a client of the brokerage and its licensees. With the client relationship the following duties are owed.

1. Perform to the terms of the written agreement

2. Exercise reasonable skill and care

3. Be available to timely present all written offers

4. Promote best interest of client in good faith, honesty, and fair dealing including but not limited to:

- Disclosing any adverse material facts actually known or reasonably should have been known;

- Seeking a buyer to purchase at a price, terms, and conditions acceptable to the seller and assisting in the negotiations;

- Seeking a property and negotiating for purchase at a price, terms and conditions acceptable to a buyer;

- When appropriate, advising a buyer/client to obtain professional inspections and seek appropriate tax, legal, and other professional advice or counsel;

- Upon written request from the seller, request reasonable proof of a buyer's financial ability to purchase property.

5. Properly account for moneys or property placed in the care and responsibility of the brokerage.

6. Maintain the confidentiality of specific client information

- Duty extends beyond termination of representation as long as information does not become generally known in the marketing community;

- Confidential information by a licensee shall remain confidential even if the licensee later associates with a different broker;

- Licensee shall inform a second client of any conflict of interest from a former client without first obtaining permission from a former client.

7. Unless agreed to in writing, no duty to verify accuracy, or completeness is required. Nor is there a duty to conduct an independent inspection to a client. In addition, unless in writing, there is not duty to conduct an independent investigation as to the financial ability to complete a real estate transaction.

8. Duties are mandatory and cannot be waived or nullified.

9. Nothing prohibits the broker from charging a separate fee for each service provided in a transaction.

10. Imputed knowledge between multiple licensees will not result when neither has reason to have such knowledge.

11. A brokerage and its licensees may represent 2 or more buyers who wish to make an offer for the same property providing such buyers have been notified in writing of such offers. However, because of confidentiality, the terms and conditions of each offer is not required to be disclosed.

**Nonagency and single agency recap**

So far we have discussed nonagency and single agency which is pretty straight forward and understandable. But what happens when a brokerage has a listing creating a client relationship with the seller and a buyer wishes to also be represented by a licensee with the same company? Can a buyer and a seller both be represented as clients within the same company?

The answer is yes, but with some conditions. When a brokerage represents both the buyer and seller in the same transaction, the agency relationship is known as Limited Dual Agency. Remember in order for this type of relationship to occur, the brokerage must acknowledge approval in their written office policy. Let's explore the duties and obligations of a limited dual agent.

**Limited Dual Agency**
IC 54-2088

## Limited Dual Agency

Only with an expressed written contract authorizing limited dual agency, can a brokerage represent both the buyer and seller. The key word is 'limited'. In order not to have conflict of interest, certain limitations will be imposed to not give one party an advantage over the other.

A brokerage acting as a limited dual agent may, at the option of the brokerage and with written consent, assign separate licensees to each client to represent and act solely for that client. Thus, the brokerage has basically allowed 'single' agency. This option could give both the client and their agent better communication without restrictions to make decisions that best meet each individual client.

The written consent to limited dual agency must have separate signatures of all clients involved in the transaction and must contain the following language:

**Mandatory language**
IC 54-2088 (3)

*CONSENT TO LIMITED DUAL REPRESENTATION AND ASSIGNED AGENCY*

*The undersigned have received, read and understand the Agency Disclosure Brochure.*

*The undersigned understand that the brokerage involved in this transaction may be providing agency representation to both the buyer and the seller.*

*The undersigned each understands that, as an agent for both buyer/client and seller/client, a brokerage will be a limited dual agent of each client and cannot advocate on behalf of one client over another, and cannot legally disclose to either client certain confidential client information concerning price negotiations, terms, or factors motivating the buyer/client to buy or the seller/client to sell without specific written permission of the client to whom the information pertains.*

The specific duties, obligations and limitations of a limited dual agent are contained in the Agency Disclosure Brochure as required in section 54-2085, Idaho Code.

The undersigned each understands that a limited dual agent does not have a duty of undivided loyalty to either client.

The undersigned further acknowledge that, to the extent the brokerage firm offers assigned agency as a type of agency representation, individual sales associates may be assigned to represent each client to act solely on behalf of the client consistent with applicable duties set forth in Section 54-2087, Idaho Code.

In an assigned agency situation, the designated broker (who supervises the sales associates) will remain a limited dual agent of the client and shall have the duty to supervise the assigned agents in the fulfillment of their duties to their respective clients, to refrain from advocating on behalf of any one client over another, and to refrain from disclosing or using, without permission, confidential information of any other client with whom the brokerage has an agency relationship.

A limited dual agent shall not disclose any of the following without express written consent:

**Shall not disclose**

- That a buyer is willing to pay more than the listing price for the property;

- That a seller is willing to accept less than the listing price for the property;

- Factors motivating the buyer to buy or the seller to sell;

- That a buyer or seller will agree to a price or financing terms other than those offered.

**Assigned agency**
IC 54-2088 (5)

If a brokerage is acting as a limited dual agent and assigns separate sales associates to act on behalf of the separate clients, the designated broker continues to act as a limited dual agent with the duty to:

- Supervise the assigned agents with their duties to their respective clients;

- Refrain from advocating on behalf of any one client over another;

- Refrain from disclosing, without permission, confidential information of any other client with whom the brokerage has an agency relationship.

If a designated broker determines confidential information of a client has been disclosed to another client and is a violation, the designated broker shall promptly provide written notice of the disclosure to the affected client.

As you can see, extra care needs to be taken when involved in a limited dual agency relationship whether assigned agency is utilized or not. Although tempting, do not disclose without written permission, any information that could be construed as confidential to anyone or anywhere including sales meetings. As an old saying goes, 'loose lips sink ships'.

| | |
|---|---|
| **Duties after agency terminates**<br>IC 54-2092 | # Requirements After Agency Termination<br>Even after a transaction closes and the agency relationship terminates there are still several duties and obligations that continue after termination.<br><br>1. Accounting for all moneys and property received during representation;<br><br>2. Maintaining confidentiality of all information defined as confidential. |
| **Fiduciary duties** | Within the real estate industry, one will hear the term, 'fiduciary' which is based on a common law system and originated in England in the Middle Ages and expanded to former colonies of the British Empire including the United States.<br><br>A fiduciary duty is the highest standard of care and revolves around trust, honesty, and good business practice. The judicial system in the United States is based on common law and the principle that it is unfair to treat similar facts differently on different occasions. To add to the complexity there can be interactions between common law, constitutional law, statutory law and regulatory law.<br><br>Like all other states, Idaho operates under the premise of common law. However, the practice of agency in real estate activities operates under statutory law. |
| **Representation not fiduciary (Idaho)**<br>IC 54-2094 | # Representation Not Fiduciary In Nature<br>Therefore, it should be noted that representation is not fiduciary in nature. While it is intended to abrogate (cancel, nullify) the common law of agency as it applies to regulated real estate transactions, a brokerage is not prohibited from entering into a written agreement with a buyer or seller which creates duties and obligations greater than the statutory requirements.<br><br>Unless such duties are expanded beyond the statutory duties, the duties and obligations are not fiduciary in nature and are not subject to equitable remedies for breach of fiduciary duty. If on the other hand a licensees duties were expanded beyond the statutory duties, then the licensee could be subject to both statutory and fiduciary duties. |

**Vicarious liability abolished**
IC 54-2093

## Vicarious Liability Abolished

Another law that may be different from other states is that vicarious liability is abolished. A buyer or seller shall not be liable for a wrongful act, error, omission or misrepresentation made by the broker or licensees.

On the other side, a brokerage or licensee representing a client shall not be liable for a wrongful act, error, or omission or misrepresentation made by the client unless the licensee should have known of the wrongful act, error, omission or misrepresentation.

**Q & A**

## Agency Questions and Answers

Q   Can a buyer who has been a buyer customer for several months change their agency relationship and become a client?

A   Yes.  It's not unusual for a buyer to be a customer and remain a customer partially out of fear of signing anything.  But once they like and trust the agent they are working with, they may desire to become a client.   Now the agent will probably work a little harder since the risk of the buyer going elsewhere is eliminated.

Q   When would it be advisable for a buyer to convert from being a customer to become a client?

A   During the customer relationship with the licensee, the buyer has unknowingly divulged several confidential issues to the licensee and really likes a listing that is with the licensee's company.  The only way confidentiality can remain confidential is with a client relationship.

Q   A buyer client has become frustrated with their agent and wants to cancel their buyer brokerage agreement.  Can they cancel?

A   Yes, anyone can cancel a contract but they need to be aware of any penalties or cancellation fees that may be associated with such act.  Unfortunately it appears there has been a communication breakdown so both the agent and the client should try to resolve the issue.

Q   Can a salesperson cancel a representation agreement with a client?

A   No, not unless they have approval from the designated broker.  Remember, the clients belong to the brokerage not the salesperson.

Q   A seller client listed and sold their property but have another separate property they would also like to sell. Are they required to list with the brokerage who had the original listing.

A   No, the agency relationship only applies to separate and individual agreements. In fact, the seller could list various separate properties with different brokerages at the same time.

Q   The owner/client has listed their property with a brokerage and later finds the roof leaks and needs replacing. They are highly motivated and reduce the price but don't want the agent to say anything about the leaking roof. What is the agent supposed to do?

A   The agent must 'disclose any adverse material fact actually known or reasonably should have been known'. The agent has no choice but to disclose.

Q   A seller/client has listed their property with a brokerage but is looking for replacement with another agent from another company. Aren't they bound by the listing company?

A   No, the seller representation agreement is a single agreement for a single act. The seller can do anything they want as far as seeking replacement property.

Q   Both the buyer and seller are represented as clients by agents at the same company. The buyer wants to make an offer on a company listing and also wants full representation with assigned agency. Is it possible?

A   Maybe. Only if the brokerage allows assigned agency in their written policy on agency and the brokerage makes the assignment with written consent of other clients. If the designated broker is directly involved as one of the agents, assigned agency cannot be utilized.

In conclusion, the real estate activity between real estate agents and the public revolves around representation. It is very important that both the licensee and the consumer know and understand the different types of representation offered.

It's also important that the licensee know and understand the duties required under each type of representation and differentiate between them.

Now that we learned about the elements for representation and different types of representation, we'll now explore client representation agreements.

# Representation Agreements

A buyer or seller desiring to be represented in a real estate transaction, must enter into a written agreement with a brokerage and the agreement must contain some required provisions.

## Seller Representation Agreement

Whether a seller enters into an exclusive (broker has total control) or a nonexclusive (seller retains the right to sell there own property without a fee) agreement, certain provisions are required to be included in the agreement.

1. Conspicuous and definite beginning and expiration dates;

2. Sufficient description of the property;

3. Price and terms;

4. All fees and commissions;

5. Signature and date of the owner or legal appointed representative.

## Buyer Representation Agreements

When a buyer elects to be represented in the purchase of property, exclusively (owes sole loyalty to the brokerage) or nonexclusively (free to buy on own without representation), certain provisions are required to be included in the agreement.

1. Conspicuous and definite beginning and expiration dates;

2. All financial obligations including fees or commissions;

3. Manner of how fee or commission will be paid to the broker;

4. Signature and date of the buyer or legal appointed representative.

**Automatic renewals prohibited**
IC 54-2050 (3)

Automatic renewal clauses of an exclusive representation agreement are prohibited.

An exception would be a completely nonexclusive agreement whereby no financial or fee obligations are due from the party signing the agreement.

**Signing parties to receive copy**

The party signing a representation agreement, offer to purchase, counteroffer, and acceptance shall receive a true and correct copy. These agreements and contracts may be electronically generated, faxed or delivered in another method and shall be enforceable as originals.

**Agency Duration**
IC 54-2091

## Duration of Agency Relationship
If an agency relationship has been established, how long does it last? The agency relationship commences on the date indicated on the written agreement and will end at the earliest of:

- Performance or completion of the representation;
- Agreement by the parties;
- Expiration of the agency relationship agreement.

**Compensation**
IC 54-2089

## Broker Compensation
Even though brokerage representation agreements for both buyer and seller discloses of all fees or commissions, a written agreement only for payment of compensation to a brokerage shall not constitute an agreement for agency.

The brokerage can offer various 'fee for service' that does not involve buying or selling representation activities.

The subject of agency need not be complex or confusing. The main thing to remember is to know what the brokerage written policy allows and follow accordingly.

It's also important to review and be familiar with the different types of agency. Each type of agency offers different requirements that need to be fully understood.

Some agents read, word for word, all the information contained on the Agency Disclosure Brochure (also known as the 'blue brochure'). This creates a good review and makes sure the consumer fully understands the different types of agency that may be available for them to choose.

**Figure 1**

# Agency Disclosure Brochure

A Consumer Guide To Understanding Agency Relationships in Real Estate Transactions

Specific duties owed by a real estate brokerage and its licensees to Idaho consumers are defined by the "Idaho Real Estate Brokerage Representation Act," Idaho Code Section 54-2082 et seq.

This informational brochure is published by the Idaho Real Estate Commission.

**Effective July 1, 2009**

## Limited Dual Agency without Assigned Agents

As a Limited Dual Agent, the brokerage and its licensees cannot advocate on behalf of one client over the other. The licensees cannot disclose confidential client information regarding negotiations, terms or factors that motivate the buyer to buy, or the seller to sell, or advocate the interests of one party over those of the other. The brokerage must otherwise promote the non-conflicting interests of both parties, perform the terms of the agency agreements with skill and care, and perform other duties required by law.

## Limited Dual Agency with Assigned Agents

If your brokerage has obtained consent to represent both parties as a Limited Dual Agent, it may assign individual licensees ("Assigned Agents") to act solely on behalf of each party. Your Assigned Agent has a duty to promote your best interests, even if your interests conflict with those of the other party, including negotiating a price, and must maintain your confidential information.

The Designated Broker of your brokerage must remain a Limited Dual Agent for both Clients. The broker will ensure the Assigned Agents fulfill their duties to their respective Clients.

## What to Look For in Any Written Agreement with a Brokerage

Any Agency Representation or Compensation Agreement should answer these questions:

- How will the brokerage get paid?
- When will this agreement expire?
- What happens to this agreement when a transaction is completed?
- Can I cancel this agreement, and if so, how?

- Can I work with other brokerages during the time of my agreement?
- What happens if I buy or sell on my own?
- Under an Agency Representation Agreement, am I willing to allow the brokerage to represent both the other party and me in my real estate transaction?

When you sign a real estate Purchase and Sale Agreement, you will be asked to confirm:

1.) This brochure was given to you, and you have read and understand its contents;

2.) The correct agency relationship, if any, between you and your brokerage.

## Real Estate Licensees Are Not Inspectors

You should not expect the brokerage or its licensees to conduct an independent inspection of the property. You should not expect your agent to independently verify any statement or representation made by a buyer, seller, or professional associated with your transaction. If the condition of the property is important to you, you should hire an appropriate professional, such as an engineer, surveyor, or home inspector.

If you have any questions about the information in this brochure, contact:

Idaho Real Estate Commission
(208) 334-3285
Toll free in Idaho (866) 447-5411
TRS (800) 377-3529
www.irec.idaho.gov

Costs associated with this publication are available from the Idaho Real Estate Commission in accordance with section 60-202, I.C.—July 2009/50k/429.

Figure 1 (2nd page)

## Right Now You Are a Customer

All real estate consumers are "Customers" under Idaho law unless a representation agreement is signed. (A real estate licensee working with a customer is called a "Non-Agent".) The law requires all real estate licensees to provide the following "Customer level" services, to everyone:

**Remember! Unless you enter a written agreement for Agency Representation, you will NOT be represented at all.**

- Perform necessary and customary acts to assist you in the purchase or sale of real estate;
- Perform these acts in good faith and with honesty and reasonable care;
- Properly account for money or other property you place in the licensee's care;
- Disclose "adverse material facts" to you which are, or should be, within the licensee's knowledge. These are facts that would significantly affect the desirability or value of the property to a reasonable person, and facts that indicate to a reasonable person that one of the parties cannot, or will not complete obligations of the contract.

**As a Customer, your brokerage will not act as your Agent and is not required to promote your best interests or keep your bargaining information confidential. If you use the services of a brokerage without a written agreement, you will remain a Customer.**

As a Customer, you may be asked to sign a Compensation Agreement, a contract that requires you to pay a fee to the broker for some service the brokerage provides you.

If you enter into a Compensation Agreement, the brokerage and its agents must also:

- Be available to receive and present written offers and counter-offers to you or from you.

The Compensation Agreement is not the same as an Agency Representation Agreement. A Compensation Agreement cannot be used to change or eliminate any Customer level services.

## You May Become a Client

If a brokerage offers agency representation and you choose to sign a representation agreement, you will become a "Client". The brokerage and its licensees must act as your "Agent". They will owe you the following duties in addition to the basic Customer level services required of all licensees:

- Perform the terms of your agency agreement with skill and care;
- Promote your best interests in good faith, honesty, and fair dealing;
- Maintain the confidentiality of some client information, including bargaining information, even after the representation has ended.

**Please Note: "Sold" prices of property are not confidential information, for either buyers or sellers, and may be disseminated by your Agent.**

## These Are Your Agency Options

### Agency Representation (Single Agency)

Under "Agency Representation" (sometimes referred to in real estate documents as "Single Agency"), your Agent may represent you, and only you, in your real estate transaction. (This representation can be modified in writing at a later date.)

**If you are a seller,** your Agent will seek a buyer to purchase your property at a price and under terms and conditions acceptable to you and will assist with your negotiations. If you make a written request, your Agent will seek reasonable proof of a prospective purchaser's financial ability to complete your transaction.

**If you are a buyer,** your Agent will seek a property for you to purchase at an acceptable price and terms and will assist with your negotiations. Your Agent will also advise you to consult with appropriate professionals, such as inspectors, attorneys, and tax advisors. If disclosed in writing, a brokerage may represent other buyers who wish to make offers on the same property.

### Limited Dual Agency

"Limited Dual Agency" means the brokerage and its agents represent both the buyer and the seller in the same transaction. You may choose Limited Dual Agency representation with your brokerage because you do not want it to be restricted in the search for suitable properties or buyers. There are two options under Limited Dual Agency.

**Each brokerage is required to have a written policy describing the types of agency representation it offers.**

RECEIPT ACKNOWLEDGED — Rev 06/01/09

Your signature below indicates a real estate licensee gave you a copy of the Idaho Real Estate Commission's "Agency Disclosure Brochure."
**Signing this document does not create an agency relationship or a contractual relationship of any kind.**

Signature ______________________ Date __________

Signature ______________________ Date __________

# Questions – Chapter 3

1. A real agent would be classified with what level of agency?

   A  Universal
   B.  General
   C.  Special
   D.  Specific

2. The Idaho Representation Act was created to identify obligations between the consumer and the:

   A.  Buyer
   B.  Seller
   C.  Real estate licensee
   D.  Real estate brokerage

3. How many types of agency can be practiced in Idaho?

   A.  One
   B.  Two
   C.  Three
   D.  Four

4. Signing the Agency Disclosure Brochure establishes what kind of agency relationship?

   A.  None
   B.  Client
   C.  Customer
   D.  Both customer and client

5. Where is the confirmation of an agency relationship contained?

   A.  Agency Disclosure Brochure
   B.  Purchase & Sale Agreement
   C.  Buyer representation agreement
   D.  Seller representation agreement

6. What is the primary difference between a customer and a client?

   A.  Disclose adverse material facts
   B.  Exercise reasonable skill and care
   C.  Maintain confidentiality
   D  Lender approval

7. When a buyer signs a representation agreement, who is the client relationship with?

   A.  The agent the buyer is working with
   B.  The real estate brokerage
   C.  Idaho Real Estate Commission
   D.  Idaho Association of Realtors®

8. When can limited dual agency with assigned agents be used?

   A.  Only with written consent of all clients in a transaction
   B.  Whenever a client desires
   C.  Is allowed at anytime
   D.  Only if Agency Disclosure Brochure states such relationship.

9. A signed and dated record of a buyer or sellers receipt of the agency disclosure brochure is kept by whom?

    A. Listing and selling agent
    B. Selling brokerage
    C. Each brokerage
    D. Both the buyer and seller

10. Each party not represented by a brokerage is a:

    A. Single buyer or seller
    B. Limited disclosed client
    C. Client
    D. Customer

11. Nonagent refers to working with or assisting a buyer or seller as a:

    A. Limited disclosed customer
    B. Client
    C. Customer
    D. Limited disclosed broker

12. Who cannot act as an assigned limited dual agent?

    A. A listing or selling agent
    B. A designated broker
    C. An associate broker
    D. A sales associate

13. An agent is working with a buyer client who makes an offer on another company's listing. The agent is practicing as:

    A. Limited dual agent
    B. Single agency
    C. Limited disclosed agent
    D. Nonagent

14. The practice of real estate and representation in Idaho is based on:

    A. Statutory law
    B. Common law
    C. Fiduciary law
    D. Federal law

15. An agent had a seller sign a representation agreement for 90 days with a automatic 30 day extension if the property didn't sell within the 90 days. The agreement is:

    A. Legal
    B. Illegal
    C. Acceptable
    D. Prohibited

16. A transaction closed and the agent represented the buyer as a client. When does confidentiality terminate?

    A. When agency confirmation signed
    B. At closing or representation cancelled
    C. Extends beyond termination until information becomes generally known in community
    D. Confidentiality never terminates unless agent changes brokerages

# Chapter 4

# Different Perspectives Of The Real Estate Market

**Diverse topography**

With such a diverse topography throughout the state, Idaho offers the opportunity to own all kinds and types of property. From the expansive desert to the forested mountain tops, the physical and economic characteristics can be very different.

Idaho has a land area of 83,642 square miles and a population of approximately 1.5 million with around 17 people per square mile. Unlike other states with higher density, Idaho offers lots of growth opportunities. From the lowest point of Lewiston, Idaho at 738 feet to the tip of Mt. Borah at 12,662 feet, a wide range of climates allow for building and living environments.

**Supply and demand**

Supply and demand creates scarcity, and parts of Idaho is no exception. Because most communities are relatively small in size, the addition or deletion of a good sized business can create wide fluctuations of supply and demand. Choosing the 'right' location can be great one moment and not so good the next, due to outside forces.

**Income**

In 2009, weekly wages in 26 of the 44 counties ranged from $500 to $599. On the upper range, 2 counties had weekly wages over $800 and 2 counties between $700 to $799. Although Idaho offers a wonderful lifestyle, it isn't a state that appeals to a labor force looking for high paying jobs.

**Taxes**

Other factors that play into supply and demand cycles are taxes. A 6% sales tax, around 7-8% state income tax, and property taxes add into the equation for competition and comparison with surrounding states.

**Land use**

Land use controls and environmental issues can lead to approval or disapproval of various kinds of development. 63% of Idaho is public land and offers wonderful recreation, hunting, fishing, winter and summer sports, together with a great climate.

**Slow but steady growth**

In spite of economic ups and downs, the above information suggests Idaho will continue to have slow but steady growth.

# Questions – Chapter 4

1. What is the approximate population of Idaho?

   A. 1,000,000
   B. 1,500,000
   C. 2,000,000
   D. 2,500,000

2. How many counties are in Idaho?

   A. 42
   B. 43
   C. 44
   D. 45

3. The state income tax rate in Idaho approximates:

   A. 5-6%
   B. 6-7%
   C. 7-8%
   D. 8-9%

4. What percentage of total land area in Idaho is private?

   A. 37%
   B. 55%
   C. 63%
   D. 77%

# Chapter 5

# Real Property and The Law

**Complex Subject**

As one can imagine, the terms real estate and real property are general terms that describe a vast and complex subject.

Just think of real property being everything from the center of the earth to the heavens above, attached or unattached to the land together with the rights to own, occupy, or use.

For a better understanding, real property needs to be broken down into different increments with separate explanations. One area known as personal property or 'chattel' is generally movable or annexed onto real property. Examples include annual growing crops, fixtures used in a trade or business, and other types of personal property that is transferable separate from real property.

The ownership transfer instrument used in real property is a deed. Personal property, on the other hand, is transferred with a *bill of sale*. In Idaho, a unique form of personal property involves water rights.

# Water Rights

**Prior Appropriation**
IC 42-103

## Prior Appropriation

Unlike the eastern United States where water rights are tied to the land through riparian rights, most of the western United States follows the doctrine of 'prior appropriation', which is based on 'first in time, first in right' principle.

Idaho is 1 of 17 states to employ prior appropriation to the exclusion of the riparian doctrine. However, it should be noted that each state operates independently of each other. Thus, the administration of the rights will differ from state to state.

All the waters of the state, when flowing in their natural channels, including the waters of all natural springs and lakes within the boundaries of the state are declared to be the property of the state.

**IDWR website**
www.idwr.idaho.gov

The Idaho Department Of Water Resources (IDWR) is the regulatory agency that administers water rights and has a duty to supervise the appropriation and allotment for beneficial purposes.

**First in time, First in right**
IC 42-106

## Priority Date

As mentioned above, 'first in time, first in right' will create a priority date. It determines who gets water when there is a shortage. If there isn't enough water to satisfy all of the water rights, then the oldest or senior water rights are satisfied first and so on in order until there is no water left. It is the new or junior water rights that do not get water when there isn't enough to satisfy all the water rights.

**½ acre limitation**
IC 42-111

## Domestic water usage

The use of water for homes and any other purpose in connection with home type use is limited to irrigation up to ½ acre of land. The total use of water is not to exceed 13,000 gallons per day.

A real estate licensee needs to be very careful when listing homes on small ranchette type properties that appear to be irrigated from a domestic well, especially if more than ½ acre is being irrigated. Infrared sensors from satellites can easily identify those parcels in which violations are occurring.

It is certainly possible that the smaller parcels are irrigated with multiple water rights for domestic uses. However, such use shall not be exercised in a manner to satisfy a single combined water use or purpose. The purpose of the limitation is to prohibit the diversion and use of water to supply a use that does not meet the domestic use definition.

**Required drilling permit**
IC 42-238

## Well drilling permit required

A well cannot be drilled in Idaho without a licensed well driller and operator of drilling equipment. In addition, a well cannot be abandoned unless a report is submitted to the director of the IDWR describing the abandonment by a licensed well driller.

**5 year rule - use**
IC 42-222 (2)

## Use it or lose it

If after the holder of the water right has ceased to put the water to a beneficial use for a period of 5 continuous years the use of the water will be lost and forfeited. Such lost right shall revert to the state and be again subject to appropriation.

| | |
|---|---|
| **Right to petition**<br>42-1701A | The water right holder shall have the right to an administrative hearing if requested in writing 15 days from the date of service of the order to petition for reinstatement. |

**Recharge water**
IC 42-4201

## Recharge ground water

Unforseen circumstances such as drought, lack of snow pack, and other situations that could jeopardize ground water basins could leave water users high and dry. Idaho's farmers have done an excellent job with water conservation and irrigation practices.

However, some of the conservation practices could in fact reduce the amount of natural recharge into the ground water.

In order to minimize excessive draw down of aquifer storage, the IDWR has the authority to appropriate recharge from the Snake River. The purpose is to replace the waters displaced from the aquifer.

**Minimum 212 degrees**
IC 42-4002

## Geothermal Energy

In Idaho, a geothermal resource is defined as ground water having a temperature of 212 degrees Fahrenheit or more in the bottom of a well. Being neither a mineral nor water resource, geothermal resources are considered *sui generis* because of the close relationship to each other.

In order to secure geothermal energy, one has to make application for a geothermal resource well permit from the Idaho Department of Water Resources.

Water has been and will continue to be a very important aspect of property ownership. It is very important that real estate licensees and the public are both aware of water law and the use of water in Idaho. In the old days, we had 'range wars'. Today, many parts of the country are experiencing 'water wars'.

**Selling water rights**
IC 42-2604

## Sale of Water Rights

All contracts and deeds for the sale of water rights shall be in the form approved by the Department of Water Resources. The contracts or deeds shall be numbered plainly and consecutively. It shall be the duty of the owner of such irrigation works to file for record in the proper county recorder's office.

The IDWR will determine the number of water rights, units or shares of water which may be sold and the number of acres which may be irrigated. The purchasers will receive a certificate in appropriate form certifying or showing the amount of water rights which may be sold. The certificate will then be recorded in the county recorder's office in each county in which the lands are located.

**MH Salesperson licensing**
IC 44-2101A (13)

## Manufactured Homes

Idaho ranks #16 in the nation with 10.9% of total housing being manufactured/mobile homes. The classification of manufactured/mobile homes is somewhat unique. They can be classified as personal property, real property, or a combination of both. Adding to the confusion, the licensing of salespeople is also a little unique. A salesperson employed with a manufactured home retailer must be licensed and can sell new or used units (personal property). However, unless that salesperson also has a real estate license, they cannot sell real property.

**Licensed real estate agents**
IC 54-2003 (3)


IC 44-2106

Licensed real estate agents, on the other hand, can sell personal property while acting on behalf of another, for compensation or the expectation of compensation: sells, lists, buys or negotiates, or offers to sell, list, buy or negotiate, the purchase or sale of a *mobile home, manufactured home or floating home* as defined by Idaho law. If the licensed real estate agent is employed with a manufactured home retailer, they must be properly licensed if they offer for resale more than 2 units per year.

**Transfer to real property**
IC 63-304

## Transfer to real property

If a manufactured/mobile home is sold as personal property, a certificate of title will be used to transfer ownership. The running gear must be removed and the land must be owned by the owner of a manufactured/mobile home. When the manufactured/mobile home is properly affixed to a permanent foundation and the owner has properly declared and recorded, in the county the manufacture/mobile home is situated, it will be reclassified as 'real' property.

# Figure 1 – Manufactured Home application to declare real property

## STATEMENT OF INTENT TO DECLARE
## MANUFACTURED HOME REAL PROPERTY

| | |
|---|---|
| Owner Name(s): | |
| Mailing Address: | |
| Property Address: | |
| Legal Description: | |

| Real Property Parcel #: | Manufactured Home Parcel #: |
|---|---|

| Land Ownership: | ☐ Deed ☐ Contract of Sale | ☐ Recorded ☐ Unrecorded |
|---|---|---|

| Manufactured Home Description: | Make: | Model: | Year: |
|---|---|---|---|

| Serial Number: | Size: | Lien Holder, if any: |
|---|---|---|

The undersigned, being duly sworn, states that the above information is true and correct, and does hereby exercise a STATEMENT OF INTENT, declaring the above manufactured home to constitute real property according to Section 63-307B, Idaho Code. The undersigned further represents that the running gear of the home has been removed and that the manufactured home will be permanently affixed to a foundation on land which is owned or being purchased by the owner or purchaser of the manufactured home.

| Signature: | Date: | Signature: | Date: |
|---|---|---|---|

STATE OF IDAHO      )
                            ) ss.
COUNTY OF ADA      )

On this _____ day of _____, 20____, before me, the undersigned notary public in and for said State, personally appeared _____ or identified to me to be the person(s) whose name(s) is/are subscribed to the within instrument, and acknowledged to me that ___he___ executed the same.

IN WITNESS WHEREOF, I have hereunto set my hand and affixed my official seal the day and year in this Statement first above written.

                    (SEAL)

Notary Public in and for the STATE of IDAHO

Residing at_____, Idaho

Commission Expires _____

Signatures - Pursuant to Section 63-307B, Idaho Code

BUILDING & ZONING DEPARTMENT OR OTHER AUTHORIZED OFFICIAL:

    A. Removal of running gear.
    B. Permanently affixed to a foundation.
      (See Idaho Code § 44-2205)

| Authorized Signature | Date |
|---|---|

COUNTY ASSESSOR

    Ownership of land and manufactured home.
    Payment of sales tax on new manufactured home verified.

| Authorized Signature | Date |
|---|---|

CONSENT OF LIENHOLDER: _____
                        Name / Company

| Authorized Signature | Date |
|---|---|

# Questions – Chapter 5

1. An example of 'chattel' is?

   A. A stand of trees
   B. A newly constructed home
   C. A building lot
   D. Annual growing crops

2. Personal property is transferred with what type of instrument?

   A. Certificate of Sale
   B. Bill of Sale
   C. Deed
   D. Title

3. Who 'own's the water in Idaho

   A. Federal government
   B. State of Idaho
   C. Irrigation districts
   D. Individual property owner

4. Domestic water usage for land irrigation is limited to?

   A. Unlimited
   B. 5 acres
   C. 1 acre
   D. ½ acre

5. Daily use of domestic water is not to exceed how many gallons per day?

   A. 1,000
   B. 5,000
   C. 10,000
   D. 13,000

6. A holder of a water right can lose a water right if not used for what continuous period of time?

   A. 1 year
   B. 3 years
   C. 5 years
   D. 7 years

7. Who is required to notify the Idaho Department of Water Resources to abandon a water well?

   A. Property owner
   B. Central Health District
   C. Licensed well driller
   D. Building permit department

8. Who has the authority to appropriate ground water recharge?

   A. Idaho Department of Water Resources
   B. State of Idaho
   C. The member's irrigation district
   D. The property owner

9. Unless declared as real property, manufactured home ownership will be transferred with:

   A. Certificate of Title
   B. Bill of Sale
   C. Deed
   D. Certificate of Sale

# Chapter 6

# Legal Descriptions

**Types of legal descriptions**

Before real estate can be transferred from one party to another, an adequate legal description must be identified. There are three different types of legal descriptions that can be used to meet Idaho requirements. They are:

- Government Rectangular Survey
- Metes and bounds
- Recorded plat (lot and block)

One of the above systems will be used to properly and completely identify the property that is to be transferred. Street address or tax parcel number alone will not meet acceptable standards to transfer property. A legal description must be able to adequately describe the exact size, shape and location of the property.

The basis for all surveys of the United States is based on a 'standardized' survey system under an ordinance of the Continental Congress passed in 1785 and officially adopted by the government in 1805.

## Government Rectangular Survey System

**Initial Point**

(Figure 1)

The rectangular survey system requires a 'initial' point from which all surveys originate. In Idaho, the 'initial' point is located on top of a lava butte one mile east of the Swan Falls Road out of Kuna, just east of the Kuna Caves. The initial point was established in 1867 and is identified with a U. S. Geological Survey brass marker.

Where the east/west base line (latitude - N43°22' 31") intersects with the north/south longitude line (longitude 116 ° 24' 15"), it serves as the initial point which is the basis of all legal descriptions in Idaho.

**Boise Meridian**

This starting point is referenced as the Boise Meridian also known as B.M. Remember, the government rectangular survey system utilizes the concept of township and range. Township 65 North (T65N) is the most northern township and Township 16 South (T65S) is the most southern township.

The western border is Range 6 West (R6W) and the eastern border is Range 46 East (R46E). Given these coordinates, one could say that Idaho is 486 miles long and 312 miles wide.

## Metes-And-Bounds

**Metes-And-Bounds**

Properties that cannot be described by the government rectangular system will be irregular in shape and described with longitude and latitude bearings in feet including tenths or hundreds of a foot. It is important to note that inches are not used at anytime to identify the length or width of property.

Identification of these irregular lots must be prepared by a licensed surveyor and a legal description prepared from the survey. The initial point of beginning (POB) will be a corner of a section or township that connects the metes-and-bounds to the government rectangular survey. The actual point of beginning will be a point of the metes-and-bounds description. In order to have a 'closed' legal description, the actual point of beginning will begin and end at the same point.

To assure accurateness, some surveyors will triangulate the legal description from two different initial points. If they both come up with the same results, the description has minimized errors.

## Recorded Plat
IC 50-1301 (15)

(Figure 2)

**Recorded Plat**

Recorded plats are used for developments that consist of multiple lots. Idaho Code describes a subdivision as a tract of land divided into 5 or more lots, parcels, or sites for the purpose of sale or building development.

A bone fide division or partition of agricultural land for agricultural purposes will be a division of land into lots, all of which are 5 acres or larger and maintained as agricultural lands.

It is important to know that cities or counties may adopt their own definition of subdivision in lieu of the state code and may be more restrictive.

After a subdivision has been formally approved and recorded in the county in which the property is located, the legal description will reference lot and block of a specified subdivision; example might read - lot 4 block 7, Sunnyside Slope, Ada County, Idaho.

Within the plat will be reference to the government rectangular description, metes and bounds description, and finally the lot and block identification. Because the plat contains all the necessary items to create a valid legal description, reference by lot and block uncomplicates the process for easier identification.

**Air Lots**
55-1504

## Air Lots

Like other legal descriptions, a licensed surveyor will prepare the plat to identify 'air lots' in which condominiums are identified. Each unit is identified by elevation but later referred to as a particular unit within an approved and recorded plat.

**Condominium**
**Elevations**
IC 55-1504 (ii)

The Condominium Property Act identifies elevations with diagrammatic floor plans in sufficient detail to identify each unit, its relative location and approximate dimensions, showing elevations where multi-level or multi-story structures are diagramed.

Most cities have a local official datum(s) for surveyors to use for an initial point of elevation. As a note, most airports (even the little ones) have a elevation point located somewhere near or on a runway for elevation verification.

Although not used directly for legal descriptions, topography or contour maps are very useful to identify elevations. Topo maps are helpful with large development plans for planned view sites, roadways, common areas, and other important factors to determine feasability.

**90 days to record**
IC 55-1901

## Recording of Surveys

After a survey has been completed, a record of survey shall be filed within 90 days after completing a survey that:

1. Discloses a material discrepancy with previous surveys of record;

2. Establishes boundary lines and/or corners not previously existing or of record;

3. Results in the setting of monuments at corners of record which were not previously monumented;

4. Produces evidence or information which varies from, or is not contained in, surveys of record relating to the public land survey, lost public land corners or obliterated land survey corners.

**Monuments**
IC 54-1234

## Survey Monuments

A land survey, performed by a licensed professional land surveyor, is to set permanent and reliable, magnetically detectable monuments. The minimum size shall be at least ½" in diameter and 2 feet long. Such monuments must be permanently marked with the license number of the surveyor placing the monument.

If any person willfully defaces or removes a survey marker, the penalty is $500 for each offence plus damages sustained by the affected parties.

**Right to use**
IC 55-603

## Easements

Because easements provide the right to use the land of another for a particular purpose, it is very important for all parties to know and understand an easement can create serious limitations. Remember, easements transfer with property.

Some examples of limitations are: ingress, egress, set back requirements, solar easements, utilities, etc. etc.

Any easements, contained within a legal description, need to be reviewed very, very carefully.

A transfer of real property passes all and creates in favor of an easement to use other real property of the person whose estate is transferred. Such property was obviously and permanently used for the benefit and by the person at the time when the transfer was agreed upon or completed.

Another issue of easements being coordinated into legal descriptions is to identify limitations or restrictions.

**View easements**

For example, hillside view lots may need protection to preserve the views with 'view easements' that basically restricts other improvements or foliage from blocking views from the subject property. These types of restrictions may not be directly addressed in the legal description but rather in the CCR's.

**Double Check Descriptions**

The transfer of real property from one party to another is evidenced by a proper and correct legal description. It is very important that real estate licensees double check legal descriptions at closing to verify exactly what is being transferred.

If property lines are important to either the buyer or the seller, perhaps a new survey would be in order to assure all parties exactly where the property lines are located. It's not unusual to have fences erected outside or inside the property lines. Accurate legal descriptions are especially important when dealing with commercial properties. Zero lot lines can often overlap causing delays and even transaction cancellations.

Figure 1 – Boise Meridian and Initial Point

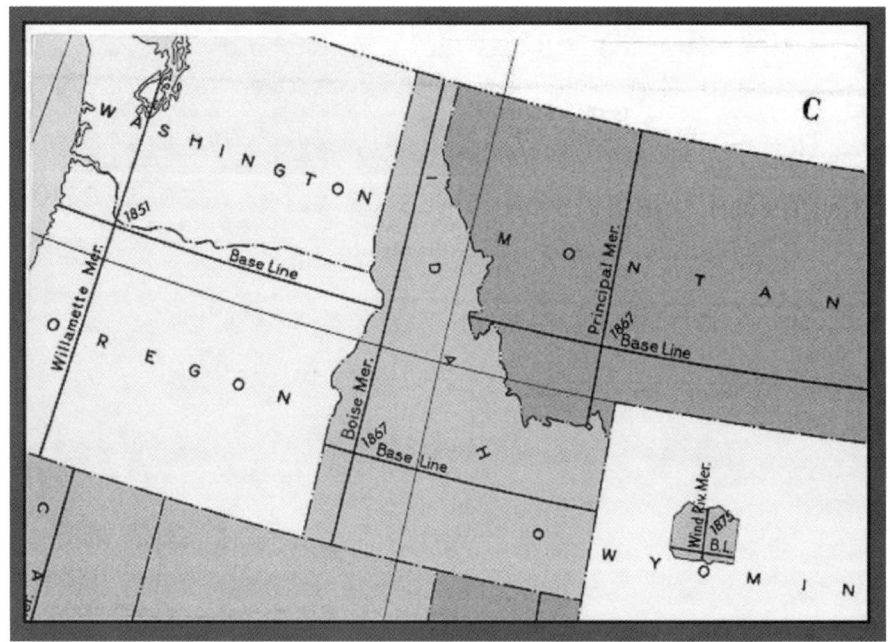

Figure 2 – Plat map and lots

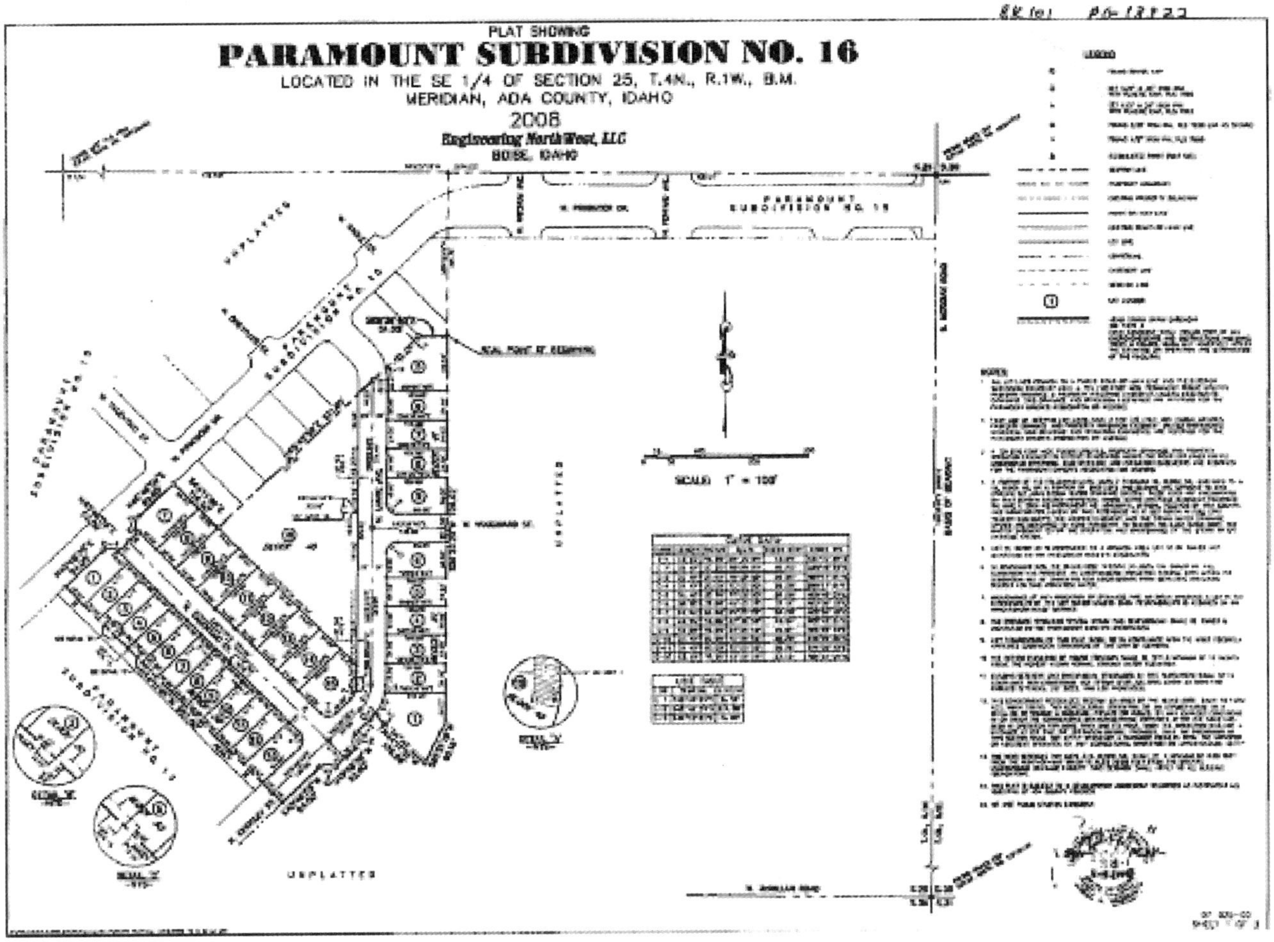

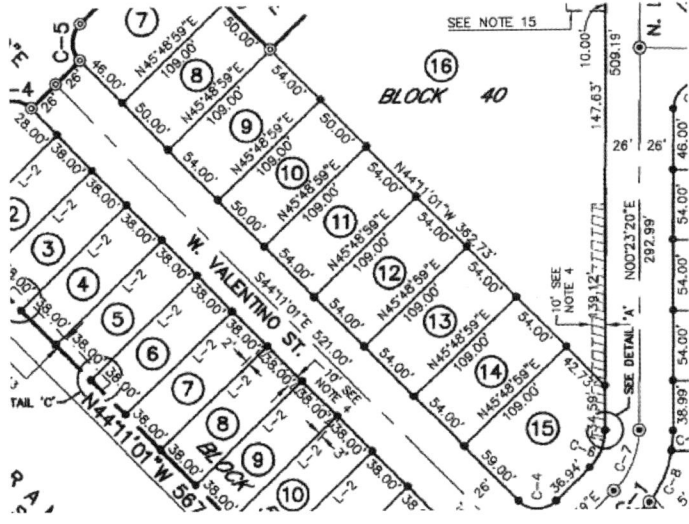

# Questions – Chapter 6

1. How many different types of surveys are recognized in Idaho.

   A. One
   B. Two
   C. Three
   D. Four

2. What type of description will not meet acceptable standards to transfer property.

   A. Tax parcel number
   B. Government Rectangular Survey
   C. Metes and Bounds
   D. Recorded plat

3. The 'initial point' (Boise Meridian) is closest to what community?

   A. Meridian
   B. Boise
   C. Nampa
   D. Kuna

4. What township borders Canada?

   A. Township 16 North
   B. Township 56 North
   C. Township 65 North
   D. Township 85 North

5. If the western border is Range 6 west and the eastern border is Range 46 east, how wide is Idaho

   A. 276
   B. 282
   C. 312
   D. 360

6. Idaho describes a subdivision as a tract of land divided into at least how many lots for the purpose of sale or development?

   A. 3
   B. 5
   C. 7
   D. 9

7. A legal description using 'lot and block' is using what method to describe the parcel?

   A. Tax parcel number
   B. Government Rectangular Survey
   C. Metes and Bounds
   D. Recorded plat

8. What period of time does a completed record of survey need to be filed?

   A. 90 days
   B. 120 days
   C. 180 days
   D. 365 days

9. The minimum size of survey pins shall be not less than:

   A. ½ inch diameter and 2 feet long
   B. ¼ inch diameter by 1 foot long
   C. ½ inch diameter by 1 foot long
   D. ⅞ inch diameter by 2 feet long

# Chapter 7

# Real Estate Interests

**Fee Simple Estate**

A fee simple estate is the highest estate possible and gives the holder all rights to the property. Unless expressed otherwise, Idaho law presumes fee simple interest will be conveyed.

But it isn't unusual to own property that is subject to various limitations with the transfer of a fee simple estate which is known as a defeasible fee estate. A defeasible fee estate, also known as fee simple qualified, is created.

**Defeasible estate**

A defeasible estate is subject to the occurrence or nonoccurrence of something happening. Words such as 'while', 'provided that', 'so long as', and 'during the period' are examples that can be incorporated by the grantor for the transfer.

**3 Limitations**

Limitations created by the grantor for a qualified fee estate fall into three categories - determinable, condition subsequent, and condition precedent.

An example of condition determinable - Mr. Harris donates a parcel of land to a school district *so long as* it is used for elementary education. But, if some other use is made, then the land reverts back to the grantor (Mr. Harris).

An example of condition subsequent - In the example above, Mr. Harris would have the right to re-enter and take the property back when it no longer is used for education.

An example of condition precedent - Transfer of ownership would not occur until a condition is performed. Using the same example above, the transfer wouldn't occur until the school is built and is actually in operation.

An estate that cannot be for a definite period of time but rather for the duration of one's life is known as a life estate.

**Life estate**

A life estate conveys an estate for the duration of someone's life that can be tied to the life of the life tenant or to a third party. Upon death, the life estate will convey to the named remainderman.  Even though a remainderman has been named, the mere possibility (based on expectation) is not transferable.

Statutory or legal estates are created by state law and include dower, curtesy, and community property.  Like most states,  Idaho has abolished dower and curtesy and advocates community property.  Idaho, together with 7 other states, (Arizona, California, Louisiana, Nevada, New Mexico, and Washington) statutorily incorporate community property.

# Homestead

**Homestead Protection**
IC 55-1003

## Homestead Protection
Another legal life estate offers homestead protection.  Homestead rights don't exist under common law but 27 states have enacted homestead protection including Idaho.

**Protects against unsecured creditors**

The home or property is protected by law from *unsecured creditors* during the occupants lifetime.  The owner can only have one homestead at a time.

**Up to $100,000 protection**

## $100,000 Maximum Protection
In Idaho, the homestead protection (exemption) includes the net value of the dwelling, manufactured home, lands, and improvements not to exceed $100,000.

**Homestead automatic**

Homestead exemption is automatic in Idaho providing:

- The property must be occupied as the principal residence;

**Minimum 6 month occupancy**

- Property must be occupied for a continuous period of at least 6 months;

- If the property is land and is not occupied, a declaration of homestead must be filed.

If the owner already resides on a parcel of property that has a claim of homestead but wants to move to another piece of property which they also own, what must they do?

The owner must file a declaration of abandonment on the property they reside and also file a declaration of homestead for the new location. The declaration(s) must be filed in the county or counties where the property(s) are located.

The declaration of homestead must contain:
1. A statement that the person making it is residing on the premises or intends to reside thereon and claims the premises as a homestead;
2. A legal description of the premises;
3. An estimate of the premises actual cash value.

The declaration of abandonment must contain:
1. A statement that the premises occupied as a residence or claimed as a homestead no longer constitutes the owner's homestead;
2. A legal description of the premises;
3. A statement of the date of abandonment.

## Leasehold Estates

The creation of occupancy with a landlord/tenant relationship becomes a contract between landlord and tenant.

**Statute of Frauds**
IC 9-505

The lease or rental agreement can be oral or in writing if the agreement is for less than one year. However, the Statute of Frauds does state that an agreement to rent or lease for longer than one year is invalid unless the agreement is in writing.

As a precaution to having an invalid contract, it would be advisable to have a rental/lease agreement in writing regardless of the time frame.

## Rental property maintenance

During the tenant's occupancy, the landlord must maintain the premises and protect the tenant's health and safety. The landlord must comply with city and county ordinances together with state laws regarding housing conditions.

Examples that could contribute to violations could include:

- Missing doors or windows
- Defective plumbing
- Exposed wiring
- Non-functioning heating
- Insect infestation
- Leaks

**Specific performance**
IC 6-323 (6) (d)

## Tenant remedies

The tenant must provide the landlord a written list of the violations in person, certified mail, or with an employee at the landlord's usual place of business.

The landlord has 3 days to fix the violations. Failure to fix the problems allows the tenant to sue for compliance. The landlord will receive a summons and complaint at least 5 days before trial.

## Landlord remedies

If the tenant damages the property through carelessness or negligence, the tenant may be required to pay the landlord for damages and may even be evicted.

Like the tenant remedies, the landlord must give written notice of the violation(s) and be delivered in person or left with a competent person at the tenant's residence or place of business If the tenant is unavailable, the landlord must post a copy of the notice in a conspicuous place on the property or leave a copy with any person living at the property and mail a copy to the tenant at the property address.

The tenant now has 3 days to fix the problem. Failure of the tenant to fix the problem gives the landlord the right to evict the tenant and recover costs for repair of the damage.

If the landlord has reasonable grounds to believe any person is or has been engaged in the unlawful delivery, production, or use of a controlled substance, the landlord can initiate immediate eviction proceedings.

**Termination**
IC 55-208

## Evictions

Proper 3 day or 30 day written notice must be given depending on the circumstances.

The 3 day notice is only available if the tenant:

- Failed to pay rent
- Violated the terms of the rental or lease agreement
- Engaged in an unlawful activity (landlord is obligated to report the crime).

**Unlawful Detainer**
IC 6-303

## Unlawful Detainer Action

If, upon proper notice to the tenant, the tenant fails to comply with the terms of the notice, the landlord must file an unlawful detainer action to force the tenant to leave the property.

A quick trial procedure is available for the landlord to regain possession within 5 to 12 days after the tenant receives notice for past due rent or illegal drug activity.

The landlord must serve the tenant with a summons and complaint for a lease violation. The tenant has 20 days to file an answer. If the tenant does not comply by a court ordered date, the sheriff, through a writ of restitution, removes the tenant, along with the tenant's property, from the rental.

**Change in lease terms**
IC 55-307

## Rent increases - month-to-month tenancy

If the landlord plans to increase the month-to-month rent, the landlord must provide a written notice at least 15 days before the increase becomes effective.

**Termination**
IC 55-208

## Termination - month to month tenancy

With a month-to-month tenancy or tenancy at will, the landlord must give the tenant written notice within a period of not less than 1 month to vacate. The tenant, in reverse, must give the landlord written notice of vacating the premises not less than 1 month from the date of such notice.

| Security deposit refund | **Security Deposits** |
|---|---|

**Security deposit refund**
IC 6-321

## Security Deposits

Deposits with the landlord other than payment for rent shall be deemed security deposits. With the exception of 'normal wear and tear', security deposit refunds shall be made within 21 days if no time is fixed by agreement. Such refund shall be made within 30 days after the surrender of the premises by the tenant.

Any amount refunded less than the deposited security deposit shall be accompanied with a detailed statement itemizing the amounts that are retained by the landlord.

# Mobile Home Park Landlord-Tenant Act

**Idaho Code - Ch. 20**
IC 55-2001 thru 2019

## Purpose

Because of the nature of a manufactured/mobile home and the fact it could be moved or relocated, the Mobile Home Park Landlord Tenant Act was created in 1980. The purpose of the act is to address issues not covered under the basic laws of the typical landlord-tenant laws between park owners and park tenants.

**Agreement required**

## Rental agreement

The landlord offering a lot for rent shall provide the prospective tenant a *written* rental agreement.

**Agreement changes**

Any changes to rent, services, utilities or rules require a 90 day notice to tenants. A rental agreement may include an escalation clause for increases or decreases in the park's taxes, utilities or other services. Rules cannot exceed one change in each category per 6 month period and shall be fairly and uniformly enforced.

**Landlord protection**

## Past due rent protection to landlord

If the tenant becomes 60 days late in rent, the landlord can notify and advise the lienholder of the liability for space rent owing. The lienholder shall be responsible for utilities from the date of notice. However, the landlord shall be entitled to a maximum of 60 days of rent due prior to notice to the lienholder.

Any and all costs then become the responsibility of the legal owner or lienholder. The manufactured/mobile home cannot be removed from the space without written landlord approval.

**Rental agreement termination**

## Rental agreement termination

Repeated violations of written rules or non payment of rent or other charges require the tenant to receive written notice of such violations. If the tenant doesn't comply within 3 days, the tenant may be given a 20 day notice to vacate.

If the tenant no longer intends to renew a rental agreement, written notice is to be provided to the landlord 30 days prior to renewal date.

If the landlord terminates the agreement by not renewing, the landlord shall give written notice to the tenant not less than 180 days prior to the expiration date of the rental agreement.

If notification is not given by either party, the rental agreement renewals are automatic.

**Retaliatory conduct**

## Retaliatory conduct by landlord

The landlord shall not terminate a tenancy, refuse to renew, increase rent, or decrease services normally supplied, or threaten repossession of a manufactured/mobile home because the tenant has complained about:
- health and safety issues
- maintenance or condition of the park
- rent charged
- rules and regulations

# Floating Homes Residency Act

### What is a moorage marina?

**IC 55-2701 thru 55-2720**

A floating home moorage marina is a waterfront facility for the moorage of 1 or more floating homes and the land and water premises on which it is located.

Some issues need to be addressed due to limited availability of moorage sites and the cost of relocating floating homes.

## Rental agreement

Any landlord offering a moorage site for rent shall provide a written agreement to be executed by both parties.

The term of a rental agreement shall be for 12 months unless the landlord and tenant agree to a lessor or longer period. The agreement shall identify the specific moorage site and remain site specific unless agreed upon by landlord and tenant.

Rental rates shall be reasonable with a minimum of 90 day written notice to increase or decrease such rates prior to expiration of any existing rental agreement. All things being equal, rental increases shall be uniform throughout the floating home marina.

If a master meter for utilities is provided, the cost of the utilities must be separately stated in each billing period. The landlord must also post the current rates charged by the utility in at least 1 conspicuous place in the marina.

If 25% or more of the tenants within a marina disagree with what may be termed 'reasonable', the dispute will be resolved by arbitration.

## Rental renewal

The landlord shall not terminate or refuse to renew a rental agreement without first giving a written notice to the tenant to remove the floating home from the marina within a period of not less than 90 days specified in the notice.

## Eviction

Grounds for eviction in which a tenancy may be terminated are:

- Conduct constituting a nuisance
- Repeated violations of reasonable rules and regulations
- Non payment of rent
- Other material breach
- Condemnation of the marina

# Questions – Chapter 7

1. Homestead protection protects the home or property from:

   A. Bankruptcy
   B. Secured lenders
   C. Automobile repossession
   D. Unsecured creditors

2. The maximum net value of the dwelling for homestead protection is:

   A. $ 50,000
   B. $ 75,000
   C. $100,000
   D. $125,000

3. To qualify for homestead protection in Idaho, the property must be occupied for a continuous period of:

   A. Only needs to be owned, not occupied
   B. Occupied 100% of the time
   C. At least 6 months out of the year
   D. Not less than 1 year

4. An owner moves from one permanent residence to another. What must the owner do to receive homestead protection.

   A. Nothing is necessary; homestead protection is automatic
   B. File for a new declaration of homestead
   C. File for abandonment
   D. File for abandonment and file a declaration for homestead for the new location.

5. An verbal lease for more than one year is:

   A. Valid
   B. Illegal
   C. Worthless
   D. Invalid

6. What kind of notice must the tenant provide the landlord to get a water heater replaced?

   A. Written notice
   B. Certified mail
   C. Leave a voice mail
   D. Email

7. Given proper notice, how long does a landlord have to resolve a violation

   A. 1 day
   B. 3 days
   C. 5 days
   D. 7 days

8. If a landlord plans to increase the rent on a month-to-month rental, how much notice must be given?

   A. At least 7 days notice
   B. At least 15 days notice
   C. At least 30 days notice
   D. Not less than 1 month

9. How much advance notice to terminate a month to month tenancy is required?

   A. At least 7 days notice
   B. At least 15 days notice
   C. At least 30 days notice
   D. Not less than one month

10. After a tenant surrenders premises, security
    deposit refunds must be made within:

    A.  10 days
    B.  21 days
    C.  30 days
    D.  60 days

11. Lot rent for a manufactured home is
    required to be:

    A.  In writing
    B.  At least verbal
    C.  Recorded in county records
    D.  Filed with county assessor

12  How much notice to tenant is required to
    increase utilities in a mobile home park?

    A.  30 days
    B.  60 days
    C.  90 days
    D.  120 days

13. How much advance notice must a landlord
    of a mobile home park give to the tenant to
    not renew a lot lease prior to expiration?

    A.  Not less than 180 days
    B.  Not less than 90 days notice
    C.  Not less than 60 days notice
    D.  Not less than 30 days notice

# Chapter 8

# Forms of Ownership and How Ownership is Held

Choosing a form of ownership and deciding on how ownership shall be held should be carefully evaluated before advising or making any decisions. If there are any questions whatsoever, competent legal and tax advisors should be consulted.

## Sole Ownership

Sole ownership is also known as severalty or to 'sever from all others' and is the simplest form of ownership since it only involves one owner or entity.

As a reminder, it should be noted that different types of business ownerships involve single entities. Some examples include:
- Partnerships
- Corporations
- Limited Liability Companies
- Real Estate Investment Trusts
- Land Trusts
- Joint Ventures

A popular type of business ownership is a limited liability company. It's not unusual to find commercial real estate to be owned by a limited liability company. Idaho has a complete chapter in the Idaho Code known as the Idaho Uniform Limited Liability Company Act.

**Title 30, Chapter 6**
**IC 30-6-201**

## Limited Liability Company

Some highlights surrounding a limited liability company in Idaho is that the company must reserve a name which the Secretary of State shall reserve for 4 months.

The formation of a limited liability company can consist of one or more persons by signing articles of organization and delivering the signed articles to the Secretary of State for filing.

**Annual report**
**IC 30-6-209**

An annual report of a limited liability company shall be delivered to the Secretary of State each year before the end of the month the company was organized.

**Failure to report**
IC 30-6-705

It is very important that the LLC not forget to file the annual report. Failure to deliver its annual report to the Secretary of State can be grounds for an administrative dissolution.

However, reinstatement is possible if application is made to the Secretary of State for reinstatement within 10 years after the effective date of the dissolution.

# Two or more owners

**2 or more owners**
IC 6-416

## Default for 2 or more owners
When 2 or more people own real estate in Idaho, the default will be tenants in common unless specified differently. The ownership interests will be equal unless stated otherwise. Tenants in common can hold unequal interest in ownership but the deed must state the percentage of ownership.

Because there are so many different types of ownership, they can result in making different ownership allocations and possible tax consequences. It is always advisable to consult legal and tax counsel if an owner is unsure of what type of ownership best suits their needs.

## Tenancy by the entirety
Because of potential conflicts with Idaho community property statutes, tenancy by the entirety cannot be used. However, it can be used on property that either spouse owns separately. The conveyance needs to state the intention to be with the right of survivorship and not as community property or another forms of co-ownership.

# Community Property

**Common Law Marriage**
IC 32-209

## Common Law Marriage
Common law marriage was outlawed on January 1, 1996 but shall not invalidate any marriage created by consenting parties prior to January 1, 1996.

Consent alone will not constitute marriage. However, with the law now requiring the issuance of a marriage license, common law marriage prior to January 1, 1996 will not be invalidated.

To be legally married, both male and female must be 18 years of age or older. If the male is at least 18, the female can be 16 years of age, provided written consent is obtained by the father, mother or guardian.

In Idaho, marriage arises out of a civil contract between a *man and woman*. Consent or mutual assumption alone will not constitute marriage. It must be followed by the issuance of a license and a solemnization as authorized by law.

**Sole and separate**
IC 32-903

## Community Property

All property of either husband or wife owned prior to marriage or received afterward as gift, bequest, or acquired with proceeds of his or her separate property shall remain his or her sole property.

**Any income community**
IC 32-906

## Income is community property

All other property acquired after marriage is community property and any income including rents and profits of all property, separate or community, is community property. The exception would be if both spouses, by written agreement, specifically state it will be treated as separate property of one of the spouses. However, any property maintained as 'sole and separate' must be just that; no co-mingling of funds for maintenance.

**One party binding another**
IC 32-912

## Binding Community Property

Either the husband or wife shall have the right to manage and control community property and either may bind the community property by contract. Neither the husband nor wife may sell, convey or encumber the community real estate unless the other joins in. However, either the husband or wife may give to the other by expressed power of attorney, the right to sell, convey or encumber community property.

**Right of Survivorship**
IC 15-6-401

## Right of Survivorship in Real Property

Effective July 1, 2008, Idaho authorized real property held by a married couple as 'community property with rights of survivorship'. The new law allows married couples an income tax basis step-up for the entire community real property and a simple title transfer through the 'joint tenancy' designation.

This allows transfer of the real estate to the surviving joint tenant by recordation of a death certificate in the county where the real estate is held, thereby avoiding a probate of such real estate. However, one should consult legal or accounting counsel to make sure there isn't conflict with estate and tax planning.

# Questions – Chapter 8

1. A partnership, 'ABC Partners', constitutes what type of ownership?

   A. Tenants in common
   B. Sole ownership
   C. Tenancy by the entirety
   D. Community property

2. The formation of a limited liability company is filed with:

   A. Secretary of State
   B. Attorney General
   C. State Tax Commission
   D. Department of Insurance

3. Failure of an LLC to file an annual report can result in:

   A. Mandatory audit from IRS
   B. State imposed fine
   C. Administrative dissolution
   D. Loss of business license

4. All property of either husband or wife acquired prior to marriage shall remain:

   A. Community property
   B. In trust
   C. Tenants in common
   D. Sole and separate

5. Unless stated otherwise, any income or profits from all property after marriage, separate or community, will be treated as:

   A. Sole and separate
   B. Community property
   C. Both sole and community property
   D. Limited liability partnership

6. When is the annual report by a limited liability company to be filed?

   A. Before the last day of the current year
   B. No later than Jan 1 of following year
   C. No later than April 15 of the following year
   D. Before the end of month company was organized

7. 'Community property with rights of survivorship' will:

   A. Avoid probate
   B. Automatically requires probate
   C. Delay probate
   D. Requires separated probate action

8. If an LLC is dissolved, an application for reinstatement may be possible if filed within what period of being dissolved?

   A. Cannot be reinstated
   B. 1 year
   C. 5 years
   D. 10 years

# Chapter 9

# Transferring Title to Real Estate

Different events can trigger the transfer of title or ownership of real estate. Examples of such events include:

- Death of an owner
- Ownership by accession
- Title by occupancy
- Voluntary and involuntary transfer

**Evidence of death**
IC 15-1-107

## Death of an owner

A certified or authenticated copy of a death certificate by an official or agency is prima facie proof of the fact, place, date, and time of death of the decedent.

The issue of a person means all of his lineal descendants of all generations, with the relationship of a parent and child of each generation, being determined by the definitions of a child and parent contained in the Idaho code.

**Intestate distribution**
IC 15-2-102

## Distribution without a will   (intestate)

Upon death of a married person living in Idaho who does not have a will, the intestate share of the surviving spouse's distribution will be as follows:

Separate Property
- If there is no surviving issue or parent of the decedent, the entire intestate estate
- If there is no surviving issue but the decedent is survived by a parent or parents, ½ of the intestate estate
- If there is no surviving issue of the deceased spouse, ½ of the intestate estate

Community Property
- ½ of community property which belongs to the decedent passes to the surviving spouse

If there is no surviving spouse, equal distribution will be made to kinship. If there is no kinship, then equal distribution to the parent or parents. If there is no surviving issue or parent, the distribution will go down the line to one or more grandparents and so on.

**Legal age**
IC 15-2 (29)

## Distribution with a will   (testate)

In Idaho, a person of legal capacity must be 18 years of age or older to make a will. A will can be prepared anytime during the property owner's lifetime but cannot take effect until the owner's death.

**Witnessed will**
IC 15-3-101

The person making the will is known as the testator. The will must be signed and witnessed by at least two persons. A verbal will (noncupative) may be made under special circumstances in immediate anticipation of the maker's death. Idaho Probate Code does not have any provision for the use or enforceability of this type of will.

## Ownership by accession

One example of accession can include shoreline property in which natural forces can increase the shoreline with soil washing up and depositing onto the shoreline. Or, if the water line is permanently reduced, the land can 'grow' in size.

Because Idaho owns all the water, it also regulates and controls the use or disposition of lands in the beds of navigable lakes, rivers and streams, to the natural or ordinary high water mark.

**High water mark**
IC 58-104 (9)

The natural or ordinary high water mark is defined to be the line which the water impresses on the soil by covering it for sufficient periods to deprive the soil of its vegetation and destroy its value for agricultural purposes.

Another example of accession is with the addition of an improvement that becomes a permanent fixture upon the land. A home, building, sidewalks, and even fences are examples of 'adding to the land'.

## Transfer by occupancy

With the adoption of the Homestead Act of 1862, a tract of unoccupied public land, 160 acres in area, could be permanently acquired after 5 years of continuous occupancy and payment of a fee. Expansion of this concept led to 'squatters rights' which in turn, works off the doctrine of possession and the statute of limitations.

In Idaho, a property must be held and possessed adversely for 20 years. A person claiming adverse possession must present clear and convincing evidence that the property has been protected by a substantial enclosure and has been usually cultivated or improved. In addition all the taxes, state, county or municipal which have been levied upon the land according to law must be paid by the party or persons, their predecessors and grantors.

**Adverse Possession**
IC 5-210

Included in the adverse possession claim, can be easement by prescription except for the payment of taxes. An easement by prescription must also be held and possessed or controlled for 20 years.

Before purchasing a property, it's a good idea to look closely for any evidence of some use that may have been created by some outside source. If something looks out of place, ask questions.

## Abandonment

Can claims of use or ownership be lost due to non use or abandonment? The answer is not only yes, but there may be specific requirements to complete the process.

**Water rights**
IC 42-222

For example, a *water right* can be lost in Idaho by abandonment or forfeiture. If the water right is not used for 5 consecutive years, the right will be forfeited unless a formal application is applied for to extend the water right. If a well is abandoned, the well must be certified by a licensed well driller of such abandonment.

**Rights-of-way**
IC 40-203

Highways and public *rights-of-way* can be abandoned but only with a proper hearing. No highway or public right-of-way shall be abandoned or vacated that leaves any real property without access to an established highway or public right-of-way.

Until abandonment is authorized by the commissioners, public use of the highway or public right-of-way may not be restricted or impeded by encroachment or installation of any obstruction restricting public use.

**New Homestead application**
IC 55-1004

## Homestead protection

The homestead protection (protection against unsecured creditors) is automatic. If the homeowner retains their homestead and moves to another home, that will become their new homestead, and the owner must file for change in homestead. The same would be true for homeowner exemption (reduction in property assessed value for tax purposes). Due to change in ownership, a *new* application must be made.

## Voluntary transfer

Anyone making a voluntary transfer of any aspect of real estate, should make sure what they are doing is legal and valid. Such voluntary transfer of use or ownership (sale, lease, deed of trust, etc.) will be discussed elsewhere in this book.

# Involuntary transfer

Unfortunately, involuntary transfer of rights or ownership occurs when one or more parties either do not want to make the transfer or the parties to the issue cannot come to agreement.

**Section 14, Article 1**

## Eminent Domain

The Idaho State Constitution states in part, 'private property may be taken for public use, but not until a just compensation, to be ascertained in the manner prescribed by law, shall be paid therefor'.

Thus, under the federal and state constitutions, private property may not be taken for public purposes without payment or just compensation. The Idaho attorney general establishes and reviews the process to assure the actions of 'a taking' do not result in an unconstitutional taking of private property.

**Forfeiture**
IC 37-2802

## Forfeiture

Violations of the uniform controlled substances act resulting in a person found guilty of, or enters a plea of guilty, shall forfeit any of the person's property used or intended to be used to facilitate the violation.

Property subject to criminal forfeiture includes: real property, including things growing on, affixed to, or found on the land. Additional property subject to criminal forfeiture includes tangible and intangible personal property, including rights, privileges, interests, claims and securities.

## Bankruptcy

Bankruptcy can be either voluntary or involuntary. Typically bankruptcy results from debts exceeding assets with little or no ability to recover. Although bankruptcies are initiated for various reasons, 3 out of 5 personal bankruptcies are due to medical debt.

A voluntary bankruptcy begins with the filing of a petition in the Bankruptcy Court. Part of the federal court system, Bankruptcy Courts are established in every state. The debtor is required to file schedules of assets and liabilities, current income and expenditures. There are different chapters for filing bankruptcy including 7, 11, 12, and 13.

Chapter 7 - results in total liquidation or 'wipe out'. All assets and non-exempt properties are turned over to a trustee who converts them into cash to pay the debtor's creditors.

Chapter 11 - is used primarily for business bankruptcies and restructuring. This chapter gives businesses the opportunity to reorganize themselves. It is far more complex and expensive than Chapter 7.

Chapter 12 - is designed for the family farmer and is less complicated and expensive than chapter 11.

Chapter 13 - is a smaller version of Chapter 11. The debtor still retains the property and may be allowed one to keep additional property that would otherwise not be exempt. Chapter 13 is designed to give a fresh start but you have to submit to the bankruptcy court how you intend to pay off your debts over a 3-5 year period of time for as little as 10 cents on the dollar. You may not incur any significant new credit obligations without consulting the trustee.

# Questions – Chapter 9

1. When one dies, evidence of death is evidenced by providing:

    A. Newspaper obituary with date and time of death
    B. Funeral notice giving date and time
    C. Legible copy of death notice
    D. Authenticated copy of death certificate

2. If a married person dies without a will, how will the decedents property be distributed?

    A. ½ community property of the decedent passes to the spouse
    B. All property passes to the spouse
    C. All property passes to the state
    D. Surviving family decides who gets what

3. When do the terms of a properly executed will of a married person take effect?

    A. When the will was signed and properly witnessed
    B. When the will was recorded
    C. Upon death of the married person
    D. When a divorce has been finalized

4. The definition of the ordinary high water mark is defined as:

    A. The normal water mark verified at any time during the year
    B. Sufficient periods water covers to deprive soil of its vegetation
    C. The highest water mark publically recorded
    D. High water mark cannot be defined

5. What period of time must a person holding and possessing a property, hold the property to claim adverse possession?

    A. 5 years
    B. 10 years
    C. 20 years
    D. 40 years

6. An easement by prescription must be held and controlled for what period of time?

    A. 5 years
    B. 10 years
    C. 20 years
    D. 40 years

7. A water right can be lost if it is not used for how many consecutive years?

    A. 5 years
    B. 10 years
    C. 20 years
    D. Once properly obtained, a water right cannot be lost due to non use.

8. Eminent domain is an example of what type of transfer?

    A. Voluntary
    B. Involuntary
    C. Illegal
    D. Transfer for private use

# Chapter 10

# Conveyance Documents

**Conveyance**
IC 55-601

A conveyance of an estate in real property may be made by an instrument in writing, subscribed by the party disposing of the property. The name of the grantee (party receiving) together with a complete mailing address must also appear on the instrument (document).

There are many documents that convey an interest or ownership in real estate including deeds, mortgages, release of mortgages, and power of attorney that has been acknowledged. Also included in conveyances are transcripts of judgments or decrees which affect the title or possession of real property including water rights.

The transfer of ownership of real property from one party to another is with a deed. With the execution of a deed, the owner transfers, conveys, and releases any interests in their ownership to another. The deed serves as evidence of ownership.

Transfers of ownership must be in writing and signed to meet the *statute of frauds* including a deed.

Although Idaho does not have a statutory deed format, one should know and understand 5 elements that make up a valid deed.

1. A deed must identify the grantor (the party giving up ownership) and a grantee (the party acquiring ownership). Because the deed is 'granting' ownership, the grantor must be of legal age and of sound mind.

2. A deed must state consideration to identify something of value is being transferred. Such statement may state, *For one thousand ($1,000) and other good and valuable consideration*, or perhaps a condensed version, *For valuable consideration* could meet the legal requirement.

3. The deed must contain a granting clause with words of conveyance. The format of the wording will identify the type of deed and to what extent ownership is being conveyed.

Examples of words of conveyance:

*"Conveys, grants and warrants"*
> Provides the most protection to the buyer and warrants encumbrances by prior owners.

*"Grant, bargain, and sell"*
> Only implies ownership transfers the implied ownership without warranty.

*"Convey, release, remiss, and forever quit claim"* Least protection of all deeds to the grantee. There are no covenants or warranties of any kind. The grantor is merely 'quitting' any claim to the property.

4. A deed must contain a legal description that cannot possibly be misunderstood. Acceptable legal descriptions can be by government survey system, metes and bounds, or recorded plat. If an easement or air right is part of the transfer, the deed should state that fact along with the legal description.

5. The signature of the grantor. In order for the deed to be recorded, the signature must be acknowledged and witnessed by someone authorized by a notary public, authorized public officer or someone approved by state law.

Once the deed is signed, it must be personally delivered or recorded in the public records and delivered to the grantee for acceptance.

**Recording in Idaho**
IC 31-2412

## Recording

The property being transferred will be recorded in the county in which the property is located. If the property is closed at a title company in the morning, it usually can be recorded the same day or the next business day.

Upon presentation to the county recorder, the recorder's office shall immediately write or stamp an instrument number. The numbers so stamped shall be consecutive in the order of filing in only one series of numbers. The priority of number shall be prima facie evidence of priority of filing in the order the instruments actually came to the recorder. If more than one instrument is received from the same source, the recorder may follow such directions as the sender may give in relation to the numbering.

**Reception book**
IC 31-2413

A reception book will be maintained by the county recorder for recorded instruments. The format consists of 8 parallel columns to enter the required information as follows:

1st column - instrument number
2nd column - day, hour, and minute of filing
3rd column - grantor or person executing instrument
4th column - grantee or person to whom executed
5th column - character of the instrument
6th column - book and page where recorded
7th column - brief description of the property
8th column - name of person to whom delivered

By the way, other resources for investigating records are the title insurance companies. They all have a 'duplicate' set of all recorded records for their use in title searching.

In fact, it may even be easier to search the title company records since they use a different formats to retain records that are very quick and efficient with cross reference information to trace a specific property back to original recordings.

**Transfer taxes**
Idaho has none

## Transfer taxes

Idaho is one of 13 states that *does not* have any transfer fees or taxes. States that have transfer taxes have rates that range from $.01/$100 (0.01%) in Colorado to as high as $.75/$100 paid by both buyer and seller (1.5%) in New Hampshire. Others may incorporate graduated scales.

Of those states that surround Idaho, only Nevada and Washington have transfer taxes. Oregon, Montana, Wyoming, and Utah do not have transfer fees.

# Questions – Chapter 10

1. The transfer of real property must be:

   A. Verbally agreed to in person
   B. Recorded at the county recorder
   C. Delivered through a title company
   D. Signed and in writing

2. Certain documents must be in writing to be enforceable to satisfy:

   A. Contract law
   B. Statute of Frauds
   C. Idaho Statutes
   D. Supreme Court decisions

3. 'Grant, bargain, and sell' transfers what type of ownership protection?

   A. The most protection to the buyer
   B. Warrants encumbrances for future owners
   C. Contains no covenants or warranties
   D. Implied ownership without warranty

4. 'Convey, release, remiss, and forever quit claim' transfers what type of ownership protection?

   A. The most protection to the buyer
   B. Warrants encumbrances for future owners
   C. Contains no covenants or warranties
   D. Implied ownership without warranty

5. How is a recorded instrument identified by priority of recording?

   A. Actual date and year of recording
   B. The year including date and hour
   C. Book where recorded
   D. Day, hour, and minute recorded

6. Along with state sales tax, what is the transfer tax in Idaho?

   A. 0.05 per cent of the value transferred
   B. 1.0 per cent of the value transferred
   C. Tax is based on property tax value
   D. There is no transfer tax

# Chapter 11

# Limitations On Rights of Ownership & Encumbrances

**Limitations of use and rights**

Perhaps a big misconception about real estate ownership is that ownership gives unlimited use and right to private property. After all, the owner of a property should be able to do as they wish. Unfortunately, this may not be true.

One by one, some of the sticks from the bundle of rights can be removed for various reasons based on limitations imposed by the powers of the government, or by the seller with deed restrictions or Homeowner Associations with Covenants, Conditions, and Restrictions.

# Dying without a will

**Unclaimed property**
IC 14-113

**Escheat**
If a person in Idaho dies without a will and has no heirs, all moneys and effects will accrue and be transferred to the public school permanent endowment fund based on the constitution of the state of Idaho.

**Holding period**
IC 15-3-914

The time frame to transfer unclaimed assets will take place in the time frame based on the 'unclaimed property act'. The time to file for a claim is to be within 1,827 days (approximately 5 years) from the date of the appointment of the personal representative.

# Easements

An easement is the right of one party to use the land of another for a special purpose consistent with the general use of the land. The use can extend from the earth below the surface to the heavens above. Thus, easements can include subsurface rights as well as air rights.

Easements of ingress and egress, such as roadways, will be discussed in another chapter. However solar and conservation easements will be included in this chapter.

## Going Green

Idaho is aware of the need to protect the ability to take advantage of alternate forms of energy. The purpose of a solar easement is to allow the exposure of solar energy to a device capable of storing such energy. Forms of solar easements are not new. A doctrine based on English law known as 'Ancient Lights' was adopted in 1832 to preserve the use of light.

**Solar Easements**
IC 55-615

Figure 1

## Solar Easements

A solar easement shall be in writing and subject to the same recording requirements as any other easement.

A solar easement shall include but not be limited to:
- Vertical and horizontal angles, expressed in degrees, at which solar easement extends over the real property subject to the solar easement;

- Any terms or conditions or both under which the solar easement is granted or will be terminated;

- Any provisions for compensation of the owner of the property benefitting from the solar easement in the event of interference with the enjoyment of the solar easement or compensation of the owner of the property subject to the solar easement for maintaining the solar easement.

**Solar lot line**

The angle in which a shadow could encroach onto another property is often referenced by the shadow that is cast on December 21 (winter solstice) between 10 am and 2 pm. The key is to keep the shadow from encroaching upon the property that has the solar capturing. Thus, if the neighbor's shadow encroaches beyond the lot line setbacks, the neighbor would be in violation of the solar easement.

Many new subdivisions incorporate solar easements in their CCR's (conditions, covenants, and restrictions).

A solar easement will attach to the property and pass with the property when title is transferred to another owner.

**Conservation Easement**
IC 55-2101

## Conservation Easement

A conservation easement is a tool that can be used between landowners and a government agency to protect natural resources including water resources and habitat, scenic views, open space, farm land. Conservation easements can limit the right to develop, now and in the future.

Conservation easements can also be used to preserve historical, architectural and cultural aspects of real property.

In addition, there are tax benefits to the landowner. The land can be bought and sold but the easement 'runs with the land' and applies to all future owners. 12 non profit land trusts hold approximately 59,000 acres in conservation easements in Idaho.

# Water Rights

## Prior Appropriation

Unlike the eastern United States where water rights are tied to the land through riparian rights, most of the western United States follows the doctrine of 'prior appropriation', which is based on 'first in time, first in right' principle.

Idaho is 1 of 17 states to employ prior appropriation to the exclusion of the riparian doctrine. However, it should be noted that each state operates independently of each other. Thus, the administration of the rights will differ from state to state.

**State owns water**
IC 42-401

All the waters of the state, when flowing in their natural channels, including the waters of all natural springs and lakes within the boundaries of the state are declared to be the property of the state.

**IDWR website**
www.idwr.idaho.gov

The Idaho Department Of Water Resources (IDWR) is the regulatory agency that administers water rights and whose duty is to supervise the appropriation and allotment for beneficial purposes.

**First in time, first in right**
IC 43-106

## Priority Date

As mentioned above, 'first in time, first in right' will create a priority date. It determines who gets water when there is a shortage. If there isn't enough water to satisfy all of the water rights, then the oldest or senior water rights are satisfied first and so on in order until there is no water left. It's the new or junior water rights that do not get water when there isn't enough to satisfy all the water rights.

## ½ acre limitation

## Domestic water usage

The use of water for homes and any other purpose in connection with home type water use is limited to irrigating up to ½ acre of land if the total use is not in excess of 13,000 gallons per day.

A real estate licensee needs to be very careful when listing homes on small ranchette type properties that appear to be irrigated from a domestic well, especially if more than ½ acre is being irrigated. Infrared sensors from satellites can easily identify those parcels in which violations are occurring.

It is certainly possible that the smaller parcels are irrigated with multiple water rights for domestic uses. However, such use shall not be exercised in a manner to satisfy a single combined water use or purpose. The purpose of the limitation is to prohibit the diversion and use of water to supply a use that does not meet the domestic use definition.

## Required drilling permit
IC 42-238

## Well drilling permit required

A well cannot be drilled in Idaho without a licensed well driller and operator of drilling equipment. In addition, a well cannot be abandoned unless a report is submitted to the director of the IDWR describing the abandonment by a licensed well driller.

## 5 year use rule
IC 42-350

## Use it or lose it

If, after the holder of the water right has ceased to put the water to a beneficial use for a period of 5 continuous years or that the licensee has willfully or intentionally failed to comply, the director of the IDWR will issue an order to show cause.

The water right holder shall have the right to an administrative hearing if requested in writing 21 days from the date of service of the order or risk losing the right to the water or forfeiting the water right.

## Water recharge
IC 42-4201

## Recharge ground water

Unforseen circumstances such as drought, lack of snow pack, and other situations that could jeopardize ground water basins could leave water users high and dry. Idaho's farmers have done an excellent job with water conservation and irrigation practices.

However, some of the conservation practices could in fact reduce the amount of natural recharge into the ground water.

The IDWR has the authority to appropriate recharge from the Snake River, or make an order to minimize excessive drawdown of aquifer storage. The purpose is to replace the waters displaced from the aquifer.

**Minimum 212 degrees F**
**IC 42-4002**

## Geothermal Energy

In Idaho, a geothermal resource is defined as ground water having a temperature of 212 degrees Fahrenheit or more in the bottom of a well. Being neither a mineral or water resource, geothermal resources are considered *sui generis* because of the close relationship to each other.

In order to secure geothermal energy, one has to make application for a geothermal resource well permit from the Idaho Department of Water Resources.

Water has been and will continue to be a very important aspect of property ownership. It is very important that real estate licensees and the public are both aware of water law and the use of water in Idaho. In the old days, we had 'range wars'. Today, we can be faced with 'water wars'.

# Land Use Controls

## Police Power

Police power is the authority of the government to adopt and enforce laws governing the use of real estate based on the need to promote public safety, health, and general welfare.

In regard to real estate, police power allows for the adoption and enforcement of various regulations, including but not limited to: zoning, building codes and environmental regulations and eminent domain.

**State land use purpose**
**IC 67-6502**

## State Land Use Planning Act

In keeping with the 'police power' concept, the Idaho land use planning purpose includes:

- Allow planned development for low cost housing
- Ensure public facilities and services at a reasonable cost
- Protect local and state economy
- Ensure that environmental features are protected
- Encourage agriculture, forestry, and food production

- Encourage urban development within cities
- Avoid undue overcrowding of population
- Ensure development on land fits physical characteristics
- Protect against natural hazards and disasters
- Protect fish, wildlife, and recreation resources
- Avoid undue water and air pollution
- Allow school districts to participate in planning

Based on the State Land Use Planning Act, counties and cities throughout Idaho have adopted local and regional comprehensive plans for local control.

The Idaho Supreme Court made a very interesting observation between planning and zoning in the case, *Giltner Dairy, LLC v Jerome County* in 2008. The Court said:

> *Planning is long range; zoning is immediate. Planning is general; zoning is specific. Planning involves political processes; zoning is a legislative function and an exercise of the police power. Planning is generally dynamic while zoning is more or less static. Planning often involves frequent changes; zoning designations should not. Planning has a speculative impact upon property values, while zoning may actually constitute a valuable property right.*

The court continued, *".....while zoning designations should generally follow and be consistent with the long range designations established in the Comprehensive Plan, there is no requirement that zoning immediately conform to the Plan. The Plan is a statement of long-range pubic intent; zoning is an exercise of police power which, in the long run, should be consistent with that intent. Planning is a determination of public policy, and zoning, to be legitimate exercise of the police power, should be in the furtherance of that policy."*

Any changes or amendments to the comprehensive plan requires at least 1 public hearing with a public notice at least 15 days prior to the hearing.

**Zoning**

## Zoning

While a comprehensive plan set the framework for future development, zoning is the 'legal' tool a municipality uses to regulate land use. Items such as height and size of buildings, size of lots, setbacks, parking, landscaping and density can be regulated to meet the needs and goals of the community.

| | |
|---|---|
| **Zoning districts** | Zoning ordinances will identify uses and density into different areas or zones for specific land use. There isn't any uniformity for the classifications but for convenience, zoning districts are often identified with abbreviations such as I or M for industrial or manufacturing, C for commercial, A for agricultural, R for residential and so on. |
| **Classifications** | Then each zoning classification may have subheadings such as R1, R2 or R3 for residential density requirements. The same may be said for commercial such as C1, C2, C3 for types of use. There can also be some special classifications such as PUD for Planned Unit Development or RPD for Residential Planned Development. |
| **Enforcement** | Within the each zoning classification are allowed uses. If the allowed uses are violated, the business or home can be shut down or 'red tagged' until the violation has been resolved. |

## Zoning changes

| | |
|---|---|
| **Grandfathered use** | Not all zoning classifications fit all situations. So mechanisms need to be available to address those special situations that might allow zoning changes. Issues such as nonconforming uses might be 'grandfathered' so the existing owner can continue the use, even though it does not conform to the new zoning. |
| **Zoning amendment** | Another example may involve an amendment to the existing zoning to be rezoned. Any zoning change requests must be sent to surrounding property owners and a public hearing must be held so the property owners and the public can both voice their opinions. |
| **Zoning variance** | A third example could address a variance allowing the owner to deviate from the current zoning requirements for a piece of property. Perhaps the owner needs a setback change to accommodate a particular structure design. |

| | |
|---|---|
| **Subdivision**<br>IC 50-1301 (12) | **Subdivision**<br>Idaho statute defines a subdivision to be a parcel of land divided into 5 or more lots for the purpose of sale or building development. However, Idaho Code excludes partitions of agricultural land for agricultural purposes.<br><br>Idaho Code also provides that cities and counties may adopt their own definition of subdivision in lieu of the state definition. It may not be unusual for local governments to define subdivision to be the division of |

land into 2 or more lots, building sites, or other divisions for the purpose of sale or building development.

**Certification of Plat**
IC 50-1309

The owner of the land shall make a certificate with the correct legal description together with a dedication of all public streets and rights-of-way on the plat. The professional land surveyor making the survey shall certify the correctness of the plat and place his seal, signature and date on the plat.

**Recording plat**

Once the plat is approved, it will be recorded in a book or file designated as 'Record of Plats'.

**Penalty for selling unplatted lots**
IC 50-1316

Any person who shall dispose of or offer any lots for sale in any city or county, before the plat has been acknowledged and recorded, shall forfeit and pay $100 for each lot and part of a lot sold or disposed of or offered for sale.

## Annexation

There are all kinds of reasons to annex land into cities including but not limited to more police or fire protection, access to water and sewer, accommodation of growth, and other public services.

**3 categories to annex**
IC 50-222

There are 3 categories in which annexation by cities can occur. Category A - requires all private landowners to consent to annexation. If all land owners have consented, the area may extend beyond the city if it is contiguous to the city and the comprehensive plan includes the area to be annexed.

Category B - addresses subject lands containing *less* than 100 separate private ownerships and platted lots of record where not all such landowners have consented to annexation or, subject lands containing *more* than 100 acres and where more than 50% of the landowners have consented to annexation prior to the annexation process.

Category C - involves annexations where the subject lands contain more than 100 separate private ownerships and where more than 50% of the area of the subject lands have not consented to annexation prior to the annexation process.

There are specific procedures to comply with each category. The implementation of any annexation proposal wherein the city council determines that annexation is appropriate, it shall be concluded with the passage of an ordinance of annexation.

After it has been decided to annex, all the property owners within the land to be considered and within 300 feet of the external boundaries of the land being considered and any additional area that may be impacted shall be notified by mail of a hearing for annexation. Notice shall also be posted on the premises not less than 1 week prior to the hearing.

At the hearing, the panel will accept both verbal and written testimony before voting.

## Building Codes

**Idaho Building Code Act IC 39-4105**

The Idaho Building Code Act has adopted the International Building Code and the International Fire Code as the basis for all construction. The purpose of the building codes is to ensure the health, safety and construction standards are adhered to with uniformity.

**Permit application**

It is unlawful for any person to allow any construction, improvement, extension or alteration of any building, residence or structure without first applying for a permit in accordance with the local government ordinance or ordinances.

Bear in mind, not all alterations or construction requires a building permit but one should check first before starting any construction project. Also, it should be noted that what may require a permit in one jurisdiction may not require a permit in another; or the construction requirements in one jurisdiction may be different in another jurisdiction.

The building permit process initiates inspections to make sure the construction meets the requirements of whatever building code(s) may be involved (construction, electrical, plumbing, gas, etc).

**Certificate of Occupancy**

After the construction is completed, a 'final' inspection will be ordered and if everything passes, the building permit will be signed off and an 'Certificate of Occupancy' will be issued which allows occupancy and habitation.

## Regulatory Takings  (eminent domain)

**Regulatory Taking IC 67-8002**

There will be issues when private property needs to be taken by the government to make way for development for public needs, roadways and highways, public parking, urban renewal, etc. The taking of private property is known as eminent domain and the process is condemnation.

If a state or local governmental entity plans to make a regulatory taking of private property, a written request for an analysis of the taking can be made by an owner of real property.

The property owner will receive compensation based on an appraisal of fair market value. The actual taking cannot be done without due process of law.

## Interstate Land Sales Full Disclosure Act

As a method to protect consumers from fraud and abuse in the sale or lease of land, Congress enacted the Interstate Land Sales Full Disclosure Act patterned after the Securities Law of 1933.

The Act requires land developers to register subdivisions of 100 or more non-exempt lots with HUD and provide each purchaser with a full disclosure document about the subdivision known as a Property Report.

Before a buyer signs a purchase and sale agreement the buyer should:
- Know the rights of a buyer
- Know something about the developer
- Know the facts about the development
- Be able to resist high pressure sales campaigns

The developer must file with HUD:
- Copy of corporate charger and financial statement
- Info on local ordinances and health regulations
- Info about the land and title opinion
- Info on facilities such as schools, hospitals, transportation
- Availability of utilities, water, sewage
- Roads, maps, plats, suppliers of water and sewer

Information that will be contained in the property report:
- Distances to nearby communities over paved or unpaved roads
- Existence of any existing mortgages or liens on the property
- Contracts to be placed in escrow and applied to purchase
- Availability and location of recreational facilities
- Availability of water, sewer, septic tanks, and wells
- Present and proposed utility services and charges
- Number of homes currently occupied
- Soil and foundation conditions and any problems with septics
- Type of title and when the buyer will receive it

Examples of dishonest sales practices (high pressure)
1. Concealing or misrepresenting facts about value
2. Failure to honor refund promises or agreements
3. Misrepresentation of facts about the subdivision
4. Failure to develop the subdivision as planned
5. Failure to deliver deeds, title insurance policies
6. Abusive treatment or high-pressure sales tactics
7. Failure to make good on sales inducements
8. 'Bait and Switch' tactics
9. Failure to grant rights under Interstate Land Disclosure Act

The information discussed is especially important to Idahoans, since Idaho is surrounded by 6 states and 1 foreign country. Add many out of state investors and developers, and the Interstate Land Sales Full Disclosure Act even becomes more important for all parties.

# Environmental Issues & the Real Estate Transaction

**Asbestos**

## Asbestos

Asbestos was considered a miracle building material in the late 19th century because of its many uses including sound insulation and its resistance to heat. As a flame-retardant and insulating factors, it was extensively used in construction. In housing, asbestos was used in ceiling insulation, fireproof drywall and drywall joint compound, flooring, roofing, and pipe insulation.

Asbestos was used outside the construction industry and was a major component for brake linings and clutches in the automotive industry.

Unfortunately the ingestion and inhalation of asbestos fibers can create serious lung disease known as asbestosis. Scarred lung tissue cannot expand and contract normally and cannot perform gas exchange. With no known cure, the disease can ultimately result in death.

Because of the serious health hazards, asbestos was outlawed in the housing industry by the EPA starting in 1977 with its use in textured paint and patching compounds used on wall and ceiling joints.

**Lead based paint**

# Lead based paint

Congress found that pre-1980 housing contained more than 3,000,000 tons of lead in the form of lead based paint. The majority of homes build before 1950 contained substantial amounts of lead based paint.

As many as 3,800,000 homes endangered the health and development of children with chipping or peeling paint. These homes afflict as many as 3,000,000 children under the age of 6, who are the most vulnerable.

As a result, the EPA outlawed lead based paint in housing in 1978. Later the Lead-Based Paint Reduction Act of 1992 was created to set some rules and guidelines to inform the purchaser or lessee of the potential hazards of housing constructed prior to 1978.

However, in 2008 the laws were strengthened with the EPA's Renovation, Repair, and Painting (RRP) Rule and HUD's Lead Safe Housing Rule which became effective on April 22, 2010.

**40 CFR 745.223**
**(Code of Federal Regulations)**

# Renovation, Repair, and Painting Rule

The purpose of the RRP is to give owners, tenants, and individuals performing renovations, better protection from lead hazards. The new ruling applies to all renovations performed for compensation in target housing and child care facilities.

If the interior surface exceeds 6 square feet or 20 square feet exterior surface is disturbed, all renovation must comply with the rule. HUD's rule still remains at 2 square feet of interior surface and 20 square feet exterior or 10% of the surface area of a small building component.

A new pamphlet, *Renovate Right: Important Lead Hazard Information for Families, Child Care Providers, and Schools* must be used exclusively for any renovations.

Individuals and firms performing renovations must be properly trained and certified. Re-certification is required every 5 years. All records of each renovation must be kept for not less than 3 years. Penalties for non compliance can be as much as $37,500 per violation, per day!

**Radon**

# Radon

As an odorless, tasteless and invisible radioactive gas created from natural deposits of uranium and radium in the soil. Radon testing was screened on 1,018 homes in Idaho. Around ⅓ of the homes had high levels of radon.

The EPA has a threshold of 4 pCi/L (picoCuries per liter). Anything over the threshold is considered dangerous. According to the Idaho Department of Health and Welfare, the average indoor radon level for Idaho is 6.4 pCi/L. In August 2005, it was reported that around 6,668 homes have reported testing results with 37% of the homes testing high for radon.

There are pockets in Idaho that have very high levels of radon present. Local building codes may require installation of radon-resistant construction by installing a pipe to remove radon gas from below a concrete floor or crawl space.

## Urea Formaldehyde

**Urea Formaldehyde**

Urea formaldehyde can be found in all kinds of products including adhesives, finishes, MDF, molded objects, foam, and insulation.

In the 1970's many homes were insulated with urea-formaldehyde foam insulation as an energy conservation measure before it was discovered that the emissions could be a dangerous health hazard.

In Idaho, many mountain cabins with high pitched roofs contain this product. Although the emissions decline over time, there can still be exposure. Early health symptoms include eye, nose, and throat irritations as well as coughing and breathing difficulties. Usually these irritants disappear once the pollutant has been removed or 'airs' out.

**Carbon Monoxide**

## Carbon Monoxide

Known as the 'silent killer', carbon monoxide is a colorless, odorless, tasteless, toxic gas created by incomplete combustion of fuel such as wood, gasoline, kerosene, propane or natural gas.

Contributing causes of carbon monoxide include:
- unvented space heaters
- leaks in furnaces and chimneys
- back drafts from gas water heaters, or furnaces
- gas ovens and ranges
- auto exhausts

Although not a federal law for residential housing, it is recommended that a CO detector be installed if the house has fuel-burning appliances. Another precaution is to crack windows when using unvented appliances and don't use gas stoves or ovens to heat your home.

**EMF's**

## Electromagnetic Fields (EMF's)

Idaho Power has monitored the issue of health effects of electromagnetic fields since the early 1970. The research has identified that EMF's exist everywhere in our modern society as invisible forces created by any electric charge. However, the forces decrease rapidly in magnitude as one moves farther away from the source.

Although some states have established EMF exposure limits, there are no federal or Idaho-established limits. However, Idaho Power has addressed several good questions.

- Q - Do underground power lines limit EMF's?
  A - Not necessarily. The maximum magnetic field will generally be higher for underground lines, but much depends on the method of construction.

- Q - Should I have an EMF strength reading done in my home?
  A - Idaho Power will measure EMF strength upon request and will discuss the results with the customer.

- Q - Should I limit my exposure to electrical appliances?
  A - The research does not suggest that people need to change the way they use electrical appliances, or limit the amount of time they use certain appliances.

**Mold**

## Mold

Many states have legislated laws surrounding toxic mold and disclosure requirements. California enacted the Toxic Mold Protection Act in 2001 to establish permissible exposure limits along with assessment standards and remediation. Other states followed California in developing regulations including New York, Massachusetts and Texas.

Additional states have adopted or created disclosure requirements for evidence of mold or excessive moisture issues. Although Idaho does not have any mandatory disclosure laws, the Idaho Association of REALTORS® has included a Moisture & Drainage Condition section in a Sellers Property Disclosure form.

**Adverse Material Facts**
IC 54-2086 (1) (d)
IC 54-2087 (4) (a)

Idaho law indirectly addresses toxic mold issues by requiring disclosure to a buyer/customer or client of *all adverse material actually known or reasonable should have been known by the licensee.*

Obviously toxic mold would be an adverse material fact and if known, must be disclosed.

**Clandestine Drug
Laboratory
Cleanup**
IDAPA 16.02.04

## Methamphetamine

Meth is highly toxic and creates extremely dangerous conditions for humans and property alike. In 2006, Idaho Administrative Code adopted very specific requirements labeled 'Clandestine Drug Laboratory Cleanup'. Part of the process requires that the contaminated home will remain vacant until such time a 'clearance sampling' renders the home safe.

The property will also be listed on a Clandestine Drug Laboratory Site Property List available to the public until it is delisted. The Idaho Department of Health and Welfare offers a lot of information including a property list, cleaning up a former meth lab, cleanup contractors, qualified industrial hygienists, and laws/rules.

**Forcible entry and
Unlawful Detainer**
IC 6-303 (5)

Idaho code does allow a landlord the use of 'rapid eviction' if any person is, has been, or engaged in the unlawful delivery, production or use of a controlled substance on the premises of the leased property.

## Underground Storage Tanks

Underground storage tanks or USTs are regulated by the U. S. Environmental Protection Agency and are required to comply with specific conditions. Not regulated as underground storage tanks are:

- Farm or residential tanks of 1,100 gallons or less storing motor fuel for non-commercial purposes
- Tanks used solely for storing fuel oil for home heating
- Tanks with a storage capacity of 110 gallons or less

**Underground
Storage Tank Act**
IC 39-8801 thru
   39-8812

The Idaho Underground Storage Tank Act addresses protection of the environment from leaking underground tanks (LUST). Leaking underground storage tanks can create huge problems with contamination of the ground water.

On-site inspections shall be conducted at least once every 3 years to determine compliance. If the Idaho Department of Environmental Quality (DEQ) conducts the inspection, it shall not charge a fee for the inspection.

Rules regulating underground storage tanks in Idaho addresses:

- Federal standards regulating underground storage tanks
- Measures to protect ground water from contamination
- Release reporting requirements
- Training requirements

- Inspections
- Delivery prohibition
- Maintenance of an underground storage tank database

Real estate practitioners should obtain a copy of a booklet titled, *Real Estate Professionals and Underground Storage Tanks*, if they work with any customers or clients who have underground storage tanks on their property.

The 12 page booklet is available at no charge from the Idaho Department of Environmental Quality and can be downloaded online. It is a great resource on how to handle a variety of issues, including the removal of home heating oil tanks.

**Hazardous Waste Management**
IC 39-4402

## Waste Disposal Sites
The purpose of Idaho's hazardous waste management laws are to protect the public health and safety from the effects of the improper, inadequate or unsound management of hazardous waste.

Based on the federal Resource, Conservation and Recovery Act of 1976, no person shall treat or store hazardous waste, nor shall any person discharge, incinerate, release, spill, place or dispose of any hazardous waste in a manner that would endanger the environment.

**Idaho DEQ**

The Idaho's Department of Environment Quality is the state agency that is delegated responsibility by the EPA to implement waste management in Idaho. The DEQ's Hazardous Waste Program issues permits, oversees inspections of facilities that generate hazardous waste, provides technical assistance and takes corrective action. The program also oversees remediation of radioactive and hazardous wastes at the Idaho National Laboratory (INL) site.

The State Response Program oversees the development and operation of municipal and non-municipal solid waste disposal sites in Idaho. It is very important that landfills in Idaho are carefully managed and regulated because more than 95% of water used by households come from ground water.

**Fair Housing**

## Fair Housing

Idaho mirrors Title VIII of the Civil Rights Act of 1968 known as the Fair Housing Act as amended. The Act prohibits discrimination in the sale, rental, and financing of dwellings. Prohibited discrimination includes:

- Race
- Religion
- Color
- Sex
- National origin
- Familial status
- Handicap

**Prohibited acts**

Under the Fair Housing Act, it is against the law to:

- Refuse to rent to you or sell you housing.
- Tell you housing is unavailable when if fact it is available.
- Show apartments or homes in certain neighborhoods only
- Advertise housing to only preferred groups of people.
- Refuse to provide you information regarding mortgage loans.
- Deny you property insurance.
- Conduct property appraisals in a discriminatory manner.
- Refuse to make certain modifications for mental or physical disability including persons recovering from alcohol and substance abuse.
- Fail to design and construct accessibility for the disabled.
- Harass, coerce, intimidate, or interfere with anyone exercising or assisting someone with their fair housing rights.

**Commission on Human Rights**
IC 67-5901
IC 76-5907

The Commission on Human Rights was created to protect individuals and their interest in personal dignity. The Commission will hear complaints of alleged discrimination within 1 year of the alleged unlawful discrimination.

**Filing a complaint with HUD**

If one feels they have been discriminated against, they can also file a formal complaint with a HUD regional office. The Fair Housing Enforcement Center for Idaho is located with the U. S. Department of HUD in Seattle, Washington.

Additional fair housing resources in Idaho include:

- Idaho Legal Aid Services,
- Idaho Human Rights Commission,
- Intermountain Fair Housing Council.

Care needs to be taken when working with any buyers or sellers, landlords or tenants when it comes to discrimination or perceived acts of discrimination.

# Encumbrances That Affect Title to Real Estate

## General information about liens
In Idaho, liens are divided into two categories, general and special.

**General Liens**

A general lien is one which the lien holder is entitled to enforce the performance of *all* obligations which exist in the favor of the lien holder against the owner of the property.

Examples include judgments, inheritance taxes, debts of a decedent and unpaid taxes to the Internal Revenue Service (IRS).

**Special Liens**

A special lien is one which the holder is entitled to enforce the performance of a *particular* act or obligation.

The liens with earlier recording dates take priority over liens recorded at a later date. For example, a first mortgage takes priority over a second mortgage and so on.

However, if one subordinates their position to a later position, the earlier position gives the junior lien holder priority. An example would be when the holder of a 1$^{st}$ mortgage gives up their position to allow a 2$^{nd}$ lien holder priority, providing all lender(s) approve. This may happen when a lender behind a 1$^{st}$ mortgage requires a 1$^{st}$ position to make a loan to protect themselves.

Voluntary special liens are offered by the owner to allow another party to secure the property as collateral for a loan. Some examples include mortgages, vendor lien, and a bail bond lien.

In Idaho, an example of a 'vendor lien' is where the owner/seller finances the property for the buyer and in essence becomes the 'bank'. Although uncommon, the act is often known as 'seller financing' with an installment contract. A deed is not delivered by the seller until the contract has been fulfilled.

**Property Bail Bond**
IC 19-2922 (1)

A bail bond lien attaches to the real estate of the person who posts bail. In Idaho, it should be noted that the lien will not be released until a verdict and sentencing has been approved by the court.

## Statutory Liens

A statutory lien are liens imposed by statute or law. Statutory law is created by legislative action. These are involuntary statutory liens and placed on the property without the owners consent. Several examples include mechanic's liens and property taxes.

**Mechanic's Lien**
IC 45-501

## Mechanic's Lien

Anyone providing labor or furnishing materials to be used in the construction, alteration or repair in connection with any land or building development or improvement shall have the right to lien the property.

Included are contractor, subcontractor, architect, builder, licensed surveyor, professional engineer or any person having charge of the construction in part or whole. The lien will attach to the property that the labor or services was delivered.

The filing of a claim shall be made within 90 days after the completion of the labor or services or furnishing of materials. The claim will identify the demand excluding all credits and offsets together with the name of the owner if known.

A true copy of the claim shall be personally served on the owner or mailed to the owner at his last known address no later than 5 business days following the filing of the claim.

**Duration of Lien**
IC 45-510

Once filed, the claim will remain on the property for no longer than 6 months at which time the claim will expire.

**Judgment lien**
**5 years**
IC 10-1110

If, prior to expiration, a judgment can be filed to extend the debt. In Idaho, a recorded judgment becomes a lien on the property of the judgment debtor in the county the property is located, or acquired afterwards, at any time prior to the expiration of the judgment.

The lien resulting from recording a judgment, other than child support, continues for 5 years from the date of the judgment.

A judgment may be renewed and recorded and shall continue for another 5 years.

**Priority of claim**
IC 45-512

It's important to know and understand the order or priority in which claims will be processed.

1. All laborers, other than contractors or subcontractors
2. All materialmen including those furnishing, renting or leasing equipment, materials or fixtures
3. Subcontractors
4. The original contractor
5. All professional engineers and licensed surveyors

The liens of all laborers, other than the original contractor or subcontractor, shall first be paid in full or pro rated if the proceeds are insufficient to pay them in full.

Then, the materialmen including those furnishing, renting or leasing equipment, materials or fixtures other than the original contractor or subcontractor shall be paid in full or pro rated if the proceeds are insufficient to pay them in full.

Out of the remainder, if any, the subcontractors shall be paid in full or pro rated and the remainder, if any, shall be paid pro rated to the original contractor. The last to receive any proceeds will be the professional engineers and licensed surveyors.

# Taxes and Other Liens

### Taxes based on market value

Like most states, real property taxes are collected to pay for the costs of local and county government services. Property taxes are based upon the *market* value of the property, real or personal.

**How property is valued**
IC 63-201 (15)

## How is property valued?

Each year, all property, real or personal, is valued on January 1 at fair market value for tax purposes. Fair market value is determined by comparing similar properties to the subject property that have sold. Market value is supposed to be equivalent to a property exchange between a willing seller, under no compulsion to sell, and an informed capable buyer given a reasonable time to consummate the sale.

Even though the value is supposed to be 'fair market' value, it is only an estimate of value based on information that isn't necessarily verified for complete accuracy.

To complicate the process, the fair market value may not be easily verifiable since Idaho is a 'non disclosure' state. The information the county appraiser can secure may or may not be accurate

**Yearly valuation**
IC 63-314

## Annual property valuation by the county assessor

All taxable property is appraised or indexed annually to reflect current market value. However, each property must be appraised at least once every 5 years. Idaho code also requires not less than 15% of taxable properties to be appraised the first year; 35% the second year; 55% the third year; 75% the fourth year; and finally 100% the fifth year. Thus, there is a partial ongoing physical appraisal each and every year. During the years an individual property isn't physically appraised, it will be indexed.

**Mass Appraisal**

Unlike the individual appraisal that usually accompanies a home to secure financing, the county assessors use a 'mass' appraisal concept. They take multiple numbers of value to arrive at an index that would equate to the ups and downs of the real estate market.

For example, a property may be appraised at $100,000 on year one and may not be physically appraised for another 4 years. However, the law requires the property to be valued each and every year. The assessor has determined, via mass appraisal techniques, that the sales values of similar properties in the area increased 2.3% for the indexed year. Thus, the $100,000 valued property would increase to $102,300 the next year.

**Index value accuracy**

This indexed value may or may not be correct. If the county appraiser hasn't physically appraised the subject property, the index can be greatly skewed. In addition, Idaho code does not require the homeowner to give inside access of their property to the county appraiser. So, it is very conceivable that the original characteristics of the property could be in error.

The homeowner may have done extensive remodeling without a permit which would have increased the value. Or, a property sold at a very low price because the inside was trashed or had deteriorated below the original characteristics contained in the county appraiser files.

Because of all the variables, assessment values for tax purposes should not be used exclusively to determine market value. Remember, the values may be collectively indexed and may not be physically appraised except for once every 5 years.

**Appraisal - Jan 1**

Value trends can also be incorrect. The data the county appraiser uses to assess each property on January 1 each year could already be a year old. If the market is increasing, it's a good bet that the assessed value could be low. If the market is declining, the assessed value could be high since it takes time for the assessed value to catch up with the market.

**Valuation notice to taxpayor**
IC 54-308

## Assessment notices sent to property owners

Even though all assessments are based on January 1 of each year, the valuation assessment notice delivery to the taxpayer shall be no later than the *first Monday in June*. The 5 month delay from January 1 to June is to allow the county assessor time to review, fine tune, and make adjustments to any or all the data they have for all properties. Thus, the value based on January 1 may or may not be the value contained in the assessment notice.

It is important to realize the assessment notice is *not* a tax notice. It is merely a notice of valuation of the property.

**Value appeal time frame**

What happens if a property owner doesn't agree with value?
The property owner will receive the assessment notice no later than the first Monday in June but only has until *fourth Monday in June* to appeal.

Although a formal written appeal is good, a phone call to the assessors office may get a quicker result if a county appraiser can come to your home and reappraise. Be careful! If the appraiser finds your home to be of greater value than the assessment notice indicates, the appraiser *must* enter the new value into their records.

Most Idaho counties have websites that will give full instructions for the appeal process. Remember the appeal is based on the value as of January 1, not later. Thus, any sales data collected should predate January 1.

# Exemptions From Taxation

Although there are many types of exemptions from taxation, we're only going to discuss two available exemptions related to home ownership.

**Primary Dwelling Exemption**
IC 63-602G

Figure 2

## Homeowner Exemption

Idaho allows for an owner/occupant exclusively using a dwelling for personal use and as their primary dwelling, the ability to receive a reduction to the market value of the home. The land surrounding the dwelling will not exceed 1 acre for value purposes. The owner only has to make one application which will be good for the duration of ownership of the dwelling being used as the primary dwelling.

**Eligibility**

In order for the claimant to be eligible for the current year, the home must have been occupied on January 1 or before April 15 of the year and occupied:

- At least 6 months during the prior year; or
- Majority of the time owned if less than 1 year; or
- Majority of time occupied if less than 1 year.

As a side note, if the claimant owned a duplex and occupied only one side as the primary dwelling, only ½ of the value would be use to calculate any reduction. The exemption does not include lessees, tenants, roomers or boarders.

Another word of caution. When a couple gets divorced and one of the spouses retains the home as their primary dwelling, ownership just changed. The 'new' owner needs to re-file for homeowner exemption, even though he/she never vacated the property. The divorced spouse/occupant is considered a new owner and thus has to be treated as such.

**Application after April 15**

What happens if a buyer purchased a property after April 15? The buyer can still apply for homeowner exemption but it won't take effect until the following year.

However, if the buyer purchased a property which already has a homeowner exemption in effect, the new owner will be able to take advantage of the previous owner's exemption.

If the owner purchased a property that was pre-owned but not occupied as a primary dwelling (it may have been a rental), then the new owner would not be eligible during the current year for the exemption but would be eligible for the next year.

**Exemption calculation**

The amount exempt from taxation will be the first $75,000 of the market value or 50% of the market value. The value is subject to and will reflect cost-of-living adjustments. These adjustments are subject to fluctuations and are tied to the annual change in the Idaho housing index determined by the United States office of federal housing enterprise oversight.

An example from the base of $75,000, the adjusted base amount for 2010 is $101,153. So, 50% of the property value or $101,153, which ever is less, is what the exemption would be for 2010. Let's say the property market value is $265,000 in 2010. 50% of $265,000 is $132,500. Since $101,153 is less, the $265,000 would be reduced and revalued to $163,847 for tax purposes.

**Circuit Breaker**

IC 63-701

Figure 3

## Circuit Breaker

Another property tax reduction program is known as the 'circuit breaker'. The maximum amount of property tax reduction that can be claimed for 2010 was $1,320.

This program is designed primarily for lower income older people. For example, to qualify for 2010, the maximum income was capped at $28,000 for 2009. The income is based on gross income less unreimbursed medical expenses.

The applicant must meet one or more criteria as of January 1:

- Age 65 or older
- Widow(er)
- Blind
- Fatherless or motherless child under 18
- Former prisoner of war/hostage
- Veteran with 10% or more service disability
- Disabled as recognized by Social Security, Railroad Retirement, or Federal Civil Service

The applicant needs to contact the assessor in the county in which the owner and property is located to receive the application form. There will be a long list of what the income guidelines are, as well as explaining medical issues.

| | |
|---|---|
| **Application deadline** | File the completed application between January 1 and April 15. This particular program must be applied for each and every year the owner is eligible. The deadline is April 15 and cannot be extended. If the application is approved, the tax reduction will appear on the December tax bill.<br><br>The monies paid by the program comes out the Idaho state general fund and are paid to the county. Thus, the county does not suffer any loss of operating income. |
| **New construction exception**<br>IC 63-602W | **New Construction Exemption**<br>New homes or improvements never occupied are exempt from property taxation. However, once residential improvements are occupied, they shall be subject to occupancy tax. |
| **Occupancy tax**<br>IC 63-317 | **Occupancy Tax**<br>An occupancy tax shall be levied upon all newly constructed and occupied residential, commercial and industrial structures, including manufactured housing. The occupancy tax shall be for that portion of the calendar year in which first occupancy occurs.<br><br>It is the obligation of the owner of any newly constructed improvement or manufactured housing to report to the county assessor that the improvement or manufactured housing has been occupied. |
| **Homeowner Exemption Application** | Upon completion of the appraisal by the county assessor, the owner will be notified of their right to apply for homeowner exemption. If done so within 30 days of receiving such notification, the exemption will be extended to the property. |
| **Penalties** | In the event the owner fails to report to the county assessor that the property is ready for occupancy, the assessor shall notify the county board of equalization. The board may impose a penalty of an additional amount equal to 5% of the tax for each month following the date of first occupancy to a maximum of a 25% penalty. |
| **Two tax bills** | The lesson learned is not to occupy, or allow to be occupied, any residential property without first notifying the county assessor.<br>As a side note, the owner will receive two tax bills for the first year; one for occupancy tax, and the other for the general tax on the land. |

# Property Taxes

## Property taxes

Property taxes are based on the total cost of operating various parts of the government, divided by the total value of the properties. All the parts that make up a tax bill are known as tax districts. Each tax district operates within a boundary limit. Thus, your home could be exactly like the home across the street but the taxes could be different. Why? Because the home across the street may be in a different taxing district.

**Tax districts**

Examples of different taxing districts could be:
> County
> City
> Fire
> School district
> Parks & Recreation
> Highway
> Special bonding
> Police
> Emergency bonding
> Ambulance
> Mosquito abatement
> Airport
> College
> Recreation center

As an example, all the taxing districts a home is located in could total 0.01375 and the property value is $100,000. Multiply the tax rate times the property value and the tax equates to $1,375.

**Assessed value vs. cost of operating government**

There's a misconception that if the assessed value of a property goes up, so will the taxes. This would not be true if the cost of operating the government didn't change. Conversely, if all the property values decreased and the government kept the cost the same from one year to the next, the taxes would still be the same. Remember, the key is the cost of operating the government. Taxes only increase when the cost of the government increases. Assessed value is only one part of the equation.

**Tax Statements**
IC 63-903

## Tax Statements

All tax statements are to be sent to all property owners no later than the *fourth Monday in November*. The owner now has until December 20 to either pay the taxes in full or elect to make two equal payments. The first half is due by *December 20* and the second half is due no later than *June 20* of the following year.

**Tax delinquency**
IC 63-1001

## Delinquency

Payment for delinquent taxes will be applied to the oldest delinquency on record. Interest on a delinquency will be charged at 1% per month calculated from January 1, following the year the tax lien attached.

Remember when we previously stated taxes can be paid in two installments? Don't be late on the second installment. The delinquency will start when the lien was first placed on the property. Let's say you were late by 2 days in making the second installment. The interest would revert back to and begin when the lien was placed; 1 year plus 5 months and 22 days; that equates to a little more than 17% interest!!!!

**Important Dates**

As one can see, it's very important to remember various dates involved with taxes. The following are helpful reminders.

| | |
|---|---|
| *January 1* | Tax lien date each year |
| *January 1* | annual assessment value on property |
| *1ˢᵗ Monday in June* | Assessment notice to owner |
| *4ᵗʰ Monday in June* | Latest date for assessment protests |
| *4ᵗʰ Monday in Nov.* | Tax notice to owner |
| *December 20* | 1ˢᵗ half taxes due |
| *June 20* | (following year) - 2ⁿᵈ half taxes due |

**Tax Deed**
IC 63-1005

## Tax Deed

If property taxes have been delinquent and not redeemed within 3 years from the date of delinquency, public notice and notice to the record owner or owners will advise them of the tax delinquency.

If the owner doesn't redeem and pay at least the taxes owed for the third year for which the property was assessed and the delinquency exists, then the owner will lose their property.

Figure 1 – December 21 Shade Point

Step 2: Determining Height of Highest Shade Producing Point

**(A) LOCATING THE POINT**

The highest shade producing point will usually be the tallest point of the structure, but not always. Whenever the roof pitch is at an angle less than 17 degrees (i.e. a 4 in 12 roof pitch or less) the highest shade producing point will be the bottom eave of the structure (see Figure 3 below). Whenever the roof pitch is 5 in 12 or greater the highest shade producing point will be the highest point of the structure. The altitude, or vertical bearing, of the sun at 10:00 a.m. and 2:00 p.m. on December 21 is 17 degrees above the horizon.

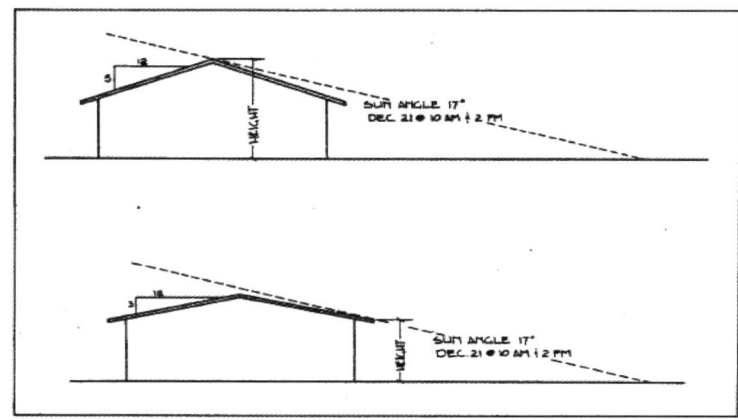

Figure 3
Location of Highest Shade Producing Point Differs with Roof Pitch

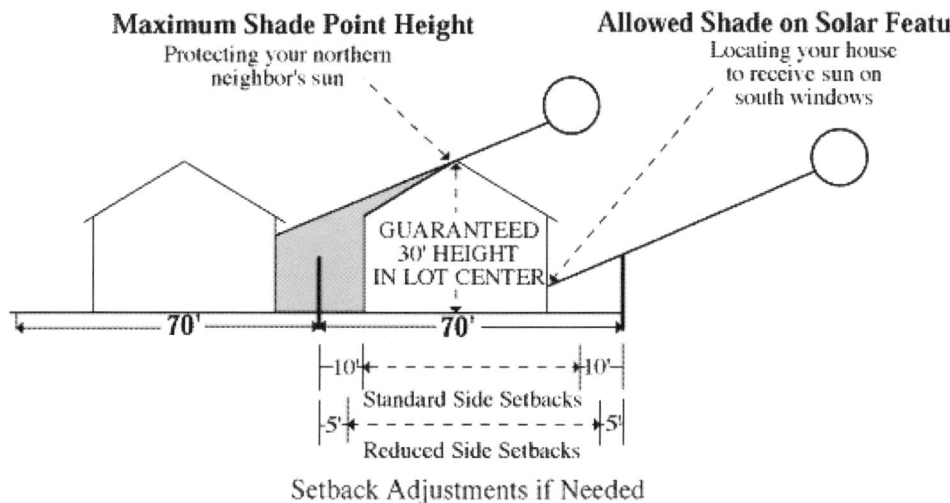

**Maximum Shade Point Height**
Protecting your northern
neighbor's sun

**Allowed Shade on Solar Feature**
Locating your house
to receive sun on
south windows

GUARANTEED
30' HEIGHT
IN LOT CENTER

70'        70'

10'        10'
Standard Side Setbacks
5'          5'
Reduced Side Setbacks

Setback Adjustments if Needed
to Meet Solar Standards

## Figure 2 – Homeowner Exemption Application

**ADA COUNTY ASSESSOR**
**Transaction Verification / Homeowner's**
**Exemption Application**

PLEASE HAND-DELIVER, MAIL
OR FAX SIGNED COPY TO
**Ada County Assessor's Office**
190 E Front St., Ste 107, Boise, ID 83702
Phone (208) 287-7200  Fax (208) 287-7209
www.adacountyassessor.org

If you would like a receipt, mark one: ☐ Fax to: _____

☐ Mail to address below

Owner(s) of Record: _____

Mailing Address _____  Property Address _____

City, State: _____  City, State: _____

Zip: _____  Zip: _____

Email Address _____  Phone No. _____

**P A R C E L #**

### Transaction Verification

1. Type of property purchased  ☐ Bare Land  ☐ Residence  ☐ Manufactured Home
2. If your purchase was a Manufactured Home, was land included in the purchase?  ☐ Yes  ☐ No
3. TOTAL PURCHASE PRICE of this property: _____
4. Date property purchased _____  5. Date property occupied _____
6. Type of sale or activity:  ☐ a typical home purchase  ☐ to refinance property
   ☐ a transfer between relatives  ☐ forced sale (e.g., in lieu of foreclosure by a court order, etc.)
   ☐ a transfer of convenience (i.e., Quit Claim deed, create life estate, name change, etc.)
7. Are you the first occupant of this dwelling?  ☐ Yes  ☐ No
8. Comments: _____

### Homeowner's Exemption Eligibility Declaration

To qualify for a **HOMEOWNER'S EXEMPTION,** Idaho Code 63-602G, this property must serve as your primary dwelling.  To receive the Homeowner's Exemption for the current year, you **must apply & have occupied the dwelling before April 15.** Applications received after this deadline will be considered for the next tax year.

1. Is there a co-signer on your loan? (a co-signer is someone that helped you qualify for the mortgage you otherwise did not qualify for on your own)
   If yes, an **Affidavit of Possessory & Security Interests** is required to obtain a full exemption.  ☐ Yes  ☐ No
2. Is this property held in title by a Trust? (other than a deed of trust)
   If yes, an **Affidavit Regarding Resident of Trust** is required to obtain exemption.  ☐ Yes  ☐ No
3. Previous Address _____
4. Previous County _____  5. Is an exemption claimed at this address?  ☐ Yes  ☐ No

*By signing this application I certify to the Ada County Assessor that I meet all of the following requirements to qualify for the Homeowner's Exemption: 1) I am a resident of Idaho. 2) I own or am purchasing under contract and I occupy as my primary dwelling place the property herein described.  3) I have not made application for Homeowner's Exemption on any other previously mentioned property in the State of Idaho, and 4) The information provided herein is true and correct.*

### ALL OWNERS CLAIMING THE EXEMPTION MUST SIGN!

_____  _____  _____  _____
Owner / Occupant Signature  Date  Owner / Occupant Signature  Date

*Pursuant to Idaho Code 63-602G(5) upon discovery of evidence indicating the existence of an improperly claimed
Homeowner's Exemption, the Assessor must assess a recovery of property taxes, plus costs, late changes and interest.*

PRINTVER 12/2009

## Figure 3 – Circuit Breaker

# APPLICATION FOR PROPERTY TAX REDUCTION FOR 2010
ALL OF THE FOLLOWING QUESTIONS MUST BE COMPLETED. ATTACH SUPPORTING DOCUMENTS.

| County | Code Area | Parcel Number |
|---|---|---|

**Section A.** 1. Ownership Information (Name, address and ZIP code)

**Section B.** Eligibility Status  As of January 1, 2010, I was (check all that apply)

☐ 65 or older  ☐ Blind  ☐ Former P.O.W.  ☐ Fatherless or Motherless Minor

☐ Widow(er):  Spouse Name_____  Date of Death_____

☐ Veteran 10-30% Service-connected disability
☐ Veteran 40-100% Service-connected disability
☐ Veteran Nonservice-connected disability with pension

Entity recognizing the disability:
Soc. Sec. Adm. ☐   Fed. Civil Svc. ☐   R/R Retirement ☐

2. Social Security Number (Claimant) | Social Security Number (Spouse)

3. Birth Date (Claimant) | Birth Date (Spouse)

4. As of January 1, 2010, you were:
☐ Single  ☐ Married  ☐ Widow(er)/Not remarried

5. Physical address of the property if different than ownership information.

6. Did you receive a Property Tax Reduction in 2009?  ☐ Yes ☐ No

7. Have you filed a claim on a different primary residence between January 1, 2010 and now?  ☐ Yes ☐ No
Where? _____

8. Did you occupy your home as your primary residence before April 15, 2010?  ☐ Yes ☐ No

9. Did you or your spouse stay in a care facility in 2009?  ☐ Yes ☐ No

10. Did you receive rental income for all or any part of this property in 2009?
If yes, please attach a copy of your rental agreement.  ☐ Yes ☐ No

11. If you used any part of this property for business or commercial use in 2009, list the percent used for business or commercial use (See instructions.) _____%.

12. Did you sell real estate, stocks, or other capital assets in 2009?  ☐ Yes ☐ No

13. This year, you or your spouse will file: (Check all that apply.)
☐ Federal Income Tax Return (Attach a copy of this return.) (If your tax information is incomplete, please contact your county assessor for instructions on completing this form.)
☐ State income tax return (List state, if other than Idaho:_____.)
☐ Idaho grocery credit form

14.                                                                     Claimant  Spouse
I certify that my Social Security number and birthdate are correct.  ☐  ☐
I certify that I am a citizen or legal permanent resident of the United States, OR  ☐  ☐
I certify that I am in the United States legally.  ☐  ☐

**Under penalty of perjury, I certify that to the best of my knowledge the information I have provided here is true, correct, and complete.**

**I grant permission to any government agency and contractor to confirm my status and to reveal to the Idaho State Tax Commission the total monetary payments made to me or my spouse during 2009.**

(Check one) ☐ Yes ☐ No

Claimant(s) (Please print.)                         Date

Signature(s) and Relationship        Telephone Number

**Section C.** Income
Household Income and Qualified Expenses
January 1 - December 31, 2009
Subsection 1

1. Federal adjusted gross income......................... $ _____
Extension filed ☐ Yes ☐ No

Subsection 2
Include all income from all sources **not** included in Section 1
(taxable and nontaxable)

2. Social Security income/SSI (Claimant)............. $ _____
3. Social Security income/SSI (Spouse)............... $ _____
4. Capital gains .................................. $ _____
5. Wages, workers' compensation, and/or unemployment ........................ $ _____
6. Pensions, retirements, annuities, and/or IRAs  $ _____
7. VA pension or compensation ......................... $ _____
8. Interest and dividends....................................... $ _____
9. Railroad retirement ...................................... $ _____
10. Other income
(Received from _____) $ _____
11. Subtotal (add lines 1 through 10) ................... $ _____
12. Principal of annuity (Attach contract.)............... $ (_____)
13. Total of nonreimbursed, paid medical expenses and medical insurance premiums.................... $ (_____)
14. Total of paid or prepaid funeral expenses
(Attach receipt - maximum allowable amount: $5,000.) $ (_____)
15. Subtotal of deductions (Add lines 12, 13, and 14)  $ (_____)
16. Total net income (Subtract line 15 from line 11) $ _____

If you would like information about property tax deferral for any remaining taxes, ask your assessor or contact the State Tax Commission for a brochure explaining this program.

### FOR COUNTY USE ONLY
Check all that apply:
☐ Single family            ☐ Sole owner
☐ Multi dwelling _____%   ☐ Community property
☐ Multi use _____%        ☐ Partial ownership _____%
                            ☐ Trust or life estate
                            ☐ LP, LLC, or Corp.
Overall claimant percentage of ownership/use _____%
I _____ certify that Property Tax
County Assessor or Deputy Assessor
Reduction benefits are only applied to the claimant's eligible portion of the net taxable value.

| Tax reduction not to exceed: | Date |
|---|---|

| Approved and verified by Assessor or Deputy Assessor: ☐ Yes ☐ No | Disapproved and verified by Assessor or Deputy Assessor: ☐ Yes ☐ No |

**THIS APPLICATION MUST BE FILED WITH YOUR COUNTY ASSESSOR BY APRIL 15, 2010**

# Questions – Chapter 11

1. The property of a person who died had no heirs and ended up as 'unclaimed property'. How long does one have to file a claim?

   A. 1 year
   B. 365 days
   C. 5 years
   D. 1827 days

2. A solar lot line is often referenced on what date?

   A. June 21
   B. September 15
   C. December 21
   D. January 16

3. Scenic views and open space can be protected with:

   A. Conservation easement
   B. Easement by prescription
   C. Solar easements
   D. Access easement

4. If there isn't enough water to satisfy all the water rights, who get the water?

   A. All water shared equally
   B. Junior water rights holder
   C. Senior water rights holder
   D. Water is shut off if there isn't any

5. Who can drill a water well?
   A. Water witcher
   B. Property owner
   C. Licensed well driller
   D. A registered well driller

6. What's required before a well can be drilled?

   A. A soil test
   B. A drilling permit
   C. A building and drilling permit
   D. A drilling permit and soil test

7. A zoning regulation is an example of:

   A. Eminent domain
   B. Police power
   C. Economic changes
   D. Federal regulations

8. Any changes to the comprehensive plan requires how many public hearings?

   A. 1
   B. 2
   C. 3
   D. 4

9. To modify the comprehensive plan, how much notice must be given prior the hearing

   A. 7 days
   B. 15 days
   C. 21 days
   D. 30 days

10. Zoning ordinances are used to identify?

   A. Population
   B. Traffic patterns
   C. Density
   D. Age groups

11. In an owner needed a setback change to accommodate a structure design, the owner would request:

A. Grandfathered use
B. Comprehensive plan change
C. Zoning amendment
D. Zoning variance

12. Who certifies the correctness of a plat for a planned subdivision?

A. City or county planning commission
B. County recorder
C. Professional land surveyor
D. The developer of the subdivision

13 What's the penalty for offering subdivision lots for sale from a preliminary plat but has not yet been approved and recorded?

A. Shut down all future subdivision sales
B. $100 for each lot
C. $500 for any lot
D. Cannot close the sale until the subdivision is approved

14. How many categories are available to cities to annex land into cities?

A. 1
B. 2
C. 3
D. 4

15. What building code has been adopted for all construction?

A. Uniform Building Code
B. State of Idaho Construction Code
C. National Building Code
D. International Building Code

16. Contractors doing major surface repairs to homes built prior to 1978 must be:

A. Certified
B. Licensed
C. Registered
D. Approved

17. A bail bond lien won't be released until?

A. A trial begins
B. A verdict has been reached
C. Court approved sentencing
D. The guilty party has served their sentence

18. A mechanic's lien shall remain on the property no longer than:

A. 1 month
B. 6 months
C. 12 months
D. 24 months

19. Who has the highest priority in which mechanic's liens will be processed?

A. Original contractor
B. Sub contractors
C. Materialmen
D. Laborers

20. How often are assessors required to make physical property valuations?

A. At least once a year
B. At least once every 2 years
C. At least once every 3 years
D. At least once every 5 years

21. All assessed property values are based on the value determined on:

    A. January 1
    B. First Monday in June
    C. Fourth Monday in June
    D. December 20

22. Homeowner Exemption is available for?

    A. Primary dwelling
    B. Agricultural purposes
    C. Second home in mountains
    D. Investment properties

23. When is the dollar amount of the Circuit Breaker program reviewed?

    A  Semi annually.
    B. Annually
    C. At least once every 5 years
    D. January 1

24. What age may qualify for Circuit Breaker?

    A. 21 or older
    B. 55 or older
    C. 65 or older
    D. 72 or older

25. Occupancy tax applies to what type of property?

    A. Any occupied residential home
    B. Recreational housing for investment
    C. Newly constructed homes not previously occupied
    D. Investment properties

26. Newly constructed homes will receive how many tax statements in the year occupied?

    A. 1 for land value only
    B. 1 for land and dwelling value combined
    C. 2 with previous and current land value
    D. 2 one for land; other for dwelling value

27. Tax statements are sent to owners no later than:

    A. June 20
    B. July 1 (Idaho fiscal year)
    C. 4ᵗʰ Monday in November
    D. December 20

28. When is the first installment of property taxes due?

    A. June 20
    B. July 1 (Idaho fiscal year)
    C. 4ᵗʰ Monday in November
    D. December 20

29. What period of time does one have to bring delinquent taxes current and not be subject to a tax sale?

    A. 1 year
    B. 2 years
    C. 3 years
    D. 4 years.

# Chapter 12

# Real Estate Contracts

A contract is an agreement between two parties or entities with an obligation to do or not to do something in return for a benefit known as consideration.

The real estate industry is founded upon the use of contracts which can involve variations of circumstances and complexities.

The Idaho Real Estate Commission encourages real estate agents to advise the parties to a transaction to seek legal counsel for any questions arising on any area of contract law. This concept is acknowledged with statutory duties - 'when appropriate, advising the client to seek appropriate tax, legal, and other professional advice or counsel when legal advice is desired or necessary'.

**Rule 303**

Furthermore, Rule 303 of the Idaho Real Estate License Law and Rules specifically states on the subject of legal opinion - 'A broker or sales associate shall *not* discourage any party to a real estate transaction from seeking the advice of an attorney'.

# Contract Requirements

**Essential elements**

## Essential elements

In order to create a valid real estate contract to purchase real estate in Idaho, there are six essential elements.

1. Legally competent parties

2. Offer and acceptance with a meeting of the minds

3. Lawful objective

4. Enforceable legal description

5. Valuable consideration

6. Written document, signed by all parties to the contract

**Competent parties**

## Legal capacity

In Idaho, a person must be 18 or older to have the legal capacity to enter into a valid contract. Persons younger than 18 are referred to as minors.

Although minors do not have the legal capacity to contract, a minor may make a contract and live up to it. The contracts created by a minor are not void, but they are voidable. This means the minor may renounce or disaffirm as long as they are still minors or within a reasonable time after they have reached age 18.

**Incompetency**

If a person has been declared by a court to be of unsound mind, any contract made by that person would be void. The reason is that such persons do not comprehend the consequences or obligations of a contract. However, an incompetent person could be represented by a parent or legally appointed guardian to assume the obligations of a contract.

**Parole board approval**

If a person has been convicted of a serious crime and enters into a contract, the contract could be considered void unless such a person has obtained expressed permission from the state parole board.

**Contracts to be in writing**
IC 9-505

## Idaho Statute of Frauds

The Idaho Statute of Frauds state that transfers of real property must be in writing. Written requirements also apply to leases for longer than 1 year.

**Commissions to be in writing**
IC 9-508

The Idaho Statute of Frauds also clearly states that no contract for the payment of any sum of money or thing of value (real estate commission) shall be valid unless the contract shall be in writing. Examples would include seller or buyer representation agreements, where a fee or commission is involved between the consumer and the brokerage.

## Mutual Agreement

The term mutual agreement may also be known as the 'meeting of the minds'. It means that there is a willingness by all parties to enter into a contract. However, mutual agreement cannot exist if the terms are ambiguous, vague, or undisclosed. Nor can mutual agreement exist if the offer does not clearly state the obligations of each party involved. Also a meeting of the minds cannot be achieved if there is an intent to deceive or failure to disclose important information such as an adverse material fact. Lastly, the offer and acceptance must be without duress or undue influence giving unfair advantage to one party over the other.

### Lawful objective

A contract cannot be made for the purpose of breaking the law or violating public policy. An example could be purchasing a property for a use such as a day care center in a residential neighborhood that violates local use code. Such a contract is void or if already in operation, it is unenforceable in a court of law.

### Enforceable legal description

The legal description should be sufficient enough that no other property will encroach or duplicate the subject property. A recorded record of survey will verify the description.

### Valuable Consideration

If consideration is lacking from any party to a transaction, the contract fails to be legally binding. Both parties give something of value to a real estate contract. Consideration does not always involve money. It can also be a promise, other property or services.

### Written document signed by all parties

It's not unusual to have additional documents accompany a offer to purchase such as: amendments, addendums, counter offers and possible required disclosures. ALL documents must be signed by ALL parties to a transaction.

# Purchase and Sale Agreements

Although real estate licensees cannot draft a contract, they are allowed to 'fill in the blanks' of a pre-printed contract or agreement. Idaho does not endorse the use of, or require any specific form or format to be used in the practice of real estate.

But a generally known contract for acquiring or selling real estate in Idaho is known as a Real Estate Purchase and Sale Agreement.

Approximately 90% of all active licensees in Idaho are members of the Idaho Association of REALTORS®, also known as the 'IAR'. Most licensees use the forms created by this trade organization for their real estate business. So, we'll also use some of the forms created by the IAR as guidelines to demonstrate what could be incorporated into a legal, valid contract.

**Seeking legal counsel**

## Disclaimer to seek counsel

At the top of the Purchase and Sale Agreement, a disclaimer clearly suggests the agreement is a legally binding contract and if any party has questions, an attorney or accountant should be consulted. It's not a bad idea for an agent to read the total disclaimer to both buyer and seller as a reminder that outside counsel could be sought.

**Unauthorized practice of law**
**IC 3-420**

## Unauthorized practice of law

It's really important that real estate licensees work hard on giving lots and lots of information instead of advice. Every contract is a legal document which adds to the confusion of whether an issue results in information or advice. Taking instructions from the buyer and/or seller and converting those instructions into the contract can create a fine line. Did the agent make the recommendation to do something or did the agent merely transcribe the desires of the buyer or seller into the contract?

The penalty for someone practicing law without a license includes a fine not to exceed $500, or be imprisoned for a period not to exceed 6 months, or both! Again, let the buyers and sellers make legal decisions based on information you can provide, not the other way around.

In addition, a real estate licensee could lose their real estate license, commission, and even face a law suit for damages.

## Fill in the blanks

Sample contracts created by private sources or trade organizations are designed to 'fill in the blanks'. Remember, not all contracts contain the same information. If one is unfamiliar with a contract, it is highly suggested that each and every line be read..

Some rules to use when completing a contract that will help assure a 'meeting of the minds' between the parties include.

*1. Fill in all the blanks*

If some of the blanks are not applicable, then fill in the blank with NA or DNA which means 'not applicable' or 'does not apply'. The key is to make the contract complete and not ambiguous.

*2. Dates*

If dates are called for, try to work with specific dates. If an activity is tied to a situation occurring and not a specific date, the interpretation of the situation timing could be contested, especially if 3rd parties are involved.

*3. Categories*

Address all the categories contained within the contract to make sure all parties are aware of and understand the printed material. If any category involves activity that is date specific, make sure the dates to perform are reasonable and achievable. An overlooked category may lead to trouble later on after a contract has been accepted by all parties.

*4. Personal Property*

If there are personal property items included, make sure there is a complete identification of each item, including model and serial numbers if possible. Specific identification eliminates the possibility of substitution of items.

*5. Mandatory disclosures*

If there are mandatory disclosures required, either state or federal, make sure they are included in the contract. As an example, lead paint disclosure is required if the residence was built prior to 1978. Or, another example would be the Idaho required Seller's Property Condition Disclosure.

*6. Addendums and attachments*
Identify each and every addendum and/or attachment with numbers in a sequential order. Do not skip numbers or mix numbers and alphabet letters.

*7. Signatures*
Make sure all parties to a transaction sign and date all of the documents relating to a transaction. Avoid using initials whenever possible, especially if they aren't accompanied by a date. This can lead to question as to who signed what and when.

**Representation Confirmation**
IC 54-2085 (4)

## Representation confirmation
Whether there is representation or not, Idaho code requires a representation confirmation to be included with any purchase and sale contract. Care needs to be exercised to make sure the agency representation is accurate and correct.

**Time is of the essence**

## Time is of the essence
If 'time is of the essence' is incorporated into a contract, performance of one party is necessary to enable that party to require performance by the other party within the time period specified in the contract.

Failure to comply within the required time frame constitutes a breach of the contract. When time is not of the essence, courts generally permit parties to perform their obligations within a reasonable time. It's important to understand what is 'reasonable' to one party may not be 'reasonable' to the other.

There can be many different time frames contained in a purchase and sale agreement; not just a closing date. Dates for financing, inspections, repairs, appraisals and possession need to be known by all parties concerned.

**Contract changes**

## Contract changes
It's not unusual for a purchase and sale agreement to incorporate changes after acceptance but prior to closing. Addendums, amendments, counter offers, exhibits, and other items can flow in and out of a transaction. The key to maintaining a 'meeting of the minds' is to accurately keep all changes in numerical sequence and dated. There needs to be a 'paper trail' with no voids.

If changes are made it is important to know the difference between an addendum and an amendment.

**Addendum**

## Addendum

It might be noteworthy to know that an addendum adds to or supplements an existing contract. For example, the original contract called for and was contingent upon a property inspection by a certain date. The inspection was completed and acknowledged with an addendum.

**Amendment**

## Amendment

An amendment, on the other hand, is a modification later to the terms of an already accepted contract. Should it be necessary to change the contract it would require the approval of *all* parties to the contract. An example would be to extend a closing date from the original accepted date. Both parties would need to agree. If one of the parties does not agree, then the original closing date would be the binding date for all parties to close the transaction.

**Counter offer**

## Counter Offer

A counter offer is a response to a previous offer that has not yet been accepted. Making a counter offer automatically rejects the original offer or prior counter offer. Because the original offer becomes 'dead' with a counter offer, sellers need to be aware that the buyer is no longer bound by the terms of the original offer.

Caution needs to be taken when a seller makes minor changes on the original offer and initials and dates the changes. Bear in mind, the seller 'changed' the original document and the changes now constitutes a counter offer requiring buyer acceptance.

Although not that unusual, these 'short cuts' are not recommended. Why?

• 1st, where is the time limit for the buyer to accept?
• 2nd, in what manner is the buyer expected to accept?
• 3rd, do changes change other parts of the original agreement? If so, how? Are the changes (usually handwritten) legible? Initialing and dating changes on the original contract can be dangerous indeed. For example, changing a price could have implications surrounding the buyers ability to finance by changing the terms of financing.

By using a separate counter offer form, confusion as to who did what and when is greatly reduced or eliminated. The counter offer form allows plenty of space to make whatever necessary changes are needed to address unanswered issues in the original offer.

With a properly executed counter offer, signatures and dates are well documented to eliminate what changes and when changes were actually made. It is very important that the counter offer makes specific reference to the original offer so all the original terms and conditions are connected to and incorporated into the counter offer. As a precaution to make sure all paperwork is incorporated, it is a good idea to have the counter offer stapled (not paper clipped) to the original offer and addendums, if any.

Also, do not use an addendum form and scratch out the word 'addendum' and add 'counter offer'. The sequence for acceptance and dates of an addendum are not adequate unless specifically referenced. Just use the counter offer form; it's much safer!

**Guideline 19 - IREC**

Finally, there often arises the issue of whether the seller is supposed to sign the original offer or counter offer. Guideline #19 from the Idaho Real Estate Commission takes the confusion out of who signs what.

If a counter offer has specific language that incorporates it into the original agreement, it is not mandatory that the seller sign both documents. The seller may sign the counter offer only. However, if there isn't any specific incorporation language, the seller must sign both the counter offer and the original purchase and sale agreement.

## Rejected or terminated contract

**Rejected offers**
IC 54-2048 (d)

If a purchase and sale contract is not accepted or is rejected, there still needs to be a record of the 'sale fail'. All offers presented to the seller and not accepted by that seller shall be clearly marked and dated as rejected. The original or a true copy of all rejected offers must be retained in the files of the selling broker. Although Idaho code does not identify who is to date and identify as 'rejected', it may be a good idea to have the seller actually date and sign as 'rejected' in their own handwriting as proof that the offer was actually presented to the seller. This would serve as proof that the rejection came from the seller and no one else.

**Rejected offers - record keeping**
IC 54-2049

All offers accepted, countered or rejected, are to be kept by the broker for 3 calendar years after the year in which the event occurred, the transaction closed, all funds were disbursed, or the agreement and any written extension expired.

## Double contracts

Double contracts, sometimes known as 'creative' financing, are prohibited, period!! You will find the term, 'double contract' used several times throughout this text as a constant reminder of this illegal activity.

**Double contract prohibited**
IC 54-2054 (5)

No licensed broker or salesperson shall use, propose the use of, agree to the use of, or knowingly permit the use of a 'double contract'. Such conduct by a licensee shall be deemed flagrant misconduct and dishonorable and dishonest dealing and shall subject the licensee to disciplinary action by the Commission.

Simply put, a 'double contract' means 2 or more written or unwritten contracts of sale, purchase and sale agreements, loan applications, or any other agreements, 1 of which is not made known to the prospective loan underwriter or the loan guarantor, to enable the buyer to obtain a larger loan than the true sales price would allow, or to enable the buyer to qualify for a loan which he or she otherwise could not obtain.

Again, this is why it is so important that all addendums and amendments be included in sequential order. No side agreements are allowed without written disclosure to the loan underwriter.

**Earnest money**
IC 54-2045 (4)

## Handling earnest money

One of the required elements of a purchase and sale agreement includes earnest money (consideration). Idaho code requires all consideration, including cash, checks held in an uncashed form and promissory notes, received by a sales associate in connection with a real estate transaction shall be *immediately* delivered to the broker or the broker's office.

**Earnest money transfer to 3rd party**
IC 54-2041

If the parties to a transaction have instructed the broker or its licensees, in writing, to transfer moneys or property to a 3rd party including but not limited to, a title, an escrow or a trust company, the broker or its licensees have no right to exercise control over the safekeeping or disposition of said moneys or property.

However, the broker shall be responsible for maintaining a record of the time and date that said moneys or property was transferred from the broker to a 3rd party.

Whoever delivers the earnest money or property to an approved 3rd party needs to get a receipt in exchange for the deposit. It's suggested that the receipt contain a date including hour and minute received. This will serve as evidence in case documents are either misplaced or lost.

# Questions – Chapter 12

1. In the subject area of legal opinions, Rule 303 states a broker or sales associate shall:

   A. Encourage the use of legal counsel
   B. Seek opinion from a title insurance company to verify their own opinion
   C. Not discourage any party from seeking advice from an attorney
   D. Obtain legal opinion from the Idaho Real Estate Commission

2. Leases must be in writing if they are longer than:

   A. 1 month
   B. 3 months
   C. 6 months
   D. 1 year

3. What's the maximum time a real estate salesperson can be imprisoned for unauthorized practice of law?

   A. 1 year
   B. 6 months
   C. 3 months
   D. Can receive a fine but not imprisoned

4. Representation Confirmation and Acknowledgment must be included with:

   A. Agency Disclosure Brochure
   B. Buyer Representation Agreement
   C. Seller Representation Agreement
   D. Purchase and Sale Agreement

5. What does a counter offer do to the original offer.

   A. Makes original offer voidable
   B. Voids the original offer
   C. Extends the terms of the original offer
   D. Makes original offer valid

6. All rejected offers must be:

   A. Maintained in broker's file for 5 years
   B. Removed from the broker's files
   C. Marked and signed as 'rejected'
   D. Marked and dated as 'rejected'

7. The use of a 'double contract' is:

   A. Encouraged
   B. Discouraged
   C. Prohibited
   D. Used as a back-up contract

8. When does earnest money need to be delivered to the broker or broker's office?

   A. Immediately
   B. Within 24 hours
   C. Within 48 hours
   D. Prior to closing

# Chapter 13

# Recording Of Title Information

## Recording concept

The concept of recording is based on English common law together with the Statute of Frauds which state certain documents must be in writing to be valid.

The difference between common law title and a Torrens title is that a Certificate of Title is absolute. An example is a Certificate of Title to an automobile.

On the other hand, common law transfer of title is based on the premise that the recording system does not determine who owns the title or interest in land. That determination is made through litigation in the courts. As a safety measure, most transfers of real property include title insurance, which will be discussed later.

With a government sponsored public recording service, public records would be open and free of charge to anyone confirms 'he who is first in time is preferred in right' which leads to the 'chain of title'.

**Idaho recording law**
Title 55, Chapter 8

All states, including Idaho, have passed recording acts to provide for the recording of every document in which an estate, interest, or right in land is created, encumbered, or transferred.

The primary purpose of recording is to give notice to others that an interest is claimed on real property to:

1. Provide constructive notice to the public of a real estate transaction;

2. Provide a perpetual history of the title to a particular parcel of land.

**Instruments to be recorded**
IC 31-2402

## Instruments that may be recorded in Idaho

Some examples of real estate related documents that can be recorded include:

Deeds
Mortgages
Deeds of trust
Power of Attorney
Leases
Judgments affecting title
    Partition action
    Water rights
    Quiet title action
    Condemnation action
U. S. Patents
Affidavits
    Facts showing marital status
    Possession through tax deed
    Plats and legal descriptions
Notices of mechanic's liens
Financing statements (UCC)
Platting
Condominium instruments
Conservation easements
Manufactured homes statement of intent
Sale of water rights

All these documents, and many more not listed above, may assist the public to determine the quality of ownership with historical information regarding any real estate.

**Constructive notice**
IC 55-811

## Constructive notice

In Idaho, recording is not part of the actual conveyance process. When the grantor delivers a properly executed deed to the grantee, and the grantee accepts the delivery, the conveyance of title to the real property is effective.

The act of recording establishes constructive notice and priority among competing interests in the same parcel of real property. An unrecorded instrument is valid as between the parties to the instrument. The Idaho Supreme Court made the following observation about the primary purpose of the recording laws:

*The primary purpose of the recording statutes is to give notice to others that an interest is claimed in real property, and thus give protection against bone fide third parties who may be dealing in the same property.*

Matheson v. Harris, 98 Idaho 758, 572, P.2nd 861, at 864 (1977)

**Recording requirements**
IC 55-707 and 32-912

## Requirements to record

The acknowledgment of an instrument must not be taken, unless the officer taking it knows, or has satisfactory evidence from a credible source, that the person making such acknowledgment is the individual who is described in, and who executed, the instrument.

It should be noted that neither the husband nor wife may sell, convey or encumber the community real estate unless the other joins in executing the sale agreement, deed or other instrument of conveyance.

It is possible that a husband or wife could own property as 'sole and separate' during marriage. However, a title company will probably require a 'quit claim' deed to make sure the property being conveyed is in fact 'sole and separate'.

Not all documents require acknowledgment. Some examples of documents that do not require proper acknowledgment are:

- Patents & other instruments recorded by the United States
- Authenticated judgments
- Notice of Lis Pendens
- Mechanics liens

**Place of recording**
IC 55-808

## Place of recording

Any instruments that affect real property must be recorded in the county recorder's office of the county where the affected real property is located. Recordable documents that do not specifically deal with real property are normally recordable in the county where the business is being conducted or a part to the document resides.

**English required**
IC 73-121 (3)

Idaho also requires that 'any document required to be filed or recorded . . . . shall be in the English language or shall be accompanied by a <u>certified</u> translation in English'.

**Endorsement**

IC 31-2410

## Endorsement and Index System

Once a properly executed instrument is deposited in the recorder's office with the proper officer to record, the recorder will endorse the document with the time it was received including the year, month, day, hour, and minute of its reception. The document will then be placed in the proper index.

**Book and page**

IC 31-2411

Also included will be the book and page or instrument number in which it is recorded and then it is delivered upon request to the party leaving the same for record.

**Indexes**

IC 31-2404

Constructive notice does not occur until the document is indexed. In Idaho, there are 27 different indexes that the county recorder must keep. They include:

1. Grantors (deeds)
2. Grantees (deeds)
3. Mortgagors
4. Mortgagees
5. Release of mortgagees
6. Release of mortgagors
7. Power of Attorney
8. Lessor
9. Lessee
10. Marriage Certificates - men
11. Marriage Certificates - women
12. Assignments of Mortgages and Leases - assignors
13. Assignments of Mortgages and Leases - assignees
14. Wills
15. Official Bonds
16. Mechanic's Liens
17. Transcripts and Judgment
18. Attachments
19. Notices of Actions
20. Separate Property of Married Women
21. Possessory Claims
22. Homesteads
23. Real Property Agreements
24. Mining Claims
25. Water Rights
26. General Index
27. Financing Statements (UCC)

Confused? You are not alone, especially when trying to research a specific parcel of land. So, consider an alternative; a title insurance company. Title insurance companies take all the information contained in the various indexes and apply the appropriate information to a particular parcel via tract books.

Tract books identify a specific parcel of property and then list every specific recorded document that affects that property. As one can see, it could take hours or maybe even days to research the county public records for the same information that could be gathered at a title insurance company in literally minutes.

Typically title insurance companies duplicates the same records that the county recorder has, on a daily basis, or at least within a week of actual recording, into their own tract records.

## Priority of recorded documents

Generally speaking, those documents first recorded take priority over subsequent recorded or unrecorded documents. However, it should be understood that some types of liens will in fact attach to property, even after the property has changed owners.

An example would be mechanic's liens. Another example could be property tax liens which attach to the property on January 1 of every year. These examples are another reason purchasers should seriously consider having an extended title insurance policy which covers liens not of public record at the time of recording.

**Abstracter bonding**
IC 54-101

## Abstract of title and title search

An abstract of title contains a condensed history of the title to a piece of land in addition to a summary of conveyances. In Idaho abstract searches will go back to 1890 and the original patents. Abstractors are required to be bonded for $10,000. It's very important that there aren't any breaks in the 'chain' of historical ownership. A break in the chain could lead to someone claiming an interest in the property and create legal issues.

# Title Insurance

## Title Insurance

Title insurance is the certification or guarantee of title or ownership, or insurance of owners of property against loss by encumbrance, defective titles, invalidity, or adverse claim to title.

In Idaho, the title insurance industry is regulated by the Idaho Department of Insurance. The Department of Insurance also requires title insurance company escrow, closing or settlement fees to be filed with them.

In addition, title insurance companies are regulated against offering illegal inducements or rebates. This includes quoting or reducing any charge for title insurance to any person for less than the currently filed rate with the Department of Insurance.

The duplicated records title insurance companies secure from the county recorder are put into 'tract' books and filed by date. A patent title plant will have records going back to the first Idaho recordings beginning in 1890.

Title insurance helps bridge the issue by performing a title search to examine all public records pertaining to the property including a "chain of title" which reviews the history of ownership starting with the current owner and going back to the original owner.

In addition, the search will reveal any title-related problems with the property and report all publicly recorded liens and encumbrances against the property.

To be within the unbroken chain of title, the instrument must be discoverable or traceable through linking conveyances from the present owner through successive owners to a common grantor. If the chain is broken, a "gap" exists in the chain, creating a "cloud" on the title. If the "cloud" cannot be resolved, it may be necessary to establish ownership by a court action called a 'suit to quiet title'.

When a title search is complete, the information is gathered on a commitment document for title insurance. This document shows any defects to the property that would be listed as exceptions to the policy plus any requirements that need to be resolved before the policy can be issued.

**Marketable title**

A title that is free from objectionable defects and encumbrances will be deemed as being 'marketable', Marketable title enables the owner to sell or freely transfer his property to others.

**Title Commitment**

## Title Commitment

Once a title insurance company is satisfied with their title search, they can offer a title commitment which is a promise to issue an insurance policy on a piece of property. A Title Commitment is equivalent to a binder for other types of insurance and identifies:

1. Who is being insured
2. The amount of the insurance
3. What is being insured
4. What is required to insure the title
5. What is not insured

## Title Policies

There are two basic types of title insurance; Owners Policy and a Lenders Policy.

**Owners Standard Policy**

Owner's or Standard Owners Policy (owner)

The Standard Owner's title insurance is usually based on the *real estate purchase price*. It is purchased for a one-time fee at closing and lasts as long as the owner has an interest in the property. The Standard Owner's policy fully protects the buyer should a problem arise with the title and it was not discovered during the title search. However, the policy only covers events prior to closing.

**Owners Extended Policy**

An Extended Owners Policy should be seriously considered if there has been recent construction or new construction. It protects the owner for future acts or claims that may have occurred prior to closing but would not be of public record until after closing. A good example of such claim could be a Mechanic's Lien. The claim took place prior to closing but was filed after closing.

| **Lenders Extended Policy** | **Lenders or Extended Lenders Policy (mortgagee policy)** |
|---|---|

**Lenders Extended Policy**

Lenders or Extended Lenders Policy (mortgagee policy)
Most lenders require a lenders policy when they issue a loan. The lenders policy is usually based on the *dollar amount of the loan*. It protects the lender's interest in the property should a problem arise with the title. The coverage decreases with the reduction in outstanding loan amount and will eventually disappear when the loan is paid off.

**Endorsements**

In addition to the basic policies, endorsements may be required which will add additional costs to the base title insurance costs. Endorsements could include: zoning, easements, encroachments, condominium compliance, planned unit development, and environmental issues.

Endorsements protect against those issues that may not be of public record but could easily have a legal effect upon the property.

## Uniform Commercial Code

The Uniform Commercial Code deals primarily with commercial transactions involving the transfer of personal property in real estate.

**UCC status**

The Secretary of State's UCC (Uniform Commercial Code) Division is the agency which receives and files liens, thereby making the liens public record, as well as providing a date and time of the filing. The UCC division also maintains a database of lien filings for future documentation, as necessary.

Various liens that can be filed with the Secretary of State's office are:

Basic lien
Commodity lien
Farm lien
IRS lien
Labor lien
Medical lien
Seed lien
Utility lien

# Questions – Chapter 13

1. When is the transfer of a deed effective?

   A. When the deed is recorded
   B. When the grantee accepts delivery
   C. When the grantor signs the deed
   D. When the grantor delivers the deed

2. Any document required to be filed or recorded shall be in what language?

   A. English only
   B. English or Spanish
   C. Any language
   D. English or certified Spanish

3. The title insurance industry is regulated by what government department?

   A. Department of Finance
   B. Department of Land
   C. Department of Insurance
   D. Department of Commerce

4. A title that is free from objectionable defects and encumbrances is deemed:

   A. Free and clear
   B. Contains no liens
   C. Saleable
   D. Marketable

5. The Uniform Commercial Code deals primarily with what type of transactions?

   A. Residential
   B. Farm land
   C. 2nd homes
   D. Business opportunities

6. What type of title insurance policy gives the most protection to a borrower?

   A. Mortgagee policy
   B. Owners standard policy
   C. Owners extended policy
   D. Extended lenders policy

7. The purpose of recording, beside giving constructive notice, is to provide:

   A. An immediate current history
   B. A history of county growth
   C. A brief history of the county
   D. A perpetual history of a parcel of land

Chapter 14

# Market Analysis

## Purpose and Function of Property Appraisal

The Uniform Standard of Professional Appraisal Practice gives a general definition of appraisal as "the act or process of estimating the value". Two important appraisal concepts are incorporated in the terms - appraisal purpose and appraisal function.

The purpose is to estimate value of a property based upon a sale. The function refers to the reason an appraisal is being made. Most often it is to help a lender decide if a property is suitable as security for a loan.

Both the purpose and function have to match in order to meet the qualifications of various financing programs.

## Market Analysis vs. Appraisal

A market analysis by a real estate licensee is often known as a Competitive Market Analysis or better known as a CMA.

Whereas an appraisal has a specific purpose and function, a market analysis is designed to evaluate the marketplace to assist the seller, and in some cases, the buyer, to establish a value to offer for sale or make a purchase of real estate.

A good market analysis should mirror the basic concepts of an appraisal since the final requirement will probably mandate an appraisal for financing purposes. Therefore, a licensed real estate agent needs to know and understand the underlying concepts of both the appraisal process and the process to put together a market analysis.

**Appraisal license**
IC 54-4103

## Regulation of Appraisal Activities

Another difference between a market analysis and a fee appraisal, is that a fee appraisal requires an appraisal license. However, there are a couple exceptions.

One exception is that a market analysis does not require a license as long as the purpose is to secure a prospective listing or sale.

**Exception requirements**
IC 54-4105

Another exception allows an active broker or associate broker to render a broker's price opinion, for a fee, providing the broker's price opinion is in writing and complies with the following requirements:

1. A statement of the intended purpose of the price opinion;

2. A brief description of the subject property and property interest to be priced;

3. The basis of reasoning used to reach the conclusion of the price, including the applicable market data and/or capitalization computation;

4. Any assumptions or limiting conditions;

5. A disclosure of any existing or contemplated interest of the broker(s) issuing the opinion;

6. The name and signature of the broker(s) issuing the price opinion and the date of its issuance;

7. A disclaimer that the report is not intended to meet the uniform standards of professional appraisal practice unless the broker is a licensed appraiser;

8. A disclaimer that the broker's price opinion is not intended to be an appraisal of the market value of the property, and if an appraisal is desired, the services of a licensed or certified appraiser should be obtained.

**Basic Appraisal Concepts**

## Applying basic concepts of appraisal

Even though a real estate agent cannot perform an appraisal without an appraisal license, the agent can apply the basic principles and concepts used in creating an appraisal and incorporate the information into a market analysis.

Some of the elements of value include: utility, scarcity, demand with purchasing power and transferability. In addition, knowledge and awareness of physical forces, economic forces, social forces, and political forces need to be carefully evaluated.

Perhaps one of the more important aspects of a market analysis revolves around the economic principle of value.

Does the property conform with the surrounding area? Does the property contribute to similar types of properties? Is the property being valued or being evaluated to include physical possible uses? What are the legally permissible uses allowed? In short, what is the highest and best use for the property being valued?

Once all the various elements of value are considered, one needs to select the cost approach, income approach, or market approach to determine best method to arrive at a value.

**Cost Approach**

## Cost approach

The cost approach is based on the cost to construct, minus depreciation, plus the value of the land to arrive at a final value.

The cost approach is best used with new construction or recently constructed properties as a check and balance with the market approach. One of the difficulties with using cost approach, is that the cost can end up either higher or lower than what the market might bear.

However, sometimes the cost approach might be the only way a property can be valued, especially if the property is unique or comparable properties cannot be found to compare with the subject property. Examples are churches, hospitals or other types of unique manufacturing or applications that have few, if any, comparable properties. Another challenge revolves around depreciation, especially when the subject property is older.

**Marshall & Swift Residential Cost Handbook**

If the cost approach is used, an excellent resource is the Marshall & Swift Residential Cost Handbook. This handbook is updated quarterly and re-evaluated annually for all areas in the United States. It has incredible amounts of information and is used by most fee appraisers.

The handbook can also offer great information to compare the component costs between the 6 different types of quality categories. Also, there is an extensive section about depreciation and how to make proper calculations.

**Income Approach**

# Income Approach

The income approach is used to create value based on income. An in-depth analysis can however, require extensive knowledge to apply the appropriate formulas to arrive at an accurate value.

Real estate agents should really take the time to fully understand all that goes into creating a good analysis before pursuing income properties.

**Market Approach**

# Market Approach

The market approach is the primary method used to determine value for residential properties and is known as a Competitive Market Analysis or better known as a CMA. The process involves getting characteristics and features about the subject property and then making the appropriate adjustments with the comparable properties that best meet the characteristics of subject property.

The primary source for the comparable properties will probably be the multiple-listing-service (MLS). Because of sophisticated MLS software, similar properties can be quickly researched electronically to secure comparable properties.

The data bases to be searched will usually be divided into three categories:
1. Properties currently on the market
2. Sold properties
3. Properties that were on the market but expired.

Most agents will use sold properties, then those on the market, and lastly those that expired. However, in a changing marketplace many agents use more than one category as a 'check and balance' to verify the value.

The comparable properties that most recently been sold will be more accurate than those that sold a long time ago due to a constantly changing market place.

Location is also an important factor, especially when similar properties are located along some busy roadways verses those that are located deep inside a platted subdivision.

Another factor is to make the appropriate adjustments for the differences in construction quality, design, and amenities.

Financing concessions can also be a factor with value especially if there are loan programs that assist in the acquisition of property.

When the CMA is completed, there will be a suggested price range. The seller can determine the price they wish to list the property for sale. A good CMA should be quite accurate and possibly duplicate the price a fee appraiser would arrive at to secure financing.

It's ultimately up to the brokerage to accept or reject listings. Overpriced properties are very difficult to sell, especially if the market is stagnating or trending downward. However, the agent shouldn't suggest a price range that would be significantly under the existing market conditions. This would not be acting in the best interest of the seller unless the seller demands to have a property priced lower than the market.

An accurate valuation of property available for sale is the primary and first step to a successful real estate transaction. A properly priced property is already "half sold"; all that is needed is a ready, willing, and able buyer together with adequate financing to complete and close the sale.

## Appraiser licensing

If one desires to become a licensed appraiser in Idaho, they can secure licensing information from the Idaho Real Estate Appraiser Board at the Bureau of Occupational Licensing in Boise, Idaho.

90 classroom hours plus an equivalent of 2,000 hours training experience is required for residential licensing. Licensing can obviously take a considerable amount of time to secure.

# Questions – Chapter 14

1. The purpose of a market analysis and giving an opinion of price is to:

   A. Secure prospective listing or sale
   B. Provide a price for a lender
   C. Verify price for financing
   D. Appraise property for the seller

2. Who can provide a price opinion for a fee?

   A. Any active real estate licensee
   B. Active or inactive real estate broker
   C. An active real estate salesperson
   D. An active associate broker

3. A written price opinion for a fee must identify?

   A. Name and signature of salesperson issuing the opinion
   B. Purpose is to satisfy lender financing requirements
   C. Intended purpose
   D. Opinion does not have any limiting conditions or assumptions

4. The 'cost approach' is based on:

   A. Total cost to build or reconstruct
   B. Total cost plus land to build
   C. Cost minus depreciation
   D. Cost less depreciation plus land

5. The cost approach will provide the most accurate value when applied to:

   A. Older properties
   B. New construction
   C. Properties with high depreciation
   D. Historical renovated properties

6. The income approach is best used with:

   A. Residential properties
   B. Recreational 2$^{nd}$ homes
   C. Apartment complexes
   D. New home construction

7. How many training hours are required to become a residential licensed appraiser?

   A. 90
   B. 120
   C. 1,000
   D. 2,000

8. How many classroom hours are required to become a licensed residential appraiser?

   A. 90
   B. 120
   C. 1,000
   D. 2,000

9. Where can information be obtained to become a real estate appraiser?

   A. Idaho Real Estate Commission
   B. Bureau of Occupational Licensing
   C. Department of Commerce
   D. Secretary of State

Chapter 15

# Working with a Buyer as a Customer or Client

# Agency Representation

**Agency Representation**
IC 54-2085 (1)

**Agency Representation - Customer/Client**
When working with a prospective buyer, one of the first issues that needs to be addressed is Agency. Idaho Code clearly states, "A licensee shall give to a prospective buyer or seller at the first *substantial business* contact the agency disclosure brochure adopted or approved by the Idaho Real Estate Commission".

**Review Agency**
Chapter 3

Always have these brochures available since one doesn't always know when a substantial business contact may occur. A review of Chapter 3 of this text book may be helpful to establish a format of when and how to bring agency into the conversation with buyers.

As a safety precaution, it may be a good idea to read line by line, the contents of the brochure to the buyer before they sign the acknowledgment.

Another tip could include providing a copy of the brokerage office policy regarding agency and what types of agency the brokerage offers.

**Buyer Customer**

**Working with the buyer as a 'customer'**
If there is no written agreement, the prospective buyer will be treated as a customer. Without any agreement, the buyer is free to work with any and all agents to meet their real estate needs.

**Customer duties**
IC 54-2086

However, there are still statutory duties the agent must comply with when working with a buyer-customer.

**Compensation Agreement**

Figure 1

As a precaution, the agent may desire to utilize a compensation agreement with the buyer to assure the brokerage it will receive an agreed upon compensation should the buyer purchase a property with the aid and assistance from an agent with the brokerage.

Such agreement needs to be carefully read and understood by all parties since it is a binding contract.

| | |
|---|---|
| **Buyer Client** | **Working with a buyer as a 'client'**<br>If a buyer signs a representation agreement with a brokerage, the buyer becomes a 'client' of that brokerage and is committed to that brokerage based on the terms and conditions of the agreement. |
| **Client duties**<br>IC 54-2087 | The statutory duties to a client are different that those duties owed a customer including the duty to maintain the confidentiality of specific client information as defined by Idaho Code. |
| **Representation requirements** | **Buyer Representation Agreement Requirements**<br>If there is a written and properly executed Buyer Representation Agreement, a client relationship has been established.<br><br>It's extremely important that the agreement (contract) is carefully and completely read and understood by the buyer before the buyer signs the agreement. |
| **Buyer Representation Agreement form**<br><br>Figure 2 | Because most real estate licensees are members of the Idaho Association of REALTORS®, the Buyer Representation Agreement (RE-14) will probably be used most of the time.<br><br>So, let's go over some of the basics of the form. Although small print, the top of the agreement identifies the form as a 'legally binding contract' and the buyer needs to fully understand possible implications that may be contained within the body of the agreement. |
| **Exclusive definition** | The agreement also identifies it as being an 'exclusive' right to represent, followed with bold printing re-emphasizing and defining the conditions of 'exclusive' representation and the type and location of the property sought. |
| **Term of agreement** | The term of the agreement has specific beginning and ending dates. |
| **Brokerage services** | The broker identifies what brokerage services will be used to locate and negotiate property for the buyer. However, the agreement also states those services the brokerage may not be qualified to advise the buyer on matters concerning real estate. |

| | |
|---|---|
| **Financial information** | Financial information, the handling of other potential buyers, and the limits of confidentiality of offers is also discussed to reduce potential conflicts or misunderstandings. |
| **Consent to limited dual representation** | A detailed explanation for consent to limited dual representation and assigned agency is given and cites Idaho Code in the explanation. To make sure there isn't any misunderstanding, the agreement addresses and seeks buyer acknowledgment with consent to release the broker from conflicting agency duties. To make sure the buyer fully understands, the buyer will need to initial acceptance of limited dual representation or retain single agency. |
| **Non-discrimination** | A non-discrimination clause is included in the agreement to address potential fair housing issues and acknowledges the brokerage will not discriminate against any prospective buyer, seller or lessor. |
| **Legal disclosures** | Some legal disclosures are addressed including: severability, singular and plural defined, and default/attorney's fees, should the buyer default under the terms of the agreement. |
| **Compensation** | The area of compensation offers various options for the brokerage to receive compensation. Not all brokerages will offer all the options available. The brokerage should let the licensees know what is acceptable and supported with a written office policy. |
| **Expiration** | It is equally important that the buyer knows what could happen after the Buyer Representation Agreement expires as far as compensation or penalties are concerned. |
| **Addendum** | Other terms and conditions not covered in the Buyer Representation Agreement can be added into the agreement. If space is not sufficient, an Addendum can be added but make sure the Addendum is addressed in the original agreement with wording such as 'see attached Addendum #1'. |
| **Fax transmission** | Facsimile transmission is o.k. but law does require such use be approved in writing so the issue is addressed in the agreement. |
| **Signatures** | The authority of signatory together with 'time is of the essence' helps bind the agreement into a legal binding contract. All that is left are the proper signatures and date. |

# Real Estate Finance

**Ability to purchase**

## Buyers ability to purchase

The ability of the buyer to purchase real estate is generally predicated on the ability of the buyer to finance the purchase.  A 2008 survey by the National Association of REALTORS® indicated that over 85% of all buyers required financing to purchase their residence.  So it's really important that the licensee and buyer know exactly how the property will be paid for and plan accordingly.

**All cash**

## All cash offer

If the buyer plans to pay cash for the property, the buyer needs to be ready to prove and verify to the seller, the availability and source of funds to purchase.  There's usually a clause in the Purchase and Sale Agreement (discussed in Chapter 17) that will ask for such verification.

**Subject to financing**

## Subject to financing

As mentioned, over 85% of residential purchase involve financing.  It's very important and good business to have the prospective buyer seek a lender who in turn can issue an approval letter indicating exactly what the buyer is qualified to do.  This necessitates applying for loan approval and is another indication that the buyer is 'willing, able, and ready' to buy property.

It is not unusual for a buyer to want to postpone going to a lender until they actually find a home they wish to make an offer on.  Although there isn't anything that disallows this to occur, the buyer should be aware there are literally hundreds of different loan programs; each with different requirements for qualifying to meet the specific needs of the buyer and property alike.

Without knowing exactly which program best fits the needs of the buyer, it is very difficult for the agent to locate a property that also fits within the parameters of the financing requirements.

Explain to the buyer, that it is in the best interest of all to get pre approved first before even looking at any property.  It will save time, money, and possibly disappointment down the road.

When the buyer contacts a lender, it is suggested that the buyer inquire about Idaho specific loan programs both local and state sponsored with a lender. Bear in mind, not all lenders are approved for or work with many local and state programs available. So the buyer might need to shop around.

# Security Instruments

There are two types of security instruments used to secure the property; a mortgage or deed of trust.

**Satisfaction of mortgage**
IC 45-915

## Mortgage

A mortgage can be used as a security instrument for any real property in Idaho. Once a mortgage has been satisfied (payed off) the holder must provide the purchaser (owner) a certificate of the discharge or 'satisfaction of mortgage' for recording.

However, if the purchaser defaults on the terms of the mortgage, the holder of the mortgage can file for foreclosure.

**'Sheriff's Sale'**

Mortgages must be foreclosed by judicial action and the court will direct the sale to be advertised. A notice of the 'sheriff's sale' must be published for 3 consecutive weeks in the county in which the property is located.

The actual sale will occur between 9 a.m. and 5 p.m. on a normal county business day. The highest bidder will receive a Certificate of Sale and not a deed due to a statutory redemption period.

**Certificate of Sale**
IC 11-310

Although anyone can bid at the sale, the lender will generally be the only bidder to protect their interest. Why? Because the holder of the Certificate of Sale cannot sell or market the property during the holding redemption period.

**Redemption**
IC 11-104

The statutory redemption period for a mortgage is:

- 1 year if the property is more than 20 acres;

- 6 months if the property is 20 acres or less or if the debtor releases their right of redemption.

If the property is redeemed, the original borrower must pay the *total* amount owing prior to the expiration of the redemption period.

**Sheriffs deed**
IC 11-403

If the redemption has not been made, the successful bidder receives a Sheriff's Deed. The recording of the Sheriff's Deed will end the foreclosure process unless there may be other pending issues in the district court to fix any deficiency judgment against the original borrowers.

**Deed of Trust**

## Deed of Trust

The security instrument of choice by virtually all lenders will be a Deed of Trust. Why? There is no period of redemption and the foreclosure window is relatively short.

**Deed of Trust limitations**
IC 45-1502 (5)

However, there are some restrictions to use a deed of trust and the use of such instrument shall be limited to:

- Any real property located within an incorporated city or village at the time of transfer

- Any property not exceeding 80 acres, regardless of its location, provided that such real property is not principally used for the agricultural production of crops, livestock, dairy or aquatic goods

- Any real property not exceeding 40 acres regardless of its use or location

When a deed of trust has been payed off a reconveyance will be issued which should be recorded to remove the lien from the public records.

However, if a deed of trust ends up in foreclosure, there are statutory laws that regulate the process as a nonjudicial foreclosure. The trustee must file a notice of default with the names of the beneficiaries and the book and page where the deed of trust is recorded.

Notice will be sent registered or certified mail to:
- Grantor (owner) or any person requesting notice
- Any successor in interest to the grantor on record
- Any person having a lien or interest subsequent

The notice of sale will identify the date, time, and place of sale in the county where the property is located.

**Notice of Sale**
IC 45-1506 (2)

The notice of sale must be published in a newspaper in each of the counties in which the property is situated (in case the property overlaps between 2 different counties) for 4 successive weeks with the last publication to be at least 30 days before the sale.

Once 'notice of sale' has been recorded the sale will take place in not less than 120 days from the date of notice. However, the sale can be postponed by the trustee up to 30 days at the time of the sale and postponed over and over; thus, delaying the actual sale.

**115 days to cure**
IC 45-1506 (12)

Although there is no redemption period for a nonjudicial foreclosure in Idaho, the debtor can 'cure' themselves by bringing the past due payments current within 115 days of the initial notice of sale was recorded. The loan will now be restored to its original terms and conditions and the foreclosure is stopped. If, by chance, the debtor comes to the table between 115 and 120 days, the total balance of the loan must be paid to restore the loan.

If the real property goes to sale, anyone can bid at the auction except the officer holding the sale and his deputy. The high bidder will be issued a 'trustees deed' upon conclusion of the sale without covenant or warranty.

# Financing Issues

2010 brought some major changes with various forms used in the world of real estate financing. The intent was to make the complex reporting easier with good faith estimates and closing statements.

- HUD's Settlement Cost Booklet
- Good Faith Estimate (GFE)
- Real Estate Settlement Statement (HUD-1)

**HUD Settlement Cost Booklet**

### HUD Settlement Cost Booklet
The HUD Settlement Cost Booklet must be given to the borrower within three days of applying for a mortgage loan. It covers everything from shopping for a home to comparing the good faith estimate with the HUD-1 loan settlement statement.

**Good Faith Estimate**

## Good Faith Estimates

For the first time ever, HUD requires lenders and brokers to provide borrowers with an easy-to-read standard Good Faith Estimate (GFE) that will clearly answer key questions that they have when applying for a mortgage including:

What's the term of the loan?

Is the interest rate fixed or can it change?

Is there a pre-payment penalty if the borrower chooses to refinance at a later date?

Is there a balloon payment?

What are the total closing costs?

**More changes**

In addition there are more changes:

The Good Faith Estimate has been reduced to 3 pages

GFE and HUD-1 can be compared line for line

Yield Spread Premiums are to be disclosed in a more meaningful way

GFE is to be provided 3 days after loan originators receipt of all necessary information

Lenders and service providers will have 30 days from closing to correct errors or violations and repay consumers for any overcharges.

GFE is now binding to 0.125% of the initial quote

The GFE that the lender presents is binding once it is issued

**HUD-1**

## HUD-1
The HUD-1 settlement statement has been reduced from 4 pages to 3 pages.

To allow consumers to compare their estimated closing costs with the actual costs, the HUD-1 includes a reference to the relevant line from the GFE. Borrowers will now be able to easily compare their estimated and actual costs.

**Offering Incentives**
IC 54-2054
Guideline #12

## Offering Incentives
Guideline #12 addresses incentives to buyers or sellers which could impact the legal aspects of securing financing. Idaho Code 54-2054 allows a broker to share any part of a commission, fee or compensation received with the buyer or seller in a real estate transaction.

However, no commission, fee or compensation may be split with any party to the transaction in a manner that would directly or indirectly create a double contract, or would otherwise mislead any broker, lender, title company or government agency involved in the transaction, regarding the source of the funds used to complete the transaction or regarding the financial resources or obligation of the buyer or seller.

Figure 1 – Compensation Agreement

# RE-15 COMPENSATION AGREEMENT WITH BUYER

THIS IS A LEGALLY BINDING CONTRACT, READ THE ENTIRE DOCUMENT, INCLUDING ANY ATTACHMENTS.
IF YOU HAVE ANY QUESTIONS, **CONSULT YOUR ATTORNEY AND/OR ACCOUNTANT** BEFORE SIGNING.

1  **1. BUYER Name(s)**_____
2  BUYER desires to purchase, lease, or option the following real estate: Type of property:
3  ☐Residential ☐Residential Income ☐Commercial ☐Vacant Land ☐Other_____
4  Applicable area, City(s), County(s), Zip Code(s), etc. _____
5  Other Description: (ie, geographical area, price, etc.)_____
6  and, whereas the undersigned parties desire to enter into this formal agreement expressing their agreement as to the payment/receipt of
7  any real estate commission resulting from the purchase and/or lease of the above described type of property. **THIS IS NOT A BROKER**
8  **REPRESENTATION AGREEMENT.** This is an agreement for compensation for services to a "customer" as defined by Idaho law. A Buyer
9  or seller is not represented by a brokerage in a regulated real estate transaction unless the buyer or seller and the brokerage agree in a
10  separate written document, to such representation. No type of agency representation may be assumed by a brokerage, buyer or seller or
11  created orally or by implication.
12
13  **2. AGENCY DISCLOSURE CONFIRMATION:** The BUYER has received, has read, and understands the AGENCY DISCLOSURE
14  BROCHURE (prepared by the Idaho Real Estate Commission.)
15
16  **3. TERM OF AGREEMENT:** The term of this Agreement shall commence on _____and will expire at
17  11:59 p.m. on date _____, or upon closing of escrow of such property purchased through this agreement.
18
19  **4. COMPENSATION OF BROKER:** Broker shall be compensated in the following ways: Check those that apply.
20  ☐ A. **If the property is subject to a listing agreement with the Broker's company or with a cooperating Broker** through the Multiple
21  Listing Service (MLS) or otherwise, the Brokerage fee shall be the amount paid by the seller to the aforementioned Brokers but not
22  less than _____% of the gross selling price or $_____dollars. BUYER agrees to pay to the Broker any
23  difference between the amount received from the aforementioned Brokers and the stated minimum.
24  ☐ B. **If the property is not subject to a Listing Agreement,** such as a For Sale By Owner or a Custom Build Job, the BUYER agrees
25  that the Broker will be paid a fee of not less than _____% of selling price or $_____ dollars. The
26  Broker shall first seek to obtain this fee through the transaction paid by the Seller. If the fee cannot be obtained through the Seller, the
27  BUYER will be responsible for such fee stated above.
28
29  This compensation shall apply to transactions made for which BUYER enters into a contract during the original term of this Agreement or during any
30  extension of such original or extended term, and shall also apply to transactions for which BUYER enters into a contract within ____ calendar days
31  (ninety [90] if left blank) after this Agreement expires or is terminated, if the property acquired by the BUYER was submitted in writing to the BUYER
32  by the Broker pursuant to Section One hereof during the original term or extension of the term of this Agreement. The fee shall be paid at closing
33  unless otherwise designated by the Broker in writing. The closing agent for this transaction is hereby authorized to pay the above mentioned
34  compensation at closing.
35
36  **5. OTHER TERMS AND CONDITIONS:** _____
37
38  **6. GENERAL PROVISIONS:** In the event either party shall initiate any suit or action or appeal on any matter relating to this Agreement the
39  defaulting party shall pay the prevailing party all damages and expenses resulting from the default, including all reasonable attorneys' fees
40  and all court costs and other expenses incurred by the prevailing party. This Agreement is made in accordance with and shall be
41  interpreted and governed by the laws of the State of Idaho. All rights and obligations of the parties hereunder shall be binding upon and
42  inure to the benefit of their heirs, personal representatives, successors and assigns.
43
44  **7. TIME IS OF THE ESSENCE IN THIS AGREEMENT.**
45
46  **8. REAL ESTATE BROKERAGE:**_____
47
48  _____     _____
49  Buyer Signature                            Date       Agent or Broker (on behalf of Brokerage) Signature      Date
50
51  _____     _____
52  Buyer Signature                            Date       Brokerage Address
53
54  _____     _____
55  Address                                               City                                State      Zip
56
57  _____     _____
58  City                      State        Zip           Brokerage Phone                   Brokerage Fax
59
60  _____     _____
61  Phone                     Fax                         Brokerage Email
62
63  _____     _____
64  Email                                                  Agent/Broker Email

JULY 2009 EDITION          RE-15 COMPENSATION AGREEMENT WITH BUYER          Page 1 of 1

Reprinted with permission from IAR

## Figure 2 – Buyer Representation Agreement - Page 1 of 3

## RE-14 BUYER REPRESENTATION AGREEMENT
### (EXCLUSIVE RIGHT TO REPRESENT)

THIS IS A LEGALLY BINDING CONTRACT, READ THE ENTIRE DOCUMENT, INCLUDING ANY ATTACHMENTS.
IF YOU HAVE ANY QUESTIONS, **CONSULT YOUR ATTORNEY AND/OR ACCOUNTANT** BEFORE SIGNING.

1  DATE:_____ AGENT: _____
2                                                    Acting as Agent for the Broker
3  **1. BUYER** _____
4
5  retains_____ Broker of _____
6  as exclusive Buyer Broker (hereinafter referred to as Broker), where the BUYER is represented by one agent only for time herein
7  set forth and for the express purpose of Representing BUYER in the purchase, lease, or optioning of real property. Further,
8  BUYER agrees, warrants and acknowledges that BUYER has not and shall not enter into any buyer representation agreement
9  with another broker in the state of Idaho as a broker for BUYER during the effective term of this agreement, unless otherwise
10 agreed to in writing by BUYER and above-listed Broker. BUYER agrees to indemnify and hold the above-listed Broker harmless
11 from any claim brought by any other broker or real estate salesperson for compensation claimed or owed during the effective
12 term of this agreement. By appointing Broker as BUYER'S exclusive agent, BUYER agrees to conduct all negotiations for
13 property through Broker, and to refer to Broker all inquiries received in any form from real estate brokers, salespersons,
14 prospective sellers, or any other source, during the time this Buyer Representation Agreement is in effect. BUYER desires to
15 purchase, lease, or option the following real estate: Type of property:
16
17 ☐Residential ☐Residential Income ☐Commercial ☐Vacant Land ☐Other_____
18 Applicable City(s)_____, Idaho; Applicable Zip Codes _____
19 Applicable County(s) _____
20 Other Description: (i.e., geographical area, price, etc.)_____
21
22 **2. TERM OF AGREEMENT:** This BUYER REPRESENTATION AGREEMENT (herein after referred to as Agreement) is in force from
23 date_____ and will expire at 11:59 p.m. on date_____, or upon closing of escrow of such property purchased
24 through this agreement.
25
26 **3. BROKER REPRESENTATIONS AND SERVICES:** The Broker and Broker's agent representing a BUYER are agents of the BUYER.
27 Broker will use reasonable efforts as BUYER'S agent to locate property as described in Section One hereof from the information available
28 in the Multiple Listing Service (MLS) and from other sources for unlisted property that the Broker may be aware of when applicable as set
29 forth in Section One. The Broker's duty to locate property for the BUYER is limited to the properties that the Broker is aware of and does
30 not include a duty to discover every unlisted property that may be privately advertised. Broker shall make submissions to BUYER
31 describing and identifying properties that substantially meet the criteria set forth in Section One, for consideration of the BUYER and Broker
32 agrees to negotiate acceptance of any offer to purchase or lease such property.
33
34 **4. TRANSACTION RELATED SERVICES DISCLAIMER:** BUYER understands that Broker is qualified to advise BUYER on general
35 matters concerning real estate, but is not an expert in matters of law, tax, financing, surveying, structural conditions, property inspections,
36 hazardous materials, or engineering. BUYER acknowledges that Broker advises BUYER to seek expert assistance for advice on such
37 matters. Broker cannot warrant the condition of property to be acquired, or guarantee that all material facts are disclosed by the Seller.
38 Broker will not investigate the condition of any property including without limitation the status of permits, zoning, location of property lines,
39 square footage, possible loss of views and/or compliance of the property with applicable laws, codes or ordinances and BUYER must
40 satisfy themself concerning these issues by obtaining the appropriate expert advice. The Broker or Broker's agent may, during the course
41 of the transaction, identify individuals or entities who perform services including **BUT NOT LIMITED TO** the following; home inspections,
42 service contracts, appraisals, environmental assessment inspections, code compliance inspections, title insurance, closing and escrow
43 services, loans and refinancing services, construction and repairs, legal and accounting services, and/or surveys. The BUYER understands
44 that the identification of service providers is solely for BUYER'S convenience and that the Broker and its agent are not guaranteeing or
45 assuring that the service provider will perform its duties in accordance with the BUYER'S expectations. BUYER has the right to make
46 arrangements with any entity BUYER chooses to provide these services. BUYER hereby releases and holds harmless the Broker and
47 Broker's agent from any claims by the BUYER that service providers breached their agreement, were negligent, misrepresented
48 information, or otherwise failed to perform in accordance with the BUYER'S expectations. In the event the BUYER requests Broker to
49 obtain any products or services from outside sources, **BUYER agrees to pay for them immediately when payment is due.** For example:
50 surveys or engineering, environmental and/or soil tests, title reports, home or property inspections, appraisals, etc.
51
52 **5. FINANCIAL INFORMATION:** BUYER agrees to provide Broker and/or Broker's agent with certain pertinent financial information
53 necessary to prove ability to purchase desired property.
54
55 **6. OTHER POTENTIAL BUYERS:** BUYER understands that other potential buyers may consider, make offers on, or purchase through
56 Broker the same or similar properties as BUYER is seeking to acquire. BUYER consents to Broker's representation of such other potential
57 buyers before, during, and after the expiration of this Agreement and further releases Broker of any conflicting Agency duties.

BUYER'S Initials (_____) (_____) Date:_____

Reprint permission from IAR

## Figure 2 – Buyer Representation Agreement - Page 2 of 3

BUYER'S NAME(S) _____

58  **7. LIMITS OF CONFIDENTIALITY OF OFFERS:** BUYER understands that an offer submitted to a seller, and the terms thereof may not be
59  held confidential by such seller or seller's representative unless such confidentiality is otherwise agreed to by the parties.

60

61  **8. CONSENT TO LIMITED DUAL REPRESENTATION AND ASSIGNED AGENCY:** The undersigned BUYER(S) have received, read and
62  understand the Agency Disclosure Brochure (prepared by the Idaho Real Estate Commission). The undersigned BUYER(S) understand
63  that the brokerage involved in this transaction may be providing agency representation to both the BUYER(S) and the Seller. The
64  undersigned BUYER(S) each understands that, as an agent for both BUYER/client and Seller/client, a brokerage will be a limited dual
65  agent of each client and cannot advocate on behalf of one client over another, and cannot legally disclose to either client certain
66  confidential client information concerning price negotiations, terms or factors motivating the BUYER/client to buy or the Seller/client to sell
67  without specific written permission of the client to whom the information pertains. The specific duties, obligations and limitations of a limited
68  dual agent are contained in the Agency Disclosure Brochure as required by §54-2085, Idaho Code. The undersigned BUYER(S) each
69  understands that a limited dual agent does not have a duty of undivided loyalty to either client.

70

71  The undersigned BUYER(S) further acknowledge that, to the extent the brokerage firm offers assigned agency as a type of agency
72  representation, individual sales associates may be assigned to represent each client to act solely on behalf of the client consistent with
73  applicable duties set forth in §54-2087, Idaho Code. In an assigned agency situation, the designated broker (the broker who supervises the
74  sales associates) will remain a limited dual agent of the client and shall have the duty to supervise the assigned agents in the fulfillment of
75  their duties to their respective clients, to refrain from advocating on behalf of any one client over another, and to refrain from disclosing or
76  using, without permission, confidential information of any other client with whom the brokerage has an agency relationship.

77

78  **BUYER NOTIFICATION AND CONSENT TO RELEASE FROM CONFLICTING AGENCY DUTIES:** BUYER acknowledges that Broker
79  as named above has disclosed the fact that at times Broker acts as agent(s) for other BUYERS and for Sellers in the sale of the property.
80  BUYER has been advised and understands that it may create a conflict of interest for Broker to introduce BUYER to a Seller Client's
81  property because Broker could not satisfy all of its Client duties to both BUYER Client and Seller Client in connection with such a showing
82  or any transaction which resulted. **Based on the understandings acknowledged, BUYER makes the following election.**
83  (Make one election only)

84
85

86  _____ / _____
87  Initials     BUYER **DOES WANT** to be introduced to Seller client's property and hereby agrees to relieve Broker of conflicting
88  **Limited Dual Agency**    agency duties, including the duty to disclose confidential information known to the Broker at the time and the duty
89  **and/or**    of loyalty to either party. Relieved of all conflicting agency duties, Broker will act in an unbiased manner to assist
90  **Assigned Agency**    the BUYER and Seller in the introduction of BUYER to such Seller client's property and in the preparation of any
91  contract of sale which may result. BUYER authorizes Broker to act in a **limited dual agency** capacity. Further,
92  BUYER agrees that Broker may offer, but is not obligated to offer, **assigned agency** representation, and if offered
93  **OR**    by the Broker, BUYER authorizes Broker to act in such capacity.

94
95

96  _____ / _____
97  Initials     BUYER DOES NOT WANT to be introduced to Seller client's property and hereby releases Broker from any
98  **Single Agency**    responsibility or duty under the agency agreement. Broker shall be under no obligation or duty to introduce the
   BUYER to any Seller client's property.

99
100

101  **9. NON-DISCRIMINATION:** The parties agree not to discriminate against any prospective Seller or Lessor because of race, religion,
102  creed, color, sex, marital status, national origin, familial, or handicapped status of such person.

103

104  **10. SEVERABILITY CLAUSE:** In the case that any one or more of the provisions contained in this Agreement, or any application thereof,
105  shall be invalid, illegal or unenforceable in any respect, the validity, legality or enforceability of the remaining provisions shall not in any way
106  be affected or impaired thereby.

107

108  **11. SINGULAR AND PLURAL** terms each include the other, when appropriate.

109

110  **12. DEFAULT / ATTORNEY'S FEES:** In the event of default by BUYER under this Agreement, Broker shall be entitled to the Fee that
111  Broker would have received had no default occurred, in addition to other available legal remedies. In the event of any suit or other
112  proceeding arising out of this Agreement, the prevailing party shall be entitled to its reasonable attorney's fees and all costs incurred
113  relative to such suit or proceeding. Venue of any action arising out of this Agreement shall be in the court of the county in which Broker's
114  office is located.

BUYER'S Initials (_____) (_____) Date:_____

Reprint permission from IAR

# Figure 2 – Buyer Representation Agreement - Page 3 of 3

BUYER'S NAME(S) _____

115 **13. COMPENSATION OF BROKER:** In consideration of the services to be performed by the Broker, BUYER agrees that broker may be
116 compensated in any of the following ways: Check all that apply.
117 ☐ A. **If the property is subject to a listing agreement with the Broker's Company or a cooperating Broker** through the Multiple
118      Listing Service (MLS) or otherwise, the fee will be the amount equal to the compensation offered by the aforementioned Brokers but
119      not less than _____% of the selling price. BUYER agrees to pay to the Broker any difference between the amount received from
120      the aforementioned Brokers and the stated minimum.
121 ☐ B. **If the property is not subject to a Listing Agreement,** such as a For Sale By Owner, the BUYER agrees that the Broker will be
122      paid a fee of not less than ☐_____% of selling price or ☐$_____. The Broker shall first seek to obtain this fee
123      through the transaction paid by the Seller. If the fee cannot be obtained through the Seller, the BUYER will be responsible for such fee
124      stated above.
125 ☐ C. **If the property is not subject to a Listing Agreement,** such as a Custom Build Job, the BUYER agrees that the Broker will be
126      paid a fee of not less than ☐_____% of selling price or ☐$_____. The Broker shall first seek to obtain this fee
127      through the transaction paid by the Seller. If the fee cannot be obtained through the Seller, the BUYER will be responsible for such fee
128      stated above.
129 ☐ D. **Retainer Fee.** BUYER will pay Broker a non-refundable retainer fee of $_____ due and payable upon signing of this
130      Agreement. Retainer fee ☐shall ☐shall not be credited against any compensation set forth in paragraph A or B.
131 ☐ E. **Hourly rate.** BUYER will pay Broker at the rate of $_____ per hour for the time spent by Broker pursuant to this
132      Agreement to be paid when billed whether or not BUYER acquires or leases property. The fee ☐shall ☐shall not be credited against
133      any compensation as set forth in paragraph A, B, or C.
134
135      This compensation shall apply to transactions made for which BUYER enters into a contract during the original term of this Agreement
136 or during any extension of such original or extended term, and shall also apply to transactions for which BUYER enters into a contract
137 within_____ calendar days (ninety [90] if left blank) after this Agreement expires or is terminated, if the property acquired by the BUYER was
138 submitted in writing to the BUYER by Broker pursuant to Section One hereof during the original term or extension of the term of this
139 Agreement. Unless otherwise indicated herein the Broker's fee shall be paid in cash at closing.
140      In the event BUYER purchases any property without using the representation of the Broker named above within the time this
141 agreement remains in force, above stated BUYER shall be liable to Broker for a cancellation fee equal to _____% of the contract or
142 purchase price of the property acquired or $_____.
143
144 **14. OTHER TERMS AND CONDITIONS:** _____
145 _____
146 _____
147 _____
148 _____
149
150 **15. FACSIMILE TRANSMISSION:** Facsimile or electronic transmission of any signed original document, and retransmission of any signed
151 facsimile or electronic transmission shall be the same as delivery of an original. At the request of either the BUYER or SELLER, or the
152 LENDER, or the Closing Agency, the BUYER and SELLER will confirm facsimile or electronic transmitted signatures by signing an original
153 document.
154
155 **16. AUTHORITY OF SIGNATORY:** If BUYER is a corporation, partnership, trust, estate, or other entity, the person executing this
156 agreement on its behalf warrants his or her authority to do so and to bind BUYER.
157
158 **17. TIME IS OF THE ESSENCE IN THIS AGREEMENT:** The terms hereof constitute the entire agreement and supersede all prior
159 agreements, negotiations and discussions between parties. This agreement may be modified only by a written agreement signed by each
160 of the parties.
161
162
163 Buyer Signature       Date       Agent or Broker (on behalf of Brokerage) Signature       Date
164
165
166 Buyer Signature       Date       Brokerage Address
167
168
169 Address       City       State       Zip
170
171
172 City       State       Zip       Brokerage Phone       Brokerage Fax
173
174
175 Phone       Fax       Brokerage Email
176
177
178 Email       Agent/Broker Email

# Questions – Chapter 15

1. When is a prospective buyer or seller to receive the agency disclosure brochure?

   A. Upon the first meeting
   B. Prior to writing a contract
   C. Before closing a transaction
   D. First substantial business contact

2. What is the purpose of the buyer or seller signing the agency disclosure brochure?

   A. To Establish a client relationship
   B. To Create a customer relationship
   C. To acknowledge receiving the brochure
   D. To secure a real estate activity

3. If a buyer is a 'customer' and not a 'client', what duties must the agent extend to the 'customer'?

   A. None, unless there is a written contract
   B. Must collect fee or commission from another party to a transaction
   C. Disclose adverse material facts
   D. Verify accuracy of statements made by a seller.

4. A Exclusive Buyer Representation Agreement will:

   A. Be binding only when an offer and acceptance has been completed
   B. Disallow the buyer from previewing property without their agent
   C. Create a legally binding contract
   D. Bind the buyer for an unlimited time

5. What does the highest bidder receive at a foreclosure sale of a mortgage?

   A. Certificate of Sale
   B. Sheriffs Deed
   C. Warranty Deed
   D. Mortgagee Deed

6. A 22 acre parcel secured with a mortgage ended up in foreclosure. What period of time is allowed for redemption?

   A. None, foreclosure secured with a mortgage is final
   B. 6 months
   C. 1 year
   D. Redemption period determined by a court decision

7. A 14 acre parcel secured with a deed of trust ended up in foreclosure. What period of time is allowed for redemption?

   A. None, foreclosure secured with a deed of trust is final upon sale
   B. 6 months
   C. 1 year
   D. Redemption period determined by a court decision

8. Once a 'notice of sale' has been recorded what period of time is given for the owner to bring the delinquency current?

   A. 60 days
   B. 90 days
   C. 115 days
   D. 120 days

9. What kind of deed does the successful bidder receive upon foreclosure of a deed of trust?

   A. Quit claim deed
   B. Trustees deed
   C. Trustors deed
   D. Sheriffs deed

10. When is the borrower supposed to receive a HUD Settlement Cost Booklet

    A. Prior to making loan application
    B. Upon loan commitment
    C. Within 1 day of loan application
    D. Within 3 days of loan application

11. A real estate agent gave a purchaser $5,000 to assist with a down payment in the form of a private loan to be forgiven after the closing of a pending transaction. This could be considered as:

    A. A nice 'gift'
    B. A good business decision
    C. An unenforceable loan
    D. A 'double contract'

# Chapter 16

# Working with a Seller as a Client or Customer

**Important Relationship**

It's critical that the relationship between the brokerage and the seller be fully understood and hopefully rational. After all, successful real estate transactions begin with having a piece or property that will meet the needs of everyone, not just the seller or agent and seller. Most residential real estate is purchased with emotion (I want it) and justified with fact (an appraisal justifies value to the lender with facts).

**Different Players**

The buyer and seller are players in the transaction but the sideline players: appraisers, lenders, inspectors, attorneys, accountants, and others also play an important part of the whole real estate transaction process. But, everything starts with the property being offered for sale.

**Two Appointments**

## Listing Appointments

If possible, it is suggested that you make two listing appointments to demonstrate your professionalism and efficiency prior to securing the listing.

**First Appointment**

## First appointment

The first appointment is to meet with the prospective seller to get acquainted and secure important information about the home so you can prepare an accurate CMA prior to securing the actual listing. Make sure the seller knows that the purpose of the first appointment is to secure information to assist with doing a CMA.

**Appointment for 2nd Meeting**

After you secure all the necessary information and make the measurements to apply to a CMA, explain to the seller the time frame it will take to provide an accurate CMA and make an appointment for the second meeting and listing presentation.

Before leaving, you might consider leaving a blank sample of a listing agreement with the seller so they can read through and have any questions ready when you meet with them on the second appointment. Also request the owner(s) be present for the 2nd appointment.

Why? If both you and the seller decide to list the property, you will want all owner signatures on the listing agreement.

**Listing Packet**

## Securing a Listing Packet

Prior to meeting with the prospective seller at their home, it is advisable to order a 'property profile' or 'listing packet' from your favorite title insurance company. Generally you can order and get a listing packet within 1 day. If time doesn't allow, then get the listing packet prior to the 2nd meeting with the seller.

The listing packet will generally contain:

Copy of recorded deed
Copy of 1 or 2 recorded financing documents
Plat map of subdivision (if in a subdivision)
Map reduced to show property and dimensions
CCR's, if any

**Deed Information**

The names on the deed should match the names of the people you will be meeting with. The financing document(s) will show what type of security instrument is used together with all the terms and conditions of such financing document(s). Read the 'fine print' and again make sure of who exactly is liable for the obligation and if there are any clauses that could adversely impact the seller upon sale.

**Subdivision Map**

The 'subdivision' map will show roadways, easements, and the 'fine print' may indicate some general restrictions to meet local code or other issues not contained in the deed or other documentation. For example, there may be reference to noise abatement if the subdivision is near an airport. Or, perhaps there could be a comment regarding height restrictions to abide with special uses nearby.

**Property Dimensions**

The map of the actual property the seller is thinking of selling will give actual dimensions together with where the corner pins are located.

**CCR's**

Finally, the CCR's (Covenants, Conditions and Restrictions) will provide the private restrictions that the homeowners are supposed to abide by. Again, read them carefully to see if there are violations, either with the subject property, or with other homeowners in the subdivision.

## Red Flags

When evaluating the marketability of a property, one needs to carefully consider issues that could adversely affect the value of the property. Issues to look for to make the appropriate adjustments include but are not limited to:

- Stigmatized issues - crime, noise, traffic, etc.
- Lead based paint
- Mold
- Sidewalks and foundations
- Drainage - soil instability
- Floodplain - or changes in water elevations
- Roofs, windows, flashings
- Septic systems
- Recreational hazards
- Encroachments
- Easements
- Private restrictions
- Crawl spaces and basements
- House alignment
- Electrical, plumbing, HVAC systems
- Glass
- Smoke detectors

**Second Appointment**

## Second Appointment

The second appointment will be to make the listing presentation together with supporting documentation to verify and justify your work. Included in your documentation, will be a CMA (Competitive Market Analysis) and a listing packet.

In addition, have a listing agreement ready and maybe even partially filled out except for price and terms.

The 2nd appointment will focus with the explanation of the CMA together with any 'back-up' documentation to assist with your verification of value and securing the actual listing if agreed upon between you and the seller.

Be patient and answer any questions or concerns the seller may have regarding all your services and the listing process. Be a good listener to build understanding and rapport.

# Competitive Market Analysis

**CMA**

The heart of the whole listing process starts with a CMA. The CMA is designed to assist the seller in establishing a price in which the property will meet the sellers needs to sell.

There are many formats to do a CMA from Multiple Listing Service forms to in-house brokerage company forms. Whatever format is used, be sure you can verify your information.

**CMA Purpose**
IC 54-4105 (2)

A CMA is perhaps better known as a condensed version of the basic items a fee appraisal contains. Remember, you are not an appraiser and cannot do an appraisal unless you are licensed to do so. But Idaho Code does allow you to give an opinion of price for the purpose of securing a prospective listing or sale.

A review of Chapter 14, Market Analysis, gives the basics of appraisal and CMA's. The market approach concept of appraisal will be used most of the time for valuing residential real estate.

**CMA Characteristics**

## CMA Characteristics

When constructing a CMA, the first task is to get all the characteristics of the subject property (the property to be sold) for comparison with comparable properties that are either:
1. On the market;
2. Recently sold, or, as a last option;
3. Were on the market but expired.

The characteristics of the subject property that should be considered but not limited to, include:

Type and age of neighborhood - single, multiple family
Zoning and allowed uses - conforming
Location of neighborhood - established, new, older, etc.
Quality of neighborhood - well maintained, deteriorating
Lot size - square footage, dimensions
Age of home - new, 1-5 yrs, 6-10 yrs, 10-20, older, etc.
Style of home - single story, multiple story, etc
Habitable square footage
Number of bedrooms
Number of baths
Condition and quality of construction - inside

Condition and quality of construction - exterior
Parking - size of garage, extra parking for RV's
Landscaping - quality and quantity
Amenities - view, extras, uniqueness, floor plan

**Securing Comps**

## Securing Comparables

Once the subject property characteristics are obtained you will now find comparable properties that best match the characteristics of the subject property (the property to be sold). If you are a member of a Multiple Listing Service (MLS) this will probably be the best resource available.

**Internet Resources**

The internet is another good resource but may have limitations. Generally speaking, you will only find those properties that are currently on the market and available for sale. 'Solds' are not easy to find on the internet. But with some deep searching you may even be able to find 'solds' through specialty sites.

To create accuracy and true comparisons, it's suggested you mirror what appraisers do and come up with a minimum of 3 comparables to work with. The goal is to find other properties that best match the subject property and then make appropriate adjustments to get as close as possible, for an accurate match.

**Making Adjustments**

## Making adjustments

Perhaps the most difficult challenge in constructing a CMA is making adjustments where there are significant differences between the subject property and the comparable.

**Market Trends**

You really need to know and understand the current market trends and personal needs and desires of the buyer in the local market. For example, a outdoor in-ground pool may cost a lot of money but the local market may not support the cost equated with the demand. Thus, there may be no adjustment, or in some cases, there may even be a deduction for a pool.

**Construction Quality**

The quality of construction and condition of the property is another challenge. Let's say you find 3 comps that all match the subject. However, one of the comps has been 'trashed' but is the same floor plan, age, size, etc. Again, you must make a judgment call and decide what the dollar amount of adjustment will be made to the home that has been 'trashed' to make it equal to the subject home.

| **Adjustments Made to Comparable Home** | Note, the adjustment is made to the comparable home; not the subject home. What we are trying to do, is make the comparable home the same, or as close as possible, as the subject home. |
|---|---|

Now comes the hard part; assigning a value to the portion of the comparable that is substantially different from the subject property.

For example, you have found a comparable that virtually matches the subject property. However, the subject property has a 3 car garage and the comparable has a 2 car garage. The question is - how much adjustment will be made for the difference between a 3 car garage and a 2 car garage. This is where 'judgment' calls are made which leads to 'opinions' as well as 'facts'.

**Minimizing Variables**

## Minimizing variables

To minimize opinion variables, agents can use different resources for various component values.

> Market trends based on supply and demand
> Actual cost to construct or reproduce
> Actual cost minus depreciation
> MLS component differentials
> Builders and remodelers
> Marshall & Swift Residential Cost Handbook
> Marshall & Swift Remodel Cost Handbook
> Awareness of International Residential Code

Remember, most properties require financing of some sort which ultimately requires an appraisal. The closer real estate licensees can 'mirror' an appraiser, the closer the properties will approximate values utilized to meet various financing programs.

**Narrowing to 3 Comps**

## Narrowing down to the best 3 comparables

Generally speaking, the goal is to have 3 comparables, including adjusted differences, with the least amount of adjustments that will best equal the characteristics of the subject property.

Each of the three best comparables will arrive at a price. But there will be differences between each of the 3 comparables. Rather than arriving at a specific price for the subject property, a price range should be considered with maybe a ± 5% variable. Now the seller can choose somewhere from low to high.

Chances are, they will choose a higher price to leave room for negotiation. Bear in mind starting high could eliminate some potential buyers from making an offer because the property is out of their price range.

**Sellers Decision**

Much of the seller's decision will be based on their personal motivation. If they need to sell, they may start in the middle or even low. If they only 'want' to sell, chances they may start high.

**Agents Acceptance?**

Remember, you have the final say as to whether you want the listing or not. Will it sell withing the listing period? How much time and effort will be required to service the listing? If it is listed 'high' will others sell against you? What will a 'over valued' listing do to your image and reputation? It's critical to know the motivation and time frame the seller expects for performance.

**Servicing Listing**
IC 54-2053 (2)

## Servicing the listing

Once the listing is secured, the marketing plan springs into action. When advertising, special attention needs to be made and rechecked to make sure the brokerage name is included with any and all advertising or promotion.

# Measuring Property

**ANSI Standard**

## ANSI Z765-2003

One area of practicing real estate that can be confusing is the proper way to measure single family houses. Prior to 1996, there was no nationwide standard in the United States. The American National Standards Institute (ANSI) has developed a standard that has been accepted by the National Association of Home Builders, The National Association of REALTORS®, Fannie Mae, Freddie Mac, and many other entities that deal with financing and appraisal methods, in 1996 and was amended in 2003.

**Measuring Highlights**

## Highlights of ANSI Z765-2003

Below are condensed highlights of how to properly measure homes with universal acceptance. Often appraisers use the MLS figures when they prepare their comparables so it's very important that everyone measure the same way.

| **Measuring** | *Measuring* |
| | Exterior dimensions only |
| | Reported to nearest inch or tenth of a foot |
| | Total measurement to the nearest whole square foot |

**Floor Openings**

*Openings to floor below*
Area of both stair treads and landings is included from which stairs descend
Staircases to unfinished basement included as 'finished'
Openings not supported by staircases are not included

**Ceiling Height**

*Ceiling height requirements*
Must have a ceiling height of at least 7 feet
Under beams or other obstructions can be 6' 4"
Sloped ceilings
At least ½ of finished footage must have vertical height of at least 7 feet
No portion can have height of less than 5 feet to be included as 'finished'

**Garages, etc.**

*Garages, unfinished, and protrusions*
No portion can be included as finished square footage
Chimneys, windows and other areas that protrude beyond exterior are not included if they do not have a floor on the same level
Finished areas above a garage are included only if connected to house by hallway

**Conversion to 10th's**

*Converting inches to $10^{ths}$ of a foot*
1" = .0833
2" = .1667
3" = .25
4" = .3333
5" = .4161
6" = .5
7" = .5833
8" = .6667
9" = .75
10" = .8333
11" = .9167
12" = 1

**Potential Errors?**

## Issues that can lead to errors

If agents don't physically measure either the subject home or comparables, errors can occur due to using inaccurate information. Examples include using assessor square footage, house plans, previous MLS information, owners information, and just mis-measuring.

**Exterior Measurements**

## Measuring exterior

Either get a surveyors tape (measures in 10th's or a regular tape that measures in 12ths) or, make the appropriate conversion.

Diagram the home on graph paper (to make it neater or easier to track). Line out squares to equal 1 foot. Then, measure and record your measurements for each length.

Once you have all the measurements make sure the home is 'square' with the parallel sides equaling each other. Once the outside dimensions are identified, break up the home into square and rectangular sections. Add up the square footage of each section. Then, total the sections to get the total square footage for the home.

Remember, measurements are based on 10th's. Most people do not know this and thus, inaccurate square footage is calculated. For example, 30' 6" is actually 30.5'; 42' 8" is actually 42.75'. The error is small but none the less an error. By the way, look at a plat map and you will see all linear measurements are in feet, tenths, and even hundredths of a foot. Interesting huh?

Most homes are not just squares and rectangles. They are made up with different angles. The math applications are:

Rectangles
   length x width

Triangles
   ½ the base x height

Trapezoid   (bay windows)
   Sum of the parallel sides ÷ in half  x  height

A good way to avoid errors is to physically measure the home twice to make sure the total square footage equals each other with both measurements. It's not unusual to 'back in' values based on square footage or just get a 'feeling' of what the value would be based on square footage. It's also not unusual to see advertising relating cost per square foot.

**Misleading Information**
IC 54-2053 (4)

Remember, Idaho Code could come into play if advertised property is misleading or if such information will deceive the persons whom it is intended to influence.

# Seller Representation Agreement

**Seller Representation Agreement**

Figure 1

## Seller Representation Agreement
The Seller Representation Agreement created by the Idaho Association of Realtors (RE 16) will generally be used by most members of this trade organization for residential listings.

When preparing the Seller Representation Agreement, the seller needs to understand exactly what an 'exclusive right to represent' really means and that the agreement is a binding contract.

**Term of Agreement**

## Term Of The Agreement
The term of the agreement should be indirectly based on the estimated time it takes to market and close a sale. Many variables enter into the equation including: broker policies, economic trends, supply and demand of customers and clients, and cost of money.

**Price Ranges To Consider**

## Price ranges
Some price ranges sell quicker than others. Understanding where price point ranges break and change, may influence which price range the seller should consider to be most effective.

**Finance Programs**

## Finance Programs

Different financing programs come with different requirements including additional costs to the seller. The agent should explain the different financing programs so the seller can choose which program best fits the seller, including the possibility of offering seller financing.

If the seller will consider 'seller financing', be very careful how the terminology is added into the agreement. You may consider adding the term, 'seller may consider .......'. This does not require the seller to accept the terms but rather 'consider' the terms.

**Brokerage Fee**

## Brokerage Fee

The brokerage fee generally is based on the brokerage office policy. It may also give the sales associate latitude to negotiate a fee different from the brokerage office policy. The seller needs to know and understand what happens once a listing has expired. Someone who saw the property, while it was listed, but makes an offer after expiration may obligate the seller to still pay a fee.

**Additional Fees**

## Additional Fees

Additional fees the brokerage may impose need to be fully explained to the seller so they aren't surprised later. If the agent pays for some items, make sure it is explained how the agent will be reimbursed. Or, if additional fees for additional services are imposed, make sure everyone knows how such fees are calculated and paid.

**Excluded Personal Items**

## Excluded Personal Items

If the seller desires to remove any items listed in the 'included items' section, such items should be so noted in the 'excluded items' section and make reference to the lines they were originally included.

**Possible Tax Consequences**

## Tax Consequences

If the seller is considering a short sale or even foreclosure, they should be encouraged to seek legal and accounting counsel before they make the decision. There can be major tax consequences not to mention credit issues and other possible penalties.

## Authorizations

Various authorizations for MLS, lockbox, internet options, and advertising need to be explained to the seller. Educating the seller regarding some of the possible implications, may result in the seller accepting or not accepting some of the authorizations.

**Sellers Property Disclosure Form**
IC 55-2508

Figure 2.1 & 2.2

## Sellers Property Disclosure Form

The Sellers Property Disclosure Form (RE 25) may have been completed by the seller on the first visit but needs to be reviewed as it is incorporated into the Sellers Representation Agreement.

Any person who intends to transfer any residential real property, including nonowner occupied rental property shall complete all applicable items contained in a property disclosure form. Idaho Code defines residential property of consisting of not less than 1 nor more than 4 dwelling units. There are however some exemptions that include:

**Exemptions**
IC 55-2505

1. Transfer pursuant to court order
2. Transfer by deed in lieu of foreclosure
3. Transfer to beneficiary of deed of trust in default
4. Transfer by foreclosure
5. Transfer under power of sale within 1 year of foreclosure
6. Transfer by mortgagee who acquired by 'deed in lieu of'
7. Transfer by fiduciary of a decedents estate
8. Transfer from one co-owner to other co-owners
9. Transfer made by spouse to more lineal persons
10. Transfer between spouses or former spouses
11. Transfer to or from the state or another govt. entity
12. Transfer of new uninhabited residential real property
13. Transfer of occupant who has occupied for at least 1 year
14. Transfer by inheritance to non occupants within 1 year
15. Transfer by relocation company within 1 year
16. Transfer from a decedents's estate

The disclosure form is *not* a warranty and the purchaser is encouraged to obtain an independent professional inspection. The seller is relaying what they know to be true but does not possess any expertise in construction or any specific areas related to the construction or condition of the improvements on the property.

**Disclosure Requirements**
Newly constructed

IC - 55-2505

Sellers of newly constructed residential real property shall disclose information regarding annexation and city services including:

1. Is the property located in an area of city impact, adjacent or contiguous to a city limits?

2. Does the property, if not within the city limits, receive any city services, thus making it legally subject to annexation by the city?

3. Does the property have a written consent to annex recorded in the county recorder's office, thus making it legally subject to annexation by the city?

**Required disclosure by all sellers**

All sellers are required to disclose the following:

4. Appliances and service systems are functioning properly except (seller needs to list and explain).

5. Specify problems with
   Basement water
   Foundation
   Roof condition and age
   Well (type)
   Septic system
   Plumbing
   Drainage
   Electrical
   Heating

6. Describe any conditions that may affect ability to clear title (encroachments, easements, zoning violations, lot line disputes, etc.)

7. Are you aware of any hazardous materials or pest infestations on the property?

8. Have any substantial additions or alterations been made without a building permit?

9. Any other problems, including legal, physical or other not listed above that you know concerning the property.

The seller certifies the information is true and correct and both the buyer and seller acknowledge receipt of the disclosure.

The Idaho Association of REALTORS® offers an excellent form that is an extension of the mandated state form. Their form expands some of the items for a much more comprehensive disclosure for both the seller and buyer alike.

**Lead Paint Disclosure Form**

Figure 3

## Lead Paint Disclosure
If the home was built prior to 1978, the seller will need to agree to provide the Lead Paint Disclosure form to be signed by all parties to the transaction including the agent's acknowledgment.

**Services Disclaimer**

## Services Disclaimer
A disclaimer should be understood by the seller that the agent is not an expert in all phases of real estate. In the event the seller requests the agent to secure products or services, the seller will reimburse the agent immediately when payment is due.

**Dual Agency Consent**

## Dual Agency Consent
In order for an agent to represent both parties in a real estate transaction, there must be written consent. Such consent should be well explained and acknowledged by the seller so there are no questions regarding the use of Limited Dual Representation and the duties of the agent.

**Seller Information**

## Seller Information
As a precaution for the agent, a clause that the information, provided by the seller, is warranted to be true and correct. However, the clause does not excuse the agent from disclosing to all parties when such information is untrue or incorrect.

Although improbable, there should be a clause that identifies what happens should a law suit be filed including attorney fees to the prevailing party. Filed law suits will be interpreted and governed by the State of Idaho.

| | |
|---|---|
| **Discrimination** | ## Discrimination Prohibited |
| | Also addressed should be a clause acknowledging by both the seller and broker that it is illegal to discriminate in the showing, sale, or leasing of the property based on race, color, national origin, religion, sex, family status or disability. |
| | |
| **Time Is Of The Essence** | ## Time Is Of The Essence |
| | 'Time Is Of The Essence' means the clause reinforces strict time issues will be adhered to, and can make a contract voidable or void if not done within the time frames agreed upon. |
| | |
| **Calculating Sellers Net Sheet** | ## Calculating a Sellers Net Sheet |
| | Obviously one of the key elements to selling a property is what the seller will net after the sale closes. A rough estimate is to add around 4% to the listing fee and the total of both costs will be what the seller might expect to be the total selling costs will be to close. But, there are more items to take into consideration. |

Basically the net proceeds will be the gross sales price minus unpaid mortgage(s) balances minus other selling costs. There could also be some 'hidden' costs such as overdue or unpaid bills not known or even judgments that have attached to the property.

Some mortgages have penalties for 'pre-paying' a mortgage early or 'recapture', so it's important the seller be aware of and know exactly what the net proceeds will be upon sale.

Closing costs that the seller will have, or may incur, include:

> First mortgage
> Second mortgage (or more)
> Home equity loan
> Prepayment penalties
> Property taxes - current year (pro-rated)
> Property taxes - from previous year(s)
> Tax service fee
> Medical bills (secured by the property)
> Home improvement assisted grants
> Seller assisted closing costs
> Brokerage commission or fee
> Title insurance - owners
> Escrow fee (usually ½ of total escrow fee)

Recording fees
Overnight delivery (mortgage payoff)
Homeowner Association Dues (HOA) - unpaid or prepaid
Irrigation fees - unpaid or prepaid
Unpaid public services - water and sewer
Special assessments
Judgments
IRS liens
Mechanic's liens
Fuel oil or propane

**IREC Guideline #1**

## Terminating a Listing Contract

Because of the confusion and possible legal ramifications, the Idaho Real Estate Commission has established a guideline to address cancellation or withdrawal of listings.

There may be circumstances in which a listing contract needs to be terminated either by the seller or the brokerage. Extreme care should be taken to make sure the seller understands the difference between the term 'withdraw' and the term 'cancel'.

There have been issues where the brokerage allowed the seller to withdraw. The seller, in turn, listed with another company only to find the seller owed two commissions; one to the original listing company and the other to the new listing company.

**Withdraw Listing**

How could this happen? If the owner withdraws, the contract remains in full force and effect. Some listing agreements specify a penalty for early withdrawal of the property from sale by the owner. Even if no penalty is specified in the contract, the court might award damages to a broker if the seller has acted unreasonably and the broker acted in good faith

**Listing Cancellation**

If the owner cancels a contract, they are essentially 'breaking' the contract. Unless the owner has sufficient legal justification to break the contract, he or she may be required to pay the losses, or damages, incurred by the broker. Such damages can include the out-of-pocket costs incurred by the broker, or the full commission to the broker would have earned had the broker not cancelled the contract.

# Figure 1 – Seller Representation Agreement - Page 1 of 4

## RE-16 SELLER REPRESENTATION AGREEMENT
### (EXCLUSIVE RIGHT TO REPRESENT)

THIS IS A LEGALLY BINDING CONTRACT, READ THE ENTIRE DOCUMENT, INCLUDING ANY ATTACHMENTS.
IF YOU HAVE ANY QUESTIONS, **CONSULT YOUR ATTORNEY AND/OR ACCOUNTANT** BEFORE SIGNING.

1  DATE:_____ AGENT: _____
2                                                                                   Acting as Agent for the Broker
3  **1. SELLER** _____
4  retains_____ Broker of _____as
5  SELLER'S exclusive Broker to sell, lease, or exchange the property described in Section 2 below, during the term of this agreement and on
6  any additional terms hereafter set forth.
7
8  **2. PROPERTY ADDRESS AND/OR LEGAL DESCRIPTION.** The property address and/or the complete legal description of the property
9  are as set forth below.
10 Address_____
11 County_____ City_____ Zip_____
12 Legal and/or Property Description_____
13 _____
14 or ☐Legal and/or Property Description Attached as addendum #_____. **(Addendum must accompany this agreement)**
15
16 **3. TERM OF AGREEMENT.** The term of this Agreement shall commence on _____and shall expire at 11:59
17 p.m. on _____ unless renewed or extended. If the SELLER accepts an offer to purchase or exchange,
18 the terms of this Agreement shall be extended through the closing of the transaction.
19
20 **4. PRICE.** SELLER agrees to sell the property for a total price of $_____
21
22 **5. FINANCING.** SELLER agrees to consider the following types of financing: *(Complete all applicable provisions).*
23        ☐FHA      ☐VA      ☐CONVENTIONAL      ☐IHFA      ☐RURAL DEVELOPMENT      ☐Exchange
24        ☐Cash      ☐Cash to existing loan(s)          ☐Assumption of existing loan(s)
25 ☐SELLER will carry contract and accept a minimum down payment of $_____ and an acceptable
26 secured note for the balance to be paid as follows: _____
27 _____
28 _____
29 Other acceptable terms _____
30 _____
31
32 **6. BROKERAGE FEE.**
33 (A) If Broker or any person, including SELLER, procures a purchaser ready, willing and able to purchase, transfer or exchange the
34 property on the terms stated herein or on any other price and terms agreed to in writing, the SELLER agrees to pay a total brokerage fee
35 of _____% of the contract or purchase price OR $_____ of which _____% of the contract or purchase price OR
36 $_____ will be shared with the cooperating brokerage unless otherwise agreed to in writing. The fee shall be paid in cash at
37 closing unless otherwise designated by the Broker in writing.
38 (B) Further, the brokerage fee is payable if the property or any portion thereof or any interest therein is, directly or indirectly, sold,
39 exchanged or optioned or agreed to be sold, exchanged or optioned within _____ calendar days (ninety [90] if left blank) following
40 expiration of the term hereof to any person who has examined, been introduced to or been shown the property during the term hereof.
41 (C) If SELLER, upon termination of this Agreement, enters into a Right to Sell Agreement to market said property with another Broker,
42 then the time period specified above in Section 6B, shall not apply and will be of no further force or effect.
43
44 **7. ADDITIONAL FEES:**_____
45 _____
46 _____
47
48 **8. INCLUDED ITEMS.** SELLER agrees to leave with the premises all seller-owned attached floor coverings, attached television antennae,
49 satellite dish, attached plumbing, bathroom and lighting fixtures, window screens, screen doors, storm doors, storm windows, window
50 coverings, garage door opener(s) and transmitter(s), exterior trees, plants or shrubbery, water heating apparatus and fixtures, attached
51 fireplace equipment, awnings, ventilating, cooling and heating systems, all ranges, ovens, built-in dishwashers, fuel tanks and irrigation
52 fixtures and equipment, all water systems, wells, springs, water, water rights, ditches and ditch rights, if any, that are appurtenant thereto
53 that are now on or used in connection with the premises and shall be included in the sale unless otherwise provided herein.
54 Also included: _____
55 _____
56 _____
57 _____

SELLER'S Initials (_____) (_____) Date:_____

# Figure 1 – Seller Representation Agreement - Page 2 of 4

PROPERTY ADDRESS:_____

| HEATING & COOLING SYSTEMS SECTION | None/Not Included | Working | Not Working | Do Not Know | Remarks |
|---|---|---|---|---|---|
| Attic Fan(s) | | | | | |
| Central Air Conditioning | | | | | |
| Room Air Conditioner(s) | | | | | |
| Evaporative Cooler(s) | | | | | |
| Fireplace(s) | | | | | |
| Fireplace Insert(s) | | | | | |
| Furnace/Heating System(s) | | | | | |
| Humidifier(s) | | | | | |
| Wood/Pellet Stove(s) | | | | | |
| Air Cleaner(s) | | | | | |

| MOISTURE & DRAINAGE CONDITIONS SECTION | Yes | No | Do Not Know | Remarks |
|---|---|---|---|---|
| Is the property located in a floodplain? | | | | |
| Are you aware of any site drainage problems? | | | | |
| Has there been any water intrusion or moisture related damage to any portion of the property, including, but not limited to, the crawlspace, floors, walls, ceilings, siding, or basement, based on flooding; moisture seepage, moisture condensation, sewer overflow/ backup, or leaking pipes, plumbing fixtures, appliances, or moisture related damage from other causes? | | | | |
| Have you had the property inspected for the existence of any types of mold? | | | | |
| If the property has been inspected for mold, is a copy of the inspection report available? | | | | |
| Are you aware of the existence of any mold-related problems on any interior portion of the property, including but not limited to, floors, walls, ceilings, basement, crawlspaces, and attics, or any mold-related structural damage? | | | | |
| Have you ever had any water intrusion, moisture related damage, mold or mold-related problems on the property remediated, repaired, fixed or replaced? | | | | |

| FUEL TANK SECTION | N/A ( )   Propane ( )   Oil ( )   Diesel ( )   Gasoline ( )   Other ( ) |
|---|---|
| Location: | Size: |
| In Use: ( )    Not In Use: ( )    Above Ground: ( )    Buried: ( )    Owned: ( )    Leased: ( ) | |

| WATER & SEWER SYSTEMS SECTION | None/Not Included | Working | Not Working | Do Not Know | Remarks |
|---|---|---|---|---|---|
| Hot Tub/Spa and Equipment | | | | | |
| Pool and Pool Equipment | | | | | |
| Plumbing System – Faucets and Fixtures | | | | | |
| Water Heater(s) | | | | | |
| Water Softener (owned) | | | | | |
| Water Softener (leased) | | | | | |
| Septic System | | | | | |
| Sump Pump/Lift Pump | | | | | |
| Landscape Sprinkler System | | | | | |

| WATER & SEWER SYSTEM TYPE SECTION | Public System | Community System | Private System | Cistern | Other |
|---|---|---|---|---|---|
| Domestic Water Provided By: | | | | | |
| Irrigation Water Provided By: | | | | | |
| Property Sewer Provided By: | | | | | |
| If Septic System, Date Last Pumped / / | | | | | |

| ROOF SECTION: Age (If known): | Yes | No | Do Not Know | Remarks |
|---|---|---|---|---|
| Is there present damage to the roof? | | | | |
| Does the roof leak? | | | | |
| SIDING SECTION: Age (If known): | | | | |
| Are there any problems with the siding? | | | | |

SELLER'S Initials (_____)(_____) Date_____      BUYER'S Initials (_____)(_____) Date_____

# Figure 1 – Seller Representation Agreement - Page 3 of 4

PROPERTY ADDRESS:_____

| HAZARDOUS CONDITIONS SECTION | Yes | No | Do Not Know | Remarks |
|---|---|---|---|---|
| Are you aware of any asbestos or other toxic or hazardous materials on the property? | | | | |
| Has the property ever been used as an illegal drug manufacturing site? | | | | |
| Are you aware of any current or previous insect, rodent or other pest infestation(s) on the property? | | | | |
| Have you ever had the property serviced by an exterminator or had the property otherwise remediated for insect, rodent or other pest infestation(s)? | | | | |
| Is there any damage due to wind, fire, or flood? | | | | |

| OTHER DISCLOSURES SECTION | Yes | No | Do Not Know | Remarks |
|---|---|---|---|---|
| Are there any conditions that may affect your ability to clear title such as encroachments, easements, zoning violations, lot line disputes, restrictive covenants, etc.? | | | | |
| Has the property been surveyed since you owned it? | | | | |
| Have you received any notices by any governmental or quasi-governmental entity affecting this property; i.e. Local improvement district (LID) or zoning changes, etc.? | | | | |
| Are there any structural problems with the improvements? | | | | |
| Are there any structural problems with the foundation? | | | | |
| Have any substantial additions or alterations been made without a building permit? | | | | |
| Has the fireplace/wood stove/chimney/flue been inspected? | | | | |
| Has the fireplace/wood stove/chimney/flue been cleaned? | | | | |
| Have you ever filed a homeowner's insurance claim on the property? | | | | |

**ADDITIONAL REMARKS AND/OR EXPLANATIONS SECTION:** Please list any other existing problems that you know of concerning the property including legal, physical, product defects or others that are not already listed. (Use additional pages if necessary.)

_____
_____
_____
_____

*The referenced property herein is exempt from the code because of Section 55-2505 for any of the following reasons:*

☐ A transfer pursuant to court order including, but not limited to a transfer ordered by a probate court during the administration of the decedent's estate, a transfer pursuant to a writ of execution, a transfer by a trustee in bankruptcy, a transfer as a result of the exercise of the power of eminent domain, and a transfer that results from a decree for a specific performance of a contract or other agreement between persons:

☐ A transfer to a mortgagee by a mortgagor by deed in lieu of foreclosure or in satisfaction of the mortgage debt:

☐ A transfer to a beneficiary of a deed of trust by trustor in default:

☐ A transfer by a foreclosure sale that follows a default in the satisfaction of an obligation secured by a mortgage:

☐ A transfer by a sale under a power of sale following a default in the satisfaction of an obligation that is secured by a deed of trust or another instrument containing a power of sale occurring within one (1) year of foreclosure on the default:

☐ A transfer by a mortgagee, or beneficiary under a deed of trust, who has acquired the residential real property at a sale conducted pursuant to a power of sale under a mortgage or deed of trust or who has acquired the residential real property by a deed in lieu of foreclosure:

☐ A transfer by a fiduciary in the course of the administration of a decedent's estate, a guardianship, a conservatorship or a trust:

☐ A transfer from one (1) co-owner to one (1) or more other co-owners:

☐ A transfer made to the transferor's spouse or to one (1) or more persons in the lineal line of consanguinity of one (1) or more of the transferors:

☐ A transfer between spouses or former spouses as a result of a decree of divorce, dissolution of marriage, annulment or legal separation or as a result of a property settlement agreement incidental to a decree of divorce, dissolution of marriage, annulment or legal separation.

☐ A transfer to or from the state, a political subdivision of the state, or another governmental entity:

☐ A transfer that involved newly constructed residential real property, that previously has not been inhabited, except as required by questions 1, 2 and 3:

☐ A transfer to a transferee who has occupied the property as a personal residence for one (1) or more years immediately prior to the transfer:

☐ A transfer from a transferor who has both not occupied the property as a personal residence within one (1) year immediately prior to the transfer and has acquired the property through inheritance or devise:

☐ A transfer by a relocation company to a transferee within one (1) year from the date that the previous owner occupied the property:

☐ A transfer from a decedent's estate:

**SELLER'S** Initials (_____)(_____) Date_____          **BUYER'S** Initials (_____)(_____) Date_____

Reprint with permission from IAR

## Figure 1 – Seller Representation Agreement - Page 4 of 4

**PROPERTY ADDRESS:**_____

The **SELLER** certifies that the information herein is true and correct to the best of the **SELLER'S** knowledge as of the date signed by the **SELLER**. The **SELLER** is familiar with the residential property and each act performed in making a disclosure of an item of information is made and performed in good faith.

**SELLER** and **BUYER** understand and acknowledge that the statements contained herein are the representations of the **SELLER** regarding the condition of the property. No statement made herein is a statement of a **SELLER'S** agent or agents, and no agent is authorized to make any statement, or verify any statement, relating to the condition of the property. **SELLER** and **BUYER** also understand and acknowledge that **SELLER** in no way warrants or guarantees the above information regarding the property. **SELLER** and **BUYER** also understand and acknowledge that, unless otherwise specifically set forth, no agent of the **SELLER** is an expert in environmental or other conditions which are or may be hazardous to human health, and which may exist on the property. **BUYER MAY, AT BUYER'S OPTION AND EXPENSE, CONSULT WITH ANY INDEPENDENT QUALIFIED INSPECTOR TO ASSESS OR DETECT THE PRESENCE OF SUCH KNOWN OR SUSPECTED HAZARDOUS CONDITIONS.**

**SELLER** and **BUYER** understand that Listing Broker and Selling Broker in no way warrant or guarantee the above information on the property.

**SELLER** hereby acknowledges receipt of a copy of this form:

_____   _____   _____   _____
SELLER                   DATE            SELLER                   DATE

**BUYER** hereby acknowledges receipt of a copy of this disclosure form and does hereby _____WAIVE _____NOT WAIVE the right to rescind the related purchase agreement within three **(3) business days** from the date of receipt of this form. **IF BUYER DOES NOT WAIVE THE RIGHT TO RESCIND** as set forth above, **BUYER** may only rescind the purchase and sale agreement within **three (3) business days** following receipt of this disclosure statement, by a written, signed and dated document that is delivered to the seller or his agents by personal delivery, ordinary or certified mail, or facsimile transmission. BUYER's rescission must be based on a specific objection to a disclosure in the disclosure statement. The notice of rescission must specifically identify the disclosure objected to by the BUYER. If no signed notice of rescission is received by the SELLER within the **three (3) business day** period, BUYER's right to rescind is waived.

_____   _____   _____   _____
BUYER                   DATE            BUYER                   DATE

**AMENDED DISCLOSURE FORM**: Subsequent to the delivery of the initial **SELLER'S** Property Condition Disclosure Form previously acknowledged, **SELLER** hereby makes the following amendments. (Attach additional pages if necessary.) Other than those amendments made below, the **SELLER** states that there have been no changes to the information contained in the initial **SELLER'S** Property Condition Disclosure Form. **IF THERE ARE NO UPDATES, THERE IS NO NEED TO SIGN BELOW.**

_____
_____
_____

**SELLER** hereby acknowledges receipt of this amended form:

_____   _____   _____   _____
SELLER                   DATE            SELLER                   DATE

**BUYER** hereby acknowledges receipt of a copy of the amended disclosure form and does hereby _____WAIVE _____NOT WAIVE the right to rescind the related purchase agreement based strictly on the amendments to the disclosure form within **three (3) business days** from the date of receipt of this amended form. **IF BUYER DOES NOT WAIVE THE RIGHT TO RESCIND** as set forth above, **BUYER** may only rescind the purchase and sale agreement within **three (3) business days** following receipt of this amended disclosure statement, by a written, signed and dated document that is delivered to the SELLER or his agents by personal delivery, ordinary or certified mail, or facsimile transmission. BUYER's rescission must be based on a specific objection to a disclosure in the disclosure statement. The notice of rescission must specifically identify the disclosure objected to by the BUYER. If no signed notice of rescission is received by the SELLER within the three **(3) business day** period, BUYER's right to rescind is waived.

_____   _____   _____   _____
BUYER                   DATE            BUYER                   DATE

Reprint with permission from IAR

## Figure 2.1 – Property Condition Disclosure - State Approved Format
### Seller Property Disclosure Form

Seller's Name and Address_____

      Section 55-2501, et seq., Idaho Code, requires Sellers of residential real property to complete a property condition disclosure form.

      PURPOSE OF STATEMENT: This is a statement of the conditions and information concerning the property known by the Seller. Unless otherwise advised, the Seller does not possess any expertise in construction, architectural, engineering or any other specific areas related to the construction or condition of the improvements on the property. Other than having lived at or owning the property, the Seller possesses no greater knowledge than that which could be obtained upon a careful inspection of the property by the potential buyer. Unless otherwise advised, the Seller has not conducted any inspection of generally inaccessible areas such as the foundation or roof. It is not a warranty of any kind by the Seller or by any agent representing any Seller in this transaction. It is not a substitute for any inspections. Purchaser is encouraged to obtain his/her own professional inspections. Notwithstanding that transfer of newly constructed residential real property that previously has not been inhabited is exempt from disclosure pursuant to section 55-2505, Idaho Code, Seller of such newly constructed residential real property shall disclose information regarding annexation and city services in the form as prescribed in questions 1., 2., and 3.

1.  Is the property located in an area of city impact, adjacent or contiguous to a city limits, and thus legally subject to annexation by the city? _____Yes _____No

2.  Does the property, if not within city limits, receive any city services, thus making it legally subject to annexation by the city? _____Yes _____No

3.  Does the property have a written consent to annex recorded in the county recorder's office, thus making it legally subject to annexation by the city? _____Yes _____No

4.  All appliances and services systems included in the sale, (such as refrigerator/freezer, range/oven, dishwasher, disposal, hood/fan, central vacuum, microwave oven, trash compactor, smoke detectors, tv antenna/dish, fireplace/wood stove, water heater, garage door opener, pool/hot tub, etc.) are functioning properly except: (please list and explain)

_____

5.  Specify problems with the following:
    Basement water _____
    Foundation _____
    Roof condition and age _____
    Well (type) _____Problem _____
    Septic system (type)_____Problem _____
    Plumbing _____
    Drainage _____
    Electrical _____
    Heating _____

6.  Describe any conditions that may affect your ability to clear title (such as encroachments, easements, zoning violations, lot line disputes etc.) _____

7.  Are you aware of any hazardous materials or pest infestations on the property_____ _____

8.  Have any substantial additions or alterations been made without a building permit? _____ _____

9.  Any other problems, including legal, physical or other not listed above that you know concerning the property?
_____

      The Seller certifies that the information herein is true and correct to the best of Seller's knowledge as of the date signed by the Seller. The Seller is familiar with the residential real property and each act performed in making the disclosure of an item of information is made performed in good faith.

      I/we acknowledge receipt of a copy of this statement.

Seller:                              Buyer:

_____         _____

Date:_____      Date: _____

_____         _____

Date: _____     Date: _____

## Figure 2.2 – Property Condition Disclosure - Page 1 of 4

# RE-25 SELLER'S PROPERTY CONDITION DISCLOSURE FORM

REALTOR

Seller's Name(s):_____ Date:_____

**Property Address:**_____

Section 55-2501, et seq., Idaho Code, requires **SELLERS** of residential real property to complete a property condition disclosure form and deliver a signed and dated copy of the completed disclosure form to each prospective transferee or his agent within ten (10) calendar days of transferor's acceptance of transferee's offer. "Residential Real Property" means real property that is improved by a building or other structure that has one (1) to four (4) dwelling units or an individually owned unit in a structure of any size. This also applies to real property which has a combined residential and commercial use. THE PURPOSE OF THE STATEMENT: This is a statement made by the **SELLER** of the conditions and information concerning the property known by the **SELLER**. <u>This is NOT a statement of any agent representing the **SELLER** and no agent is authorized to make representations, or verify representations, concerning the condition of the property.</u> Unless otherwise advised, the **SELLER** does not possess any expertise in construction, architectural, engineering or any other specific areas related to the construction or condition of the improvements on the property. Other than having lived at or owning the property, the **SELLER** possesses no greater knowledge than that which could be obtained upon careful inspection of the property by the potential **BUYER**. Unless otherwise advised, the **SELLER** has not conducted any inspection of generally inaccessible areas such as the foundation or roof. <u>This disclosure is not a warranty</u> of any kind by the **SELLER** or by any agent representing the **SELLER** in this transaction. It is not a substitute for any inspections. The **BUYER** is encouraged to obtain his/her own professional inspections.

Notwithstanding that transfer of newly constructed residential real property that previously has not been inhabited is exempt from disclosure pursuant to section 55-2505, Idaho Code, **SELLERS** of such newly constructed and existing residential real property shall disclose information regarding annexation and city services in the form as prescribed in questions **1, 2, and 3**.

1. *Is the property located in an area of city impact, adjacent or contiguous to a city limit, and thus legally subject to annexation by the city?*
   ☐Yes  ☐No  ☐Do Not Know  ☐**The property is already within city limits**

2. *Does the property, if not within city limits, receive any city services, thus making it legally subject to annexation by the city?*
   ☐Yes  ☐No  ☐Do Not Know  ☐**The property is already within city limits**

3. *Does the property have a written consent to annex recorded in the county recorder's office, thus making it legally subject to annexation by the city?*
   ☐Yes  ☐No  ☐Do Not Know  ☐**The property is already within city limits**

### THE FOLLOWING ARE IN THE CONDITIONS INDICATED:

| APPLIANCES SECTION | None/Not Included | Working | Not Working | Do Not Know | Remarks |
|---|---|---|---|---|---|
| Built-in Vacuum System | | | | | |
| Clothes Dryer | | | | | |
| Clothes Washer | | | | | |
| Dishwasher | | | | | |
| Disposal | | | | | |
| Refrigerator | | | | | |
| Kitchen Vent Fan/Hood | | | | | |
| Microwave Oven | | | | | |
| Oven(s)/ Range(s)/Cook top(s) | | | | | |
| Trash Compactor | | | | | |
| Freezer (chest or upright) | | | | | |

| ELECTRICAL SYSTEMS SECTION | None/Not Included | Working | Not Working | Do Not Know | Remarks |
|---|---|---|---|---|---|
| Air Purifier | | | | | |
| Security System(s) | | | | | |
| Ceiling Fan(s) | | | | | |
| Garage Door Opener(s)/Control(s) | | | | | |
| Inside Telephone Wiring/Jacks | | | | | |
| Aluminum Wiring | | | | | |
| Intercom System | | | | | |
| Light Fixtures | | | | | |
| Sauna | | | | | |
| Smoke Detector(s)/Fire Alarm(s) | | | | | |
| Bath Vent Fan(s) | | | | | |
| 220 Volt Outlet(s) | | | | | |
| TV Antenna/Dish/Controls | | | | | |
| Switches and Outlets | | | | | |

**SELLER'S** Initials (_____)(_____) Date_____     **BUYER'S** Initials (_____)(_____) Date_____

Reprint with permission from IAR

## Figure 2-2 – Property Condition Disclosure - Page 2 of 4

PROPERTY ADDRESS:_____

| HEATING & COOLING SYSTEMS SECTION | None/Not Included | Working | Not Working | Do Not Know | Remarks |
|---|---|---|---|---|---|
| Attic Fan(s) | | | | | |
| Central Air Conditioning | | | | | |
| Room Air Conditioner(s) | | | | | |
| Evaporative Cooler(s) | | | | | |
| Fireplace(s) | | | | | |
| Fireplace Insert(s) | | | | | |
| Furnace/Heating System(s) | | | | | |
| Humidifier(s) | | | | | |
| Wood/Pellet Stove(s) | | | | | |
| Air Cleaner(s) | | | | | |

| MOISTURE & DRAINAGE CONDITIONS SECTION | Yes | No | Do Not Know | Remarks |
|---|---|---|---|---|
| Is the property located in a floodplain? | | | | |
| Are you aware of any site drainage problems? | | | | |
| Has there been any water intrusion or moisture related damage to any portion of the property, including, but not limited to, the crawlspace, floors, walls, ceilings, siding, or basement, based on flooding; moisture seepage, moisture condensation, sewer overflow/ backup, or leaking pipes, plumbing fixtures, appliances, or moisture related damage from other causes? | | | | |
| Have you had the property inspected for the existence of any types of mold? | | | | |
| If the property has been inspected for mold, is a copy of the inspection report available? | | | | |
| Are you aware of the existence of any mold-related problems on any interior portion of the property, including but not limited to, floors, walls, ceilings, basement, crawlspaces, and attics, or any mold-related structural damage? | | | | |
| Have you ever had any water intrusion, moisture related damage, mold or mold-related problems on the property remediated, repaired, fixed or replaced? | | | | |

| FUEL TANK SECTION | N/A ( ) Propane ( ) Oil ( ) Diesel ( ) Gasoline ( ) Other ( ) |
|---|---|
| Location: | Size: |
| In Use: ( ) Not In Use: ( ) Above Ground: ( ) Buried: ( ) Owned: ( ) Leased: ( ) | |

| WATER & SEWER SYSTEMS SECTION | None/Not Included | Working | Not Working | Do Not Know | Remarks |
|---|---|---|---|---|---|
| Hot Tub/Spa and Equipment | | | | | |
| Pool and Pool Equipment | | | | | |
| Plumbing System – Faucets and Fixtures | | | | | |
| Water Heater(s) | | | | | |
| Water Softener (owned) | | | | | |
| Water Softener (leased) | | | | | |
| Septic System | | | | | |
| Sump Pump/Lift Pump | | | | | |
| Landscape Sprinkler System | | | | | |

| WATER & SEWER SYSTEM TYPE SECTION | Public System | Community System | Private System | Cistern | Other |
|---|---|---|---|---|---|
| Domestic Water Provided By: | | | | | |
| Irrigation Water Provided By: | | | | | |
| Property Sewer Provided By: | | | | | |
| If Septic System, Date Last Pumped __/__ | | | | | |

| ROOF SECTION: Age (If known): | Yes | No | Do Not Know | Remarks |
|---|---|---|---|---|
| Is there present damage to the roof? | | | | |
| Does the roof leak? | | | | |

| SIDING SECTION: Age (If known): | | | | |
|---|---|---|---|---|
| Are there any problems with the siding? | | | | |

SELLER'S Initials (_____)(_____) Date_____    BUYER'S Initials (_____)(_____) Date_____

# Figure 2-2 – Property Condition Disclosure - Page 3 of 4

PROPERTY ADDRESS:_____

| HAZARDOUS CONDITIONS SECTION | Yes | No | Do Not Know | Remarks |
|---|---|---|---|---|
| Are you aware of any asbestos or other toxic or hazardous materials on the property? | | | | |
| Has the property ever been used as an illegal drug manufacturing site? | | | | |
| Are you aware of any current or previous insect, rodent or other pest infestation(s) on the property? | | | | |
| Have you ever had the property serviced by an exterminator or had the property otherwise remediated for insect, rodent or other pest infestation(s)? | | | | |
| Is there any damage due to wind, fire, or flood? | | | | |

| OTHER DISCLOSURES SECTION | Yes | No | Do Not Know | Remarks |
|---|---|---|---|---|
| Are there any conditions that may affect your ability to clear title such as encroachments, easements, zoning violations, lot line disputes, restrictive covenants, etc.? | | | | |
| Has the property been surveyed since you owned it? | | | | |
| Have you received any notices by any governmental or quasi-governmental entity affecting this property; i.e. Local improvement district (LID) or zoning changes, etc.? | | | | |
| Are there any structural problems with the improvements? | | | | |
| Are there any structural problems with the foundation? | | | | |
| Have any substantial additions or alterations been made without a building permit? | | | | |
| Has the fireplace/wood stove/chimney/flue been inspected? | | | | |
| Has the fireplace/wood stove/chimney/flue been cleaned? | | | | |
| Have you ever filed a homeowner's insurance claim on the property? | | | | |

**ADDITIONAL REMARKS AND/OR EXPLANATIONS SECTION:** Please list any other existing problems that you know of concerning the property including legal, physical, product defects or others that are not already listed. (Use additional pages if necessary.)

_____
_____
_____
_____
_____

*The referenced property herein is exempt from the code because of Section 55-2505 for any of the following reasons:*

☐ A transfer pursuant to court order including, but not limited to a transfer ordered by a probate court during the administration of the decedent's estate, a transfer pursuant to a writ of execution, a transfer by a trustee in bankruptcy, a transfer as a result of the exercise of the power of eminent domain, and a transfer that results from a decree for a specific performance of a contract or other agreement between persons:

☐ A transfer to a mortgagee by a mortgagor by deed in lieu of foreclosure or in satisfaction of the mortgage debt:

☐ A transfer to a beneficiary of a deed of trust by trustor in default:

☐ A transfer by a foreclosure sale that follows a default in the satisfaction of an obligation secured by a mortgage:

☐ A transfer by a sale under a power of sale following a default in the satisfaction of an obligation that is secured by a deed of trust or another instrument containing a power of sale occurring within one (1) year of foreclosure on the default:

☐ A transfer by a mortgagee, or beneficiary under a deed of trust, who has acquired the residential real property at a sale conducted pursuant to a power of sale under a mortgage or deed of trust or who has acquired the residential real property by a deed in lieu of foreclosure:

☐ A transfer by a fiduciary in the course of the administration of a decedent's estate, a guardianship, a conservatorship or a trust:

☐ A transfer from one (1) co-owner to one (1) or more other co-owners:

☐ A transfer made to the transferor's spouse or to one (1) or more persons in the lineal line of consanguinity of one (1) or more of the transferors:

☐ A transfer between spouses or former spouses as a result of a decree of divorce, dissolution of marriage, annulment or legal separation or as a result of a property settlement agreement incidental to a decree of divorce, dissolution of marriage, annulment or legal separation:

☐ A transfer to or from the state, a political subdivision of the state, or another governmental entity:

☐ A transfer that involved newly constructed residential real property, that previously has not been inhabited, except as required by questions 1, 2 and 3:

☐ A transfer to a transferee who has occupied the property as a personal residence for one (1) or more years immediately prior to the transfer:

☐ A transfer from a transferor who has both not occupied the property as a personal residence within one (1) year immediately prior to the transfer and has acquired the property through inheritance or devise:

☐ A transfer by a relocation company to a transferee within one (1) year from the date that the previous owner occupied the property:

☐ A transfer from a decedent's estate:

**SELLER'S** Initials (_____)(_____) Date_____    **BUYER'S** Initials (_____)(_____) Date_____

# Figure 2-2 – Property Condition Disclosure - Page 4 of 4

PROPERTY ADDRESS:_____

The **SELLER** certifies that the information herein is true and correct to the best of the **SELLER'S** knowledge as of the date signed by the **SELLER**. The **SELLER** is familiar with the residential property and each act performed in making a disclosure of an item of information is made and performed in good faith.

**SELLER and BUYER** understand and acknowledge that the statements contained herein are the representations of the **SELLER** regarding the condition of the property. No statement made herein is a statement of a **SELLER'S** agent or agents, and no agent is authorized to make any statement, or verify any statement, relating to the condition of the property. **SELLER and BUYER** also understand and acknowledge that **SELLER** in no way warrants or guarantees the above information regarding the property. **SELLER and BUYER** also understand and acknowledge that, unless otherwise specifically set forth, no agent of the SELLER is an expert in environmental or other conditions which are or may be hazardous to human health, and which may exist on the property. **BUYER MAY, AT BUYER'S OPTION AND EXPENSE, CONSULT WITH ANY INDEPENDENT QUALIFIED INSPECTOR TO ASSESS OR DETECT THE PRESENCE OF SUCH KNOWN OR SUSPECTED HAZARDOUS CONDITIONS.**

**SELLER and BUYER** understand that Listing Broker and Selling Broker in no way warrant or guarantee the above information on the property.

**SELLER** hereby acknowledges receipt of a copy of this form:

_____  _____  _____  _____
**SELLER**                     **DATE**         **SELLER**                    **DATE**

**BUYER** hereby acknowledges receipt of a copy of this disclosure form and does hereby _____WAIVE _____NOT WAIVE the right to rescind the related purchase agreement within three **(3) business days** from the date of receipt of this form. **IF BUYER DOES NOT WAIVE THE RIGHT TO RESCIND** as set forth above, **BUYER** may only rescind the purchase and sale agreement within **three (3) business days** following receipt of this disclosure statement, by a written, signed and dated document that is delivered to the seller or his agents by personal delivery, ordinary or certified mail, or facsimile transmission. BUYER's rescission must be based on a specific objection to a disclosure in the disclosure statement. The notice of rescission must specifically identify the disclosure objected to by the BUYER. If no signed notice of rescission is received by the SELLER within the **three (3) business day** period, BUYER's right to rescind is waived.

_____  _____  _____  _____
**BUYER**                  **DATE**         **BUYER**                    **DATE**

**AMENDED DISCLOSURE FORM**: Subsequent to the delivery of the initial **SELLER'S** Property Condition Disclosure Form previously acknowledged, **SELLER** hereby makes the following amendments. (Attach additional pages if necessary.) Other than those amendments made below, the **SELLER** states that there have been no changes to the information contained in the initial **SELLER'S** Property Condition Disclosure Form. **IF THERE ARE NO UPDATES, THERE IS NO NEED TO SIGN BELOW.**

_____
_____
_____
_____

**SELLER** hereby acknowledges receipt of this amended form:

_____  _____  _____  _____
**SELLER**                     **DATE**         **SELLER**                    **DATE**

**BUYER** hereby acknowledges receipt of a copy of the amended disclosure form and does hereby _____WAIVE _____NOT WAIVE the right to rescind the related purchase agreement based strictly on the amendments to the disclosure form within **three (3) business days** from the date of receipt of this amended form. **IF BUYER DOES NOT WAIVE THE RIGHT TO RESCIND** as set forth above, **BUYER** may only rescind the purchase and sale agreement within **three (3) business days** following receipt of this amended disclosure statement, by a written, signed and dated document that is delivered to the SELLER or his agents by personal delivery, ordinary or certified mail, or facsimile transmission. BUYER's rescission must be based on a specific objection to a disclosure in the disclosure statement. The notice of rescission must specifically identify the disclosure objected to by the BUYER. If no signed notice of rescission is received by the SELLER within the three **(3) business day** period, BUYER's right to rescind is waived.

_____  _____  _____  _____
**BUYER**                  **DATE**         **BUYER**                    **DATE**

Reprint with permission from IAR

Figure 3 – Lead Paint Brochure

# Questions – Chapter 16

1. What's the purpose of the first listing appointment?

   A. Gather information
   B. Present a listing packet
   C. Secure the listing
   D. Discuss MLS requirements

2. What type of comparable properties are generally used as the basis of a CMA?

   A. On market
   B. Recently sold
   C. Expired listings
   D. For sale by owner properties

3. What information must be included with all advertising of listed properties?

   A. Agent's name
   B. Broker's name
   C. Seller's name
   D. Brokerage business name

4. What is the minimum ceiling height based on ANSI Z765-2003?

   A. 5'
   B. 6'
   C. 7'
   D. 8'

5. Based on ANSI Z765-2003, no portion of a ceiling height can be less that:

   A. 5'
   B. 6'
   C. 7'
   D. 8'

6. The Sellers Property Disclosure must be completed by the:

   A. Agent
   B. Buyer
   C. Seller
   D. Lender

7. Sellers of newly constructed residential real property shall disclose information regarding:

   A. Annexation
   B. Contractor licensing
   C. Mechanic's liens
   D. Occupancy tax

8. Covenants, Conditions, and Restrictions (CCR's) impose what kind of restrictions?

   A. Public
   B. Private
   C. Personal
   D. Popular

# Chapter 17

# Writing and Presenting Purchase & Sale Agreements

When the prospective buyer has made the decision to make an offer on a property, the next step is to prepare a Purchase and Sale Agreement providing the buyer is ready, willing, and able.

Both the agent and the buyer need to set aside enough time so the contract can be completed in it's entirety with plenty of time to explain and answer any questions.

**Use Current Versions**

If using a pre-printed Purchase and Sale Agreement and other incorporated forms, make sure the most recent version is used. Occasionally changes in the law require changes in various forms. The Idaho Association of REALTORS® carefully reviews all their forms annually and any revisions usually are accompanied with new forms around June or July. Unless a law is declared an emergency in Idaho, legislated law changes take place on July 1 of the year the law was passed.

Only active members of the Idaho Association of REALTORS® can use their forms and use by any other person is prohibited.

**Good Business Practices**

## Good Business Practices

Some good business practices regarding the completion of the Purchase and Sale Agreement or any other incorporated forms include:

- Write legibly
- Refrain from using ambiguous language or phrases
- Refrain from using abbreviations
- Fill in all the blanks
- Use 'na' or 'dna' for 'not applicable' or 'does not apply'
- Use reasonable time frames to complete contingencies
- Use reasonable dates to meet 3rd party requirements
- Double check that stated dollar amounts are correct
- Properly identify included addendums or amendments
- Include agency representation confirmation - IC 54-2085
- Secure signatures of *all* parties to the transaction

| | |
|---|---|
| **Purchase and Sale Agreement** | # Real Estate Purchase and Sale Agreement |
| Figure 1 | Because the majority of real estate licensees are members of the Idaho Association of REALTORS®, they will use forms created by this trade organization. The RE-21 form is generally used for the purchase of residential real estate and will be used as an example in this text book to address some of the clauses that should or could be included in any Purchase and Sale Agreement. |

**Disclaimer**

## Disclaimer

Regardless of what form(s) are used, it should be clearly noted that the Purchase and Sale Agreement is a legal binding contract and if anyone has any questions, an attorney or accountant should be consulted before signing.

**Buyer**

## Buyer

Identify the buyer(s) by a full name. If more than one buyer will be purchasing, separate each buyer from the other. Example: John L. Jones and Mary Sue Jones, not John and Mary Jones.

**Purchase Price**

## Purchase Price

Make sure the filled in blanks are very legible, both numerically and spelled out.

**Earnest Money**

## Consideration

There isn't any rule regarding the amount of consideration or better known as earnest money. However, the amount of earnest money should be sufficient enough to compensate the seller should the contract be cancelled or not completed by the buyer.

Generally speaking, the buyer will tender a personal check which will be deposited either upon receipt or upon acceptance as stated in the Purchase and Sale Agreement as well as who will hold the earnest money.

**Earnest Money Delivery**
IC 54-2045 (4)

All consideration received shall be immediately delivered to the broker or broker's office

**Time of Deposit**
IC 54-2045 (1)

All moneys received by a broker for another in a real estate transaction are to be deposited on or before the banking day immediately following the receipt day of such funds, unless written instructions signed by the party or parties having an interest in the funds direct the broker to do otherwise.

If the broker or associate receives a check to be held for later deposit a ledger card needs to be created upon receiving the check in an uncashed form.

**Return of Earnest Money**
IC 54-2045 (3)

If the earnest money is returned before deposit, a ledger record must also be created. A written and dated notation must be placed on both the Purchase and Sale Agreement, offer or other document dealing with the consideration, and on the ledger record. No consideration is to be returned without the knowledge and consent of the broker.

**Financial Terms**

## Financial Terms

If the purchase requires financing, it's important to make sure all the dollar blanks add up to the purchase price. If they don't, there isn't a 'meeting of the minds'.

The financing terms and conditions need to be carefully reviewed to make sure all the 't's are crossed and the 'i's dotted, especially when it comes to the time frames.

The RE-21 clearly states, in part, that the seller is to receive *written* confirmation that funds are sufficient to close and if such written confirmation is not received by the sellers within the *strict* time allotted, the sellers may at their option *cancel* the agreement. Sloppiness or failure to adhere to the language contained in the Purchase and Sale Agreement can lead to great disappointment.

**Additional Terms**

## Additional Terms and Conditions

If additional terms or conditions are needed, this clause allows insertion of such terms and conditions. It helps avoid using a separate addendum or amendment and keeps everything nicely contained in the original Purchase and Sale Agreement. Make sure whatever is inserted is legible and unambiguous.

| Addendum | If there is not enough room on the Purchase and Sale agreement |
| Figure 2 | then use an addendum that makes reference to the Purchase and |
| | Sale agreement. |

## Included/Excluded Items — Included and Excluded Items

**Included/Excluded Items**

There are pre-printed items that are included with the transaction and the seller needs to know and understand what goes with the property. If there are additional items to be included, they need to be inserted to include model and/or serial numbers if possible. Model and serial numbers help eliminate any confusion regarding specific items that accompany a sale.

**Bill of Sale**

It's also a good business practice to get a bill of sale; especially if the personal items are of great value. Examples might be expensive riding lawn mowers, tractors, refrigerators, washers and dryers, swing sets, etc.

If, on the other hand, items are to be excluded or replaced, they should also be so noted and even tagged to eliminate any confusion upon closing with what items are or are not included with the sale.

**Title Insurance**

## Title Insurance Provider

Typically the buyer chooses the title insurance company when making an offer but then the seller changes the title company to their choice. This can happen when the seller could receive a discount or perhaps a builder has their own favorite title insurance company to work with.

**RESPA Procedures**

However, reference to the United States Code states:

| Title 12 | - Banks and banking, |
| Chapter 27 | - Real Estate Settlement Procedures, |
| Section 2608 | - Title Companies; liability of seller |

*(a) No seller of property that will be purchased with the assistance of a federally related mortgage loan shall require directly or indirectly, as a condition to selling the property, that title insurance covering the property be purchased by the buyer from a particular title company.*

**Penalty For Violation**

*(b) Any seller who violates the provisions of subsection (a) of this section shall be liable to the buyer in an amount equal to three times all charges made for such title insurance.*

Because the title insurance is for the benefit of the buyer (regardless of who pays), it's reasonable that the buyer should be able to choose the title insurance company of their choice.

However, if both parties agree otherwise, then whatever title insurance company is chosen by both parties will meet the law. The key word is 'require' as opposed to 'agree'.

**Inspections**

Figure 3

## Inspections

If the buyer chooses to have a home inspection, the time frame to conduct the inspections should be reasonable for not only the initial inspections but also for any time necessary to repair any defects.

It's also important to make sure everyone knows who is paying for what. If multiple inspections are agreed upon, each specific inspection should be identified separately with who is responsible for any required repairs. Make sure all time frames are adhered to and completed as agreed.

**Lead Paint Disclosure**

## Lead Paint Disclosure

If the home was built prior to 1978, make sure the buyer has been provided the pamphlet, 'Protect Your Family From Lead in Your Home' and agrees to waive or not waive the right to have the property tested for lead based paint. It is not required to have any property tested; it is an elective choice.

**Square Footage Verification**

## Square Footage Verification

Even though there may be a disclaimer that it is the buyer's responsibility to verify square footage if it is a material fact for the purchase, there could still be liability should the square footage be grossly misrepresented. However, the disclaimer is to remind the buyer of their responsibilities.

**Property Condition Disclosure Form**
IC 54-2501

## Sellers Property Condition Disclosure Form

Based on Idaho Code, the Sellers Property Disclosure Form shall be delivered to the buyer or buyer's agent within 10 days of execution of an agreement.

**CC&R's**

## Covenants, Conditions, and Restrictions

The buyer is responsible for obtaining and reviewing and approving the CC&R's. Some CC&R's are very lengthy and the agent needs to encourage the buyer to take the time to do a close review and look for any items that could adversely affect the buyer.

**HOA information**

## Homeowner's Association Information

It's also important that the buyer review the declaration and by-laws of the homeowner association if there is one. Included is the financial stability of the HOA as well and pending law suits. The buyer should also fully understand what the HOA fees are and what they include. When was the last time the HOA increased fees and are there any future plans for future increases?

**Who Pays Costs?**

## Who Pays What Costs?

Although some loan programs requires the seller to pay specific costs, most loan programs allow for closing costs to be negotiable between buyer and seller. Whether the Idaho Association of REALTORS® Purchase and Sale Agreement is used or some other form of purchase agreement is used, various costs should be addressed as to who pays what including but not limited to:

> Appraisal fee
> Appraisal re-inspection fee
> Closing escrow fee
> Lender document preparation fee
> Tax service fee
> Flood Certification and tracking fee
> Lender required inspections
> Attorney contract preparation or review
> Title insurance - standard owners policy
> Title insurance - standard owners extended policy
> Title insurance - lenders policy (mortgagee)
> Fuel oil or propane in tank
> Well test
> Septic inspection
> Septic pumping
> Survey

**Occupancy**

## Occupancy

It's important that the buyer fully understand the Occupancy clause in that if it is to be the buyer's primary residence, it will be the buyer's primary residence. If the buyer doesn't plan to occupy, the buyer should say so.

The purpose of this disclosure is to verify how the financing will be arranged. There are different rules for occupied and non-occupied residences.

**Walk Through**

## Final Walk Through

The primary purpose of the final walk through is to make sure any repairs scheduled were properly completed and that the property is in substantially the same condition as the acceptance date of the Purchase and Sale Agreement. It should be noted that it is the responsibility of the seller to make sure the utilities are turned on in the event the property is vacant. This takes pre-planning and needs to be addressed before the walk through is scheduled.

**Risk of Loss**

## Risk of Loss

All risk of loss will be borne by the seller. This is another indirect reason that early occupancy is risky. If the property is materially destroyed prior to closing, the buyer has the option to void the contract.

**Foreclosure Notice**
IC 15-1602

## Foreclosure Notice

If the property is involved in foreclosure, a Notice Required By Idaho Law must be in writing and be accompanied with the Purchase and Sale Agreement. The RE-42 Property Foreclosure Disclosure Form is available to members of the Idaho Association of REALTORS® for acknowledgment. If there are questions relating to the foreclosure process, an attorney or financial professional should be contacted.

**General Contractor Disclosure**
IC 45-525

## General Contractor Disclosure

If a General Contractor plans to enter into construction or make improvements to real property in an amount exceeding $2,000 or for the purchase and sale of newly constructed property, a Disclosure Statement must be given to the homeowner prior to entering into a contract.

The Disclosure Statement must contain:

- Homeowner or purchaser has the right at reasonable expense to require that the General Contractor obtain lien waivers from any subcontractors providing services or materials to the General Contractor;

- Homeowner or purchaser has the right to receive proof of general liability insurance including worker's compensation insurance for the General Contractor employees;

- Homeowner or purchase'r right to require at homeowner or purchaser's expense, a surety bond in the amount of the construction project;

- Homeowner or purchaser has right to purchase an expanded title insurance policy covering certain unfiled or unrecorded liens.

**Sales Price Information**
IC 54-2083 (6) (d)

## Sales Price Information

Idaho, not being a 'full disclosure' state, does not require sales information to be of public record. Even though 'sold' prices are not required to be disclosed, such 'sold' information is not considered confidential client information.

**Business and Calendar Days**
IC 73-108

## Business Days and Calendar Days

A business day is defined to be Monday through Friday between 8:00 A.M. and 5:00 P.M. in the local time zone where the subject property is physically located. This can be important when doing business between northern Idaho and southern Idaho where there are two different time zones; especially for recording purposes.

Business days also do not include legal holidays recognized by Idaho Code 73-108.

A calendar day is defined as Monday through Sunday, midnight to midnight in the local time zone where the subject property is located. If business and calendar days are not pre-printed in a Purchase and Sale Agreement it would be suggested they be included in an addendum to avoid confusion.

| | |
|---|---|
| **Default** | ## Default |
| | What happens if the buyer defaults? What happens if the seller defaults? A detailed default clause should be included in the Purchase and Sale Agreement so everyone knows what consequences and possible penalties might occur should one party default against the other party including brokerage fees. |
| **Representation Confirmation** | ## Representation Confirmation |
| | Idaho Code mandatorily requires Representation Confirmation to be contained in any Purchase and Sale Agreement regardless of the type of property being sold. |
| **Closing Date** | ## Closing Date |
| | There are many different definitions of what closing means. Closing means the date on which all documents are either recorded or accepted by an escrow agent and the sale proceeds are available to the seller. Closing does not mean when one or the other party signs their respective documents. |
| | The scheduled closing date can be very important especially if the transaction cannot close on or before the specified date. A written, not verbal, extension needs to be approved by all parties if the closing date is to be extended. Remember, Time Is Of The Essence! |
| | Also be careful to have a closing date at the end of the month. If for some reason, the closing extends over to the beginning of the following month, all kinds of things happen; all new pro-rates have to be calculated and the buyer could have to come up with additional closing costs which they may not have! |
| **Possession** | ## Possession |
| | Another critical area of the Purchase and Sale Agreement involves a possession date. Some forethought needs to be taken to meet the needs of both the buyer and seller. |
| | For example, when does the seller need to make their move? Is the seller going to use a moving company to move their belongings? How much advance notice is required? |

Try to coordinate between buyer and seller so both aren't moving at the same time.

Also, if possible, try to allow time for the seller to 'reclean' the home after they have moved so the buyer won't have to clean before they move in.

**Early Possession**

Never, never, never, allow early possession unless there is an emergency. All kinds of challenges can occur including the buyer demanding more things to be fixed or cleaned. Or, last minute issues that could cancel the transaction and now the buyer is in possession. Liability issues could fall back on the seller since they are still in title.

If, for some reason, early possession is allowed, it is suggested both parties seek legal counsel to address issues like personal liability issues, insurance issues, default issues by either party, and damages, just to name a few concerns before actual possession is allowed. If early possession is allowed, confirmed written approval must be acknowledged by both buyer and seller.

**Presenting the Offer**
IC 54-2051 (1)

## Presenting the Offer

Once an offer has been completed and signed by the purchaser(s) the offer must be delivered to the seller. A broker or sales associate shall, as promptly as practicable, tender to the seller every written offer to purchase obtained on the real estate involved, up until the time of closing.

There are many ways to get the offer to the seller. The usual way is to deliver the offer to the listing agent and have them deliver it to the seller. The selling agent may or may not accompany the offer to the seller via the listing agent. The key is to get the offer to the seller as soon as possible.

If the offer is faxed or electronically delivered to the listing agent, care should be taken to assure the confidentiality of the buyer.

**Multiple Offers**
Guideline #16

## Multiple Offers

Should multiple offers be made on the subject property, the listing agent should be diligent in informing the seller about any offers on the property that might materially affect the seller/client's decisions about the sale of the property.

It's advisable to have the listing agent discuss the possibility of multiple offers prior to or upon securing the listing.

On occasion, a seller who has accepted an offer is presented with a better offer from a different buyer at a later time. In such cases, the licensee should advise the seller to seek legal advice before attempting to terminate the existing contract, and before becoming obligated under the second contract. The licensee may not give the seller legal advice; but the licensee can state that failing to perform the terms of the contract, or obligating oneself under two contracts, can have serious legal consequences for the seller.

If issues arise on any area of contract law, such as if and when effective acceptance or revocation of an offer or counteroffer will take place, it is in the agent's best interest to advise the seller or buyer to seek legal counsel.

# Seller Options

**Seller Options**

When an offer is presented to the seller, the seller has 3 options; accept, reject, or counter the offer.

**Acceptance**

## Acceptance
If the offer is accepted, the acceptance needs to be immediately conveyed to the agent representing the buyer who will in turn, relay it to the buyer. Remember, the buyer can withdraw an offer anytime prior to acceptance by the seller. So, Time Is Of The Essence.

**Rejected Offers**
IC 54-2048 (3) (d)

## Rejection
If the offer is rejected, the offer must be clearly marked and dated as rejected. All rejected offers must be retained in the files of the selling broker.

**Counteroffer**
Guideline #19

## Counteroffer
A counteroffer can be made when the seller likes most of the offer but dislikes something. So the seller prepares a counter offer to present back to the buyer. In an effort to avoid illegible alternations on the Purchase and Sale Agreement, 'counteroffer'

Figure 4

forms should be used to make any changes to the original offer.

Do not confuse the addendum form with a counteroffer form. An addendum is just that; adding to an existing contract.

The counteroffer form voids the original offer and creates a brand new offer from the seller to the buyer but may or will incorporate the terms and conditions of the original offer except for what is changed in the counter offer.

Once a counter offer is made, the buyer is under no obligation to accept and may in fact, make a second counter offer.

It should be noted that when a counter offer is made and the price is modified, a written statement should be inserted into the counteroffer to have the buyer and seller acknowledge the down payment and/or loan amount could change if the purchase price is changed.

Once the counteroffer is signed and accepted by all parties, a legally binding contract is now in place.

**Follow-up**

## Follow-up After Acceptance

After acceptance, all parties need to keep on top of all the terms and conditions of the Purchase and Sale Agreement and attachments. Make a list of everything that is needs to be accomplished prior to closing and take immediate action if something isn't going according to the terms of the agreement.

Once a preliminary title report is provided, check for any discrepancies. If something shows up that needs attention, notify all parties of the issue and take action.

Keep in constant contact with escrow to make sure all tasks are being resolved within the time frames indicated in the agreement.

Figure 1 – Purchase and Sale Agreement - Page 1 of 7

# RE-21 REAL ESTATE PURCHASE AND SALE AGREEMENT

THIS IS A LEGALLY BINDING CONTRACT, READ THE ENTIRE DOCUMENT, INCLUDING ANY ATTACHMENTS.
IF YOU HAVE ANY QUESTIONS, **CONSULT YOUR ATTORNEY AND/OR ACCOUNTANT** BEFORE SIGNING.

REALTOR®

1  ID#_____    DATE_____

2

3  **LISTING AGENCY**_____ Office Phone #_____ Fax #_____
4  Listing Agent_____ E-Mail_____ Phone #_____
5  **SELLING AGENCY**_____ Office Phone #_____ Fax #_____
6  Selling Agent_____ E-Mail_____ Phone #_____

7

8  **1. BUYER**:_____
9  (Hereinafter called "**BUYER**") agrees to purchase, and the undersigned SELLER agrees to sell the following described real estate hereinafter referred to
10 as "PROPERTY" **COMMONLY KNOWN AS**_____
11 _____ City_____ County, ID, Zip_____ legally described as:_____
12 _____
13 **OR** Legal Description Attached as addendum #_____ **(Addendum must accompany original offer.)**

14

15 **2. $**_____ **PURCHASE PRICE:**_____ **DOLLARS,**
16 payable upon the following **TERMS AND CONDITIONS** (not including closing costs):

17

18 **3. FINANCIAL TERMS: Note: A+C+D+E must add up to total purchase price.**

19

20 **(A). $**_____ **EARNEST MONEY:** BUYER hereby deposits_____
21 DOLLARS as Earnest Money evidenced by: ☐cash ☐personal check ☐cashier's check ☐note (due date):_____
22 ☐other_____ and a receipt is hereby acknowledged. Earnest Money to
23 be deposited in trust account ☐upon receipt, or ☐upon acceptance by all parties and shall be held by: ☐Listing Broker ☐Selling Broker
24 ☐other_____. for the benefit of the parties hereto.
25 **THE RESPONSIBLE BROKER SHALL BE:**_____

26

27 **(B). ALL CASH OFFER:** ☐NO ☐YES If this is an all cash offer do not complete Sections 3C and 3D, fill blanks with "**0**" (ZERO). **IF CASH**
28 **OFFER, BUYER'S OBLIGATION TO CLOSE SHALL NOT BE SUBJECT TO ANY FINANCIAL CONTINGENCY.** BUYER agrees to provide SELLER
29 within_____ business days (five [5] if left blank) from the date of acceptance of this agreement by all parties, evidence of sufficient funds and/or proceeds
30 necessary to close transaction. Acceptable documentation includes, but is not limited to, a copy of a recent bank or financial statement or contract(s) for
31 the sale of BUYER'S current residence or other property to be sold.

32

33 **(C). $**_____ **NEW LOAN PROCEEDS:** This Agreement is contingent upon BUYER obtaining the following financing:
34 ☐**FIRST LOAN** of $_____ not including mortgage insurance, through ☐FHA, ☐VA, ☐CONVENTIONAL, ☐IHFA, ☐RURAL
35 DEVELOPMENT, ☐OTHER_____ with interest not to exceed_____% for a period of
36 _____ year(s) at: ☐Fixed Rate ☐Other_____. BUYER shall pay no more than _____ point(s) plus origination fee if any. SELLER shall pay
37 no more than _____ point(s). Any reduction in points shall first accrue to the benefit of the ☐BUYER ☐SELLER ☐Divided Equally ☐N/A.

38

39 ☐**SECOND LOAN** of $_____ with interest not to exceed_____% for a period of _____ year(s) at: ☐Fixed Rate
40 ☐Other_____. BUYER shall pay no more than _____ point(s) plus origination fee if any. SELLER shall pay no more than
41 _____ point(s). Any reduction in points shall first accrue to the benefit of the ☐BUYER ☐SELLER ☐Divided Equally ☐N/A.

42

43 **LOAN APPLICATION:** BUYER ☐has applied ☐shall apply for such loan(s) within_____ business days (five [5] if left blank) of SELLER'S acceptance.
44 Within_____ business days (ten [10] if left blank) of final acceptance of all parties, BUYER agrees to furnish SELLER with **a written confirmation**
45 **showing lender approval of credit report, income verification, debt ratios, and evidence of sufficient funds and/or proceeds necessary to**
46 **close transaction in a manner acceptable to the SELLER(S) and subject only to satisfactory appraisal and final lender underwriting.** If such
47 written confirmation is not received by SELLER(S) within the strict time allotted, SELLER(S) may at their option cancel this agreement by notifying
48 BUYER(S) in writing of such cancellation within_____ business days (three [3] if left blank) after written confirmation was required. If SELLER does not
49 cancel within the strict time period specified as set forth herein, SELLER shall be deemed to have accepted such written confirmation of lender approval
50 and shall be deemed to have elected to proceed with the transaction. SELLER'S approval shall not be unreasonably withheld. **If an appraisal is**
51 **required by lender, the PROPERTY must appraise at not less than purchase price** or BUYER'S Earnest Money may be returned at BUYER'S
52 request. BUYER may also apply for a loan with different conditions and costs and close transaction provided all other terms and conditions of this
53 Agreement are fulfilled, and the new loan does not increase the costs or requirements to the SELLER.
54 **FHA / VA:** If applicable, it is expressly agreed that notwithstanding any other provisions of this contract, BUYER shall not be obligated to complete the
55 purchase of the PROPERTY described herein or to incur any penalty or forfeiture of Earnest Money deposits or otherwise unless BUYER has been
56 given in accordance with HUD/FHA or VA requirements a written statement by the Federal Housing Commissioner, Veterans Administration or a Direct
57 Endorsement lender setting forth the appraised value of the PROPERTY of not less than the sales price as stated in the contract. SELLER agrees to pay
58 fees required by FHA or VA.

59

60 **(D). $**_____ **ADDITIONAL FINANCIAL TERMS:**
61 ☐ Additional financial terms are specified under the heading "OTHER TERMS AND/OR CONDITIONS" (Section 4).
62 ☐ Additional financial terms are contained in a **FINANCING ADDENDUM** of same date, attached hereto, signed by both parties.

63

64 **(E). $**_____ **APPROXIMATE FUNDS DUE FROM BUYERS AT CLOSING** *(Not including closing costs)*: **Cash at**
65 **closing** to be paid by BUYER at closing in GOOD FUNDS, includes: **cash, electronic transfer funds, certified check or cashier's check. NOTE:** *If*
66 *any of above loans being Assumed or taken "subject to", any net differences between the approximate balances and the actual balance of said loan(s)*
67 *shall be adjusted at closing of escrow in:* ☐Cash ☐Other_____.

**BUYER'S** Initials (_____)(_____) Date_____    **SELLER'S** Initials (_____)(_____) Date_____

JULY 2009 EDITION          RE-21 REAL ESTATE PURCHASE AND SALE AGREEMENT          Page 1 of 7

Reprint with permission from IAR

## Figure 1 – Purchase and Sale Agreement - Page 2 of 7

PROPERTY ADDRESS:_____ ID#:_____

**4. OTHER TERMS AND/OR CONDITIONS:** This Agreement is made subject to the following special terms, considerations and/or contingencies which must be satisfied prior to closing _____
_____
_____
_____
_____
_____
_____
_____
_____
_____

**5. ITEMS INCLUDED & EXCLUDED IN THIS SALE:** All existing fixtures and fittings that are attached to the PROPERTY are **INCLUDED IN THE PURCHASE PRICE** (unless excluded below), and shall be transferred free of liens. These include, but are not limited to, all seller-owned attached floor coverings, attached television antennae, satellite dish, attached plumbing, bathroom and lighting fixtures, window screens, screen doors, storm doors, storm windows, window coverings, garage door opener(s) and transmitter(s), exterior trees, plants or shrubbery, water heating apparatus and fixtures, attached fireplace equipment, awnings, ventilating, cooling and heating systems, all ranges, ovens, built-in dishwashers, fuel tanks and irrigation fixtures and equipment, that are now on or used in connection with the PROPERTY and shall be included in the sale unless otherwise provided herein. BUYER should satisfy himself/herself that the condition of the included items is acceptable. It is agreed that any item included in this section is of nominal value less than $100.

**(A). ADDITIONAL ITEMS SPECIFICALLY INCLUDED IN THIS SALE:** _____
_____
_____
_____

**(B). ITEMS SPECIFICALLY EXCLUDED IN THIS SALE:** _____
_____
_____
_____

**6. MINERAL RIGHTS:** Any and all mineral rights appurtenant to the PROPERTY are included in and are part of the sale of this PROPERTY unless otherwise agreed to by the parties in writing.

**7. WATER RIGHTS:** Any and all water rights including but not limited to water systems, wells, springs, lakes, streams, ponds, rivers, ditches, ditch rights, and the like, if any, appurtenant to the PROPERTY are included in and are a part of the sale of this PROPERTY unless otherwise agreed to by the parties in writing.

**8. TITLE CONVEYANCE:** Title of SELLER is to be conveyed by warranty deed, unless otherwise provided, and is to be marketable and insurable except for rights reserved in federal patents, state or railroad deeds, building or use restrictions, building and zoning regulations and ordinances of any governmental unit, and rights of way and easements established or of record. Liens, encumbrances or defects to be discharged by SELLER may be paid out of purchase money at date of closing. No liens, encumbrances or defects which are to be discharged or assumed by BUYER or to which title is taken subject to, exist unless otherwise specified in this Agreement.

**9. TITLE INSURANCE: There may be types of title insurance coverages available other than those listed below and parties to this agreement are advised to talk to a title company about any other coverages available that will give the BUYER additional coverage.**

**(A). PRELIMINARY TITLE COMMITMENT:** Prior to closing the transaction, ☐SELLER or ☐BUYER shall furnish to BUYER a preliminary commitment of a title insurance policy showing the condition of the title to said PROPERTY. BUYER shall have _____ business days (five [5] if left blank) from receipt of the preliminary commitment or not fewer than twenty-four (24) hours prior to closing, within which to object in writing to the condition of the title as set forth in the preliminary commitment. If BUYER does not so object, BUYER shall be deemed to have accepted the conditions of the title. It is agreed that if the title of said PROPERTY is not marketable, or cannot be made so within _____ business days (five [5] if left blank) after notice containing a written statement of defect is delivered to SELLER, BUYER'S Earnest Money deposit will be returned to BUYER and SELLER shall pay for the cost of title insurance cancellation fee, escrow and legal fees, if any.

**(B). TITLE COMPANY:** The parties agree that _____ Title Company located at_____ shall provide the title policy and preliminary report of commitment.

**(C). STANDARD COVERAGE OWNER'S POLICY:** SELLER shall within a reasonable time after closing furnish to BUYER a title insurance policy in the amount of the purchase price of the PROPERTY showing marketable and insurable title subject to the liens, encumbrances and defects elsewhere set out in this Agreement to be discharged or assumed by BUYER unless otherwise provided herein. **The risk assumed by the title company in the standard coverage policy is limited to matters of public record.** BUYER shall receive a ILTA/ALTA Owner's Policy of Title Insurance. A title company, at BUYER's request, can provide information about the availability, desirability, coverage and cost of various title insurance coverages and endorsements. If BUYER desires title coverage other than that required by this paragraph, BUYER shall instruct Closing Agency in writing and pay any increase in cost unless otherwise provided herein.

**(D). EXTENDED COVERAGE LENDER'S POLICY (Mortgagee policy):** The lender may require that BUYER (Borrower) furnish an Extended Coverage Lender's Policy. This extended coverage lender's policy considers matters of public record and additionally insures against certain matters not shown in the public record. **This extended coverage lender's policy is solely for the benefit of the lender and only protects the lender.**

BUYER'S Initials (_____)(._____) Date _____     SELLER'S Initials (_____)(_____) Date _____

JULY 2009 EDITION     **RE-21 REAL ESTATE PURCHASE AND SALE AGREEMENT**     Page 2 of 7

Reprint with permission from IAR

# Figure 1 – Purchase and Sale Agreement - Page 3 of 7

PROPERTY ADDRESS:_____ ID#:_____

**10. INSPECTION:**

**(A). BUYER chooses** ☐to have inspection ☐not to have inspection. If BUYER chooses not to have inspection, skip Section 10C. BUYER shall have the right to conduct inspections, investigations, tests, surveys and other studies at **BUYER'S expense**. BUYER shall, within _____ business days (ten [10] if left blank) of acceptance, complete these inspections and give to SELLER written notice of disapproved items. BUYER is strongly advised to exercise these rights and to make BUYER'S own selection of professionals with appropriate qualifications to conduct inspections of the entire PROPERTY. SELLER shall make PROPERTY available for inspection and agrees to accept the responsibility and expense for making sure all the utilities are turned on for the inspection except for phone and cable. Some inspections, investigations, tests, surveys and other studies may require additional days to complete. The parties agree that unless specifically set forth below, the above timeframe for investigations, tests, surveys and other studies shall govern.

Additional inspections/timeframes:_____
_____
_____
_____
_____
_____
_____
_____
_____
_____
_____
_____
_____

**(B). FHA INSPECTION REQUIREMENT,** If applicable: "For Your Protection: Get a Home Inspection", HUD 92564-CN must be signed on or before execution of this agreement.

**(C). SATISFACTION/REMOVAL OF INSPECTION CONTINGENCIES:**

1). If BUYER **does not** within the strict time period specified give to SELLER written notice of disapproved items, BUYER shall conclusively be deemed to have: (a) completed all inspections, investigations, review of applicable documents and disclosures; (b) elected to proceed with the transaction and (c) assumed all liability, responsibility and expense for repairs or corrections other than for items which SELLER has otherwise agreed in writing to repair or correct.

2). If BUYER **does** within the strict time period specified give to SELLER written notice of disapproved items, **BUYER shall provide to SELLER pertinent section(s) of written inspection reports**. SELLER shall have _____ business days (three [3] if left blank) in which to **respond in writing**. The SELLER, at their option, may correct the items as specified by the BUYERS in their letter or may elect not to do so. If the SELLER agrees to correct the items asked for in the BUYERS letter, then both parties agree that they will continue with the transaction and proceed to closing. **This will remove the BUYER'S inspection contingency.**

3). If the SELLER elects not to correct the disapproved items, or does not respond in writing within the strict time period specified, then the BUYER(S) have the option of either continuing the transaction without the SELLER being responsible for correcting these deficiencies or giving the SELLER written notice within _____ business days (three [3] if left blank) that they will not continue with the transaction and will receive their Earnest Money back.

4). If BUYER **does not** give such written notice of cancellation within the strict time periods specified, BUYER shall conclusively be deemed to have elected to proceed with the transaction without repairs or corrections other than for items which SELLER has otherwise agreed in writing to repair or correct. BUYER shall make the PROPERTY available for all Inspections. BUYER shall keep the PROPERTY free and clear of liens; indemnify and hold SELLER harmless from all liability, claims, demands, damages and costs; and repair any damages arising from the inspections. No inspections may be made by any governmental building or zoning inspector or government employee without the prior consent of SELLER unless required by local law.

**11. LEAD PAINT DISCLOSURE:** The subject PROPERTY ☐is ☐is not defined as "Target Housing" regarding lead-based paint or lead-based paint hazards. The term lead-based paint hazards is intended to identify lead-based paint and all residential lead-containing dusts and soils **regardless of the source of the lead**. If yes, BUYER hereby acknowledges the following: (a) BUYER has been provided an EPA approved lead-based paint hazard information pamphlet, "Protect Your Family From Lead in Your Home", (b) receipt of SELLER'S Disclosure of Information and Acknowledgment Form and have been provided with all records, test reports or other information, if any, related to the presence of lead-based paint hazards on said PROPERTY, (c) that this contract is contingent upon BUYERS right to have the PROPERTY tested for lead-based paint hazards to be completed no later than _____ or the contingency will terminate, (d) that BUYER hereby ☐waives ☐does not waive this right, (e) that if test results show unacceptable amounts of lead-based paint on the PROPERTY, BUYER has the right to cancel the contract subject to the option of the SELLER (to be given in writing) to elect to remove the lead-based paint and correct the problem which must be accomplished before closing, (f) that if the contract is canceled under this clause, BUYER'S earnest money deposit will be returned to BUYER.

**12. SQUARE FOOTAGE VERIFICATION: BUYER IS AWARE THAT ANY REFERENCE TO THE SQUARE FOOTAGE OF THE REAL PROPERTY OR IMPROVEMENTS IS APPROXIMATE. IF SQUARE FOOTAGE IS MATERIAL TO THE BUYER, IT MUST BE VERIFIED DURING THE INSPECTION PERIOD.**

**13. SELLER'S PROPERTY CONDITION DISCLOSURE FORM:** If required by Title 55, Chapter 25 Idaho Code SELLER shall within ten (10) calendar days after execution of this Agreement provide to BUYER or BUYER'S agent, "Seller's Property Condition Disclosure Form" or other acceptable form. BUYER has received the "Seller's Property Condition Disclosure Form" or other acceptable form prior to signing this Agreement: ☐Yes ☐No ☐N/A

**BUYER'S** Initials (_____)(_____) Date _____      **SELLER'S** Initials (_____)(_____) Date _____

# Figure 1 – Purchase and Sale Agreement - Page 4 of 7

PROPERTY ADDRESS:_____ ID#:_____

205 **14. COVENANTS, CONDITIONS AND RESTRICTIONS (CC&Rs):** As part of the BUYER'S inspection of the PROPERTY as set forth in Section 10,
206 BUYER is responsible for obtaining and reviewing a copy of any CC&Rs which may affect the PROPERTY. BUYER shall have _____ business days (ten
207 [10] if left blank) (but in no event shall such time period exceed that time period set forth for inspections in Section 10) to review and approve of any such
208 CC&Rs that may affect the PROPERTY. Unless BUYER delivers to SELLER a written and signed objection to the terms of any applicable CC&Rs with
209 particularity describing BUYER's reasonable objections within such time period as set forth above, BUYER shall be deemed to have conclusively waived any
210 objection to the terms of any CC&Rs affecting the PROPERTY.

212 **15. SUBDIVISION HOMEOWNER'S ASSOCIATION:** BUYER is aware that membership in a Home Owner's Association may be required and
213 BUYER agrees to abide by the Articles of Incorporation, Bylaws and rules and regulations of the Association. BUYER is further aware that the PROPERTY
214 may be subject to assessments levied by the Association described in full in the Declaration of Covenants, Conditions and Restrictions. BUYER has
215 reviewed Homeowner's Association Documents: ☐Yes ☐No ☐N/A. Association fees/dues are $_____ per_____.
216 ☐BUYER ☐SELLER ☐N/A to pay Homeowner's Association **SET UP FEE of $_____** and/or **PROPERTY TRANSFER FEES of $_____** at closing.

218 **16. HOME WARRANTY PLAN:** Home Warranty Plans available for purchase can vary in many respects including, but not limited to, scope of coverage,
219 options, exclusions, limitations, service fees, and pre-existing conditions. BUYER and SELLER are advised to investigate Home Warranty Plans before
220 purchasing a plan and BUYER and SELLER acknowledge that Home Warranty Plans vary from plan to plan. Further, BUYER and SELLER acknowledge
221 that a Home Warranty Plan is separate and apart from any terms contained within this Real Estate Purchase and Sale Agreement and does not create any
222 warranties, including, without limitation, any warranty of habitability, agreements or representations not expressly set forth herein.
223 A Home Warranty Plan ☐will ☐will not be included in this transaction.
224 ☐BUYER ☐SELLER shall order a Home Warranty Plan which shall be issued by a company selected by ☐BUYER ☐SELLER.
225 The cost of the Home Warranty Plan shall not exceed $_____ and shall be paid for at closing by ☐BUYER ☐SELLER.

227 **17. COSTS PAID BY:** Costs in addition to those listed below may be incurred by BUYER and SELLER unless otherwise agreed herein, or provided by
228 law or required by lender, or otherwise stated herein. The below costs will be paid as indicated. Some costs are subject to loan program requirements. This
229 section relates ONLY to the costs to be paid by the parties. None of the costs to be paid by the parties in this section create an inspection or performance
230 obligation other than strictly for the payment of cost.

| | BUYER | SELLER | Shared Equally | N/A | | BUYER | SELLER | Shared Equally | N/A |
|---|---|---|---|---|---|---|---|---|---|
| Appraisal Fee | | | | | Title Ins. Standard Coverage Owner's Policy | | | | |
| Appraisal Re-Inspection Fee | | | | | Title Ins. Extended Coverage Lender's Policy – Mortgagee Policy | | | | |
| Closing Escrow Fee | | | | | Additional Title Coverage | | | | |
| Lender Document Preparation Fee | | | | | Fuel in Tank – Dollar Amount to be Determined by Supplier | | | | |
| Tax Service Fee | | | | | Domestic Well Water Potability Test | | | | |
| Flood Certification/Tracking Fee | | | | | Domestic Well Water Productivity Test | | | | |
| Lender Required Inspections | | | | | Septic Inspections | | | | |
| Attorney Contract Preparation or Review Fee | | | | | Septic Pumping | | | | |
| | | | | | Survey | | | | |
| | | | | | | | | | |

231 SELLER agrees to pay up to $_____ of lender required repair costs only.
232 BUYER or SELLER has the option to pay any lender required repair costs in excess of this amount.

234 **18. OCCUPANCY:** BUYER ☐does ☐does not intend to occupy PROPERTY as BUYER'S primary residence.

236 **19. FINAL WALK THROUGH:** The SELLER grants BUYER and any representative of BUYER reasonable access to conduct a final walk through
237 inspection of the PROPERTY approximately _____ calendar days (three [3] if left blank) prior to close of escrow, NOT AS A CONTINGENCY OF THE
238 SALE, but for purposes of satisfying BUYER that any repairs agreed to in writing by BUYER and SELLER have been completed and PROPERTY are in
239 substantially the same condition as on acceptance date of this contract. SELLER shall make PROPERTY available for the final walk through and agrees to
240 accept the responsibility and expense for making sure all the utilities are turned on for the walk through except for phone and cable. If BUYER does not
241 conduct a final walk through, BUYER specifically releases the SELLER and Broker(s) of any liability.

243 **20. RISK OF LOSS:** Prior to closing of this sale, all risk of loss shall remain with SELLER. In addition, should the PROPERTY be materially
244 damaged by fire or other destructive cause prior to closing, this agreement shall be void at the option of the BUYER.

**BUYER'S** Initials (_____)(_____) Date _____    **SELLER'S** Initials (_____)(_____) Date _____

# Figure 1 – Purchase and Sale Agreement - Page 5 of 7

PROPERTY ADDRESS:_____ ID#:_____

**21. SINGULAR AND PLURAL** terms each include the other, when appropriate.

**22. FORECLOSURE NOTICE:** If the PROPERTY described above is currently involved in a foreclosure proceeding (pursuant to Idaho Code §45-1506) any contract or agreement with the owner or owners of record that involves the transfer of any interest in residential real property, as defined in §45-525(5)(b), Idaho Code, subject to foreclosure must be in writing and must be accompanied by and affixed to RE-42 Property Foreclosure Disclosure Form.

**23. MECHANIC'S LIENS - GENERAL CONTRACTOR DISCLOSURE STATEMENT NOTICE:** BUYER and SELLER are hereby notified that, subject to Idaho Code §45-525 *et seq.*, a "General Contractor" must provide a Disclosure Statement to a homeowner that describes certain rights afforded to the homeowner (e.g. lien waivers, general liability insurance, extended policies of title insurance, surety bonds, and sub-contractor information). The Disclosure Statement must be given to a homeowner prior to the General Contractor entering into any contract in an amount exceeding $2,000 with a homeowner for construction, alteration, repair, or other improvements to real property, or with a residential real property purchaser for the purchase and sale of newly constructed property. Such disclosure is the responsibility of the General Contractor and it is not the duty of your agent to obtain this information on your behalf. You are advised to consult with any General Contractor subject to Idaho Code §45-525 *et seq.* regarding the General Contractor Disclosure Statement.

**24. SALES PRICE INFORMATION:** Pursuant to Idaho Code §54-2083(6)(d), a "sold" price of real property is not confidential client information.

**25. FACSIMILE TRANSMISSION:** Facsimile or electronic transmission of any signed original document, and retransmission of any signed facsimile or electronic transmission shall be the same as delivery of an original. At the request of either the BUYER or SELLER, or the LENDER, or the Closing Agency, the BUYER and SELLER will confirm facsimile or electronic transmitted signatures by signing an original document.

**26. BUSINESS DAYS:** A business day is herein defined as Monday through Friday, 8:00 A.M. to 5:00 P.M. in the local time zone where the subject real PROPERTY is physically located. A business day shall not include any Saturday or Sunday, nor shall a business day include any legal holiday recognized by the state of Idaho as found in Idaho Code §73-108. The time in which any act required under this agreement is to be performed shall be computed by excluding the date of execution and including the last day. The first day shall be the day after the date of execution. If the last day is a legal holiday, then the time for performance shall be the next subsequent business day.

**27. CALENDAR DAYS:** A calendar day is herein defined as Monday through Sunday, midnight to midnight, in the local time zone where the subject real PROPERTY is physically located. A calendar day shall include any legal holiday. The time in which any act required under this agreement is to be performed shall be computed by excluding the date of execution and including the last day, thus the first day shall be the day after the date of execution. Any reference to "day" or "days" in this agreement means the same as calendar day, unless specifically enumerated as a "business day."

**28. ATTORNEY'S FEES:** If either party initiates or defends any arbitration or legal action or proceedings which are in any way connected with this Agreement, the prevailing party shall be entitled to recover from the non-prevailing party reasonable costs and attorney's fees, including such costs and fees on appeal.

**29. DEFAULT:** **If BUYER defaults** in the performance of this Agreement, SELLER has the option of: (1) accepting the Earnest Money as liquidated damages or (2) pursuing any other lawful right and/or remedy to which SELLER may be entitled. If SELLER elects to proceed under (1), SELLER shall make demand upon the holder of the Earnest Money, upon which demand said holder shall pay from the Earnest Money the costs incurred by SELLER'S Broker on behalf of SELLER and BUYER related to the transaction, including, without limitation, the costs of title insurance, escrow fees, appraisal, credit report fees, inspection fees and attorney's fees; and said holder shall pay any balance of the Earnest Money, one-half to SELLER and one-half to SELLER'S Broker, provided that the amount to be paid to SELLER'S Broker shall not exceed the Broker's agreed to commission. SELLER and BUYER specifically acknowledge and agree that if SELLER elects to accept the Earnest Money as liquidated damages, such shall be SELLER'S sole and exclusive remedy, and such shall not be considered a penalty or forfeiture. If SELLER elects to proceed under (2), the holder of the Earnest Money shall be entitled to pay the costs incurred by SELLER'S Broker on behalf of SELLER and BUYER related to the transaction, including, without limitation, the costs of brokerage fee, title insurance, escrow fees, appraisal, credit report fees, inspection fees and attorney's fees, with any balance of the Earnest Money to be held pending resolution of the matter. **If SELLER defaults**, having approved said sale and fails to consummate the same as herein agreed, BUYER'S Earnest Money deposit shall be returned to him/her and SELLER shall pay for the costs of title insurance, escrow fees, appraisals, credit report fees, inspection fees, brokerage fees and attorney's fees, if any. This shall not be considered as a waiver by BUYER of any other lawful right or remedy to which BUYER may be entitled.

**30. EARNEST MONEY DISPUTE / INTERPLEADER:** Notwithstanding any termination of this contract, BUYER and SELLER agree that in the event of any controversy regarding the Earnest Money and things of value held by Broker or closing agency, unless mutual written instructions are received by the holder of the Earnest Money and things of value, Broker or closing agency shall not be required to take any action but may await any proceeding, or at Broker's or closing agency's option and sole discretion, may interplead all parties and deposit any monies or things of value into a court of competent jurisdiction and shall recover court costs and reasonable attorney's fees.

**31. COUNTERPARTS:** This Agreement may be executed in counterparts. Executing an agreement in counterparts shall mean the signature of two identical copies of the same agreement. Each identical copy of an agreement signed in counterparts is deemed to be an original, and all identical copies shall together constitute one and the same instrument.

**32. "NOT APPLICABLE" DEFINED:** The letters "n/a," "N/A," "n.a.," and "N.A." as used herein are abbreviations of the term "not applicable." Where this agreement uses the term "not applicable" or an abbreviation thereof, it shall be evidence that the parties have contemplated certain facts or conditions and have determined that such facts or conditions do not apply to the agreement or transaction herein.

BUYER'S Initials (_____)(_____) Date _____      SELLER'S Initials (_____)(_____) Date _____

Reprint with permission from IAR

# Figure 1 – Purchase and Sale Agreement - Page 6 of 7

PROPERTY ADDRESS:_____ ID#:_____

309 **33. SEVERABILITY:** In the case that any one or more of the provisions contained in this Agreement, or any application thereof, shall be invalid, illegal or
310 unenforceable in any respect, the validity, legality or enforceability of the remaining provisions shall not in any way be affected or impaired thereby.
311
312
313 **34. REPRESENTATION CONFIRMATION:** Check one (1) box in Section 1 and one (1) box in Section 2 below to confirm that in this transaction, the
314 brokerage(s) involved had the following relationship(s) with the BUYER(S) and SELLER(S).
315
316 Section 1:
317      ☐ A. **The brokerage working with the BUYER(S) is acting as an AGENT for the BUYER(S).**
318      ☐ B. **The brokerage working with the BUYER(S) is acting as a LIMITED DUAL AGENT for the BUYER(S), without an ASSIGNED AGENT.**
319      ☐ C. **The brokerage working with the BUYER(S) is acting as a LIMITED DUAL AGENT for the BUYER(S) and has an ASSIGNED AGENT**
320          **acting solely on behalf of the BUYER(S).**
321      ☐ D. **The brokerage working with the BUYER(S) is acting as a NONAGENT for the BUYER(S).**
322
323 Section 2:
324      ☐ A. **The brokerage working with the SELLER(S) is acting as an AGENT for the SELLER(S).**
325      ☐ B. **The brokerage working with the SELLER(S) is acting as a LIMITED DUAL AGENT for the SELLER(S), without an ASSIGNED AGENT.**
326      ☐ C. **The brokerage working with the SELLER(S) is acting as a LIMITED DUAL AGENT for the SELLER(S) and has an ASSIGNED AGENT**
327          **acting solely on behalf of the SELLER(S).**
328      ☐ D. **The brokerage working with the SELLER(S) is acting as a NONAGENT for the SELLER(S).**
329
330 Each party signing this document confirms that he has received, read and understood the Agency Disclosure Brochure adopted or approved by the Idaho
331 real estate commission and has consented to the relationship confirmed above. In addition, each party confirms that the brokerage's agency office policy
332 was made available for inspection and review. EACH PARTY UNDERSTANDS THAT HE IS A "CUSTOMER" AND IS NOT REPRESENTED BY A
333 BROKERAGE UNLESS THERE IS A SIGNED WRITTEN AGREEMENT FOR AGENCY REPRESENTATION.
334
335
336 **35. CLOSING:** On or before the closing date, BUYER and SELLER shall deposit with the closing agency all funds and instruments necessary to complete
337 this transaction. **Closing means the date on which all documents are either recorded or accepted by an escrow agent and the sale proceeds are**
338 **available to SELLER.** The closing shall be no later than (Date)_____.
339
340 The parties agree that the **CLOSING AGENCY** for this transaction shall be _____
341
342 located at_____.
343
344 If a long-term escrow / collection is involved, then the long-term escrow holder shall be _____.
345
346
347 **36. POSSESSION:** BUYER shall be entitled to possession ☐upon closing or ☐date_____ time _____ ☐A.M. ☐P.M. Property
348 taxes and water assessments (using the last available assessment as a basis), rents, interest and reserves, liens, encumbrances or obligations assumed,
349 fuel in fuel tank, and utilities shall be prorated as of _____.
350
351
352 **37. ASSIGNMENT:** This Agreement and any rights or interests created herein may be sold, transferred or otherwise assigned.
353
354
355 **38. ENTIRE AGREEMENT:** This Agreement contains the entire Agreement of the parties respecting the matters herein set forth and supersedes all prior
356 Agreements between the parties respecting such matters. No warranties, including, without limitation, any warranty of habitability, agreements or
357 representations not expressly set forth herein shall be binding upon either party.
358
359
360 **39. TIME IS OF THE ESSENCE IN THIS AGREEMENT.**
361
362
363 **40. AUTHORITY OF SIGNATORY:** If BUYER or SELLER is a corporation, partnership, trust, estate, or other entity, the person executing this
364 agreement on its behalf warrants his or her authority to do so and to bind BUYER or SELLER.
365
366
367 **41. ACCEPTANCE:** This offer is made subject to the acceptance of SELLER and BUYER on or before (Date)_____ at (Local Time in
368 which PROPERTY is located)_____ ☐A.M. ☐P.M. If acceptance of this Agreement is not received within the time specified, the offer is
369 withdrawn and the entire Earnest Money, if any, shall be refunded to BUYER on demand.

BUYER'S Initials (_____)(_____) Date _____      SELLER'S Initials (_____)(_____) Date _____

Reprint with permission from IAR

## Figure 1 – Purchase and Sale Agreement - Page 7 of 7

PROPERTY ADDRESS:_____ ID#:_____

370 **42. BUYER'S SIGNATURES:**
371
372 ☐SEE ATTACHED BUYER'S ADDENDUM(S): _____ (Specify number of BUYER addendum(s) attached.)
373
374
375 **BUYER Signature**_____ **BUYER (Print Name)**_____
376
377
378 Date _____ Time _____ ☐A.M. ☐P.M.  Phone # _____ Cell #_____
379
380
381 Address_____ City_____ State _____ Zip _____
382
383
384 E-Mail_____ Fax #_____
385
386 - - - - - - - - - - - - - - - - - - - - - - - - - - - - - - - - - - - - - - - - - - - - - - - - - - - - - - - - - - - - - - - - - - - - - -
387
388
389 **BUYER Signature**_____ **BUYER (Print Name)**_____
390
391
392 Date _____ Time _____ ☐A.M. ☐P.M.  Phone # _____ Cell #_____
393
394
395 Address_____ City_____ State _____ Zip _____
396
397
398 E-Mail_____ Fax #_____
399
400
401
402 **43. SELLER'S SIGNATURES:**
403 On this date, I/We hereby approve and accept the transaction set forth in the above Agreement and agree to carry out all the terms thereof on the part of the
404 SELLER.
405
406 ☐SIGNATURE(S) SUBJECT TO ATTACHED COUNTER OFFER
407
408 ☐SIGNATURE(S) SUBJECT TO ATTACHED ADDENDUM(S) # _____
409
410 **SELLER Signature**_____ **SELLER (Print Name)**_____
411
412
413 Date _____ Time _____ ☐A.M. ☐P.M.  Phone # _____ Cell #_____
414
415
416 Address_____ City_____ State _____ Zip _____
417
418
419 E-Mail_____ Fax #_____
420
421
422 - - - - - - - - - - - - - - - - - - - - - - - - - - - - - - - - - - - - - - - - - - - - - - - - - - - - - - - - - - - - - - - - - - - - - -
423
424
425 **SELLER Signature**_____ **SELLER (Print Name)**_____
426
427
428 Date _____ Time _____ ☐A.M. ☐P.M.  Phone # _____ Cell #_____
429
430
431 Address_____ City_____ State _____ Zip _____
432
433
434 E-Mail_____ Fax #_____
435
436
437 **CONTRACTOR REGISTRATION # (if applicable)**_____

Reprint with permission from IAR

## Figure 2 – Addendum

**RE-11 ADDENDUM #**_____ (1,2,3, etc.)

THIS IS A LEGALLY BINDING CONTRACT, READ THE ENTIRE DOCUMENT, INCLUDING ANY ATTACHMENTS.
IF YOU HAVE ANY QUESTIONS, **CONSULT YOUR ATTORNEY AND/OR ACCOUNTANT** BEFORE SIGNING.

1  Date:_____

2

3  This is an **ADDENDUM** to the ☐Purchase and Sale Agreement ☐Other_____

4  ("Addendum" means that the information below is added material for the agreement {such as lists or descriptions} and/or means the form is being

5  used to change, correct or revise the agreement {such as modification, addition or deletion of a term}).

6

7  **AGREEMENT DATED:**_____ **ID #**_____

8

9  **ADDRESS:**_____

10

11  **BUYER(S):**_____

12

13  **SELLER(S):**_____

14

15  The undersigned parties hereby agree as follows:

16  _____

17  _____

18  _____

19  _____

20  _____

21  _____

22  _____

23  _____

24  _____

25  _____

26  _____

27  _____

28  _____

29  _____

30  _____

31  _____

32  _____

33  _____

34  _____

35  _____

36  _____

37  _____

38  _____

39  _____

40  _____

41  _____

42  _____

43  _____

44  _____

45  _____

46  _____

47

48  To the extent the terms of this ADDENDUM modify or conflict with any provisions of the Purchase and Sale Agreement including all prior

49  Addendums or Counter Offers, these terms shall control. **All other terms of the Purchase and Sale Agreement including all prior**

50  **Addendums or Counter Offers not modified by this ADDENDUM shall remain the same.** Upon its execution by both parties, this agreement

51  is made an integral part of the aforementioned Agreement.

52

53

54  **BUYER:** _____  Date: _____

55

56  **BUYER:** _____  Date: _____

57

58

59  **SELLER:** _____  Date: _____

60

61  **SELLER:** _____  Date: _____

Reprint with permission from IAR

# Figure 3 – Inspection Contingency

**RE-10 INSPECTION CONTINGENCY RELEASE ADDENDUM #**_____ (1,2,3 etc.)

THIS IS A LEGALLY BINDING CONTRACT, READ THE ENTIRE DOCUMENT, INCLUDING ANY ATTACHMENTS.
IF YOU HAVE ANY QUESTIONS, **CONSULT YOUR ATTORNEY AND/OR ACCOUNTANT** BEFORE SIGNING.

1 This is an ADDENDUM to the Purchase and Sale Agreement Dated:_____

3 ADDRESS:_____ ID#:_____

5 BUYER:_____

7 SELLER:_____

9 ☐This is a BUYER Addendum.      ☐This is a SELLER Addendum.

11 **1. ITEMS IN NEED OF REPAIR.** The SELLER agrees to service, repair or replace, in a good and workmanlike manner, the following items
12 on or in the property prior to closing, as set forth in the Purchase and Sale Agreement. BUYER reserves the right to have **only the items**
13 **which are specifically set forth in this paragraph** re-inspected prior to closing to satisfy the BUYER that such service, repair or
14 replacement is acceptable to the BUYER. BUYER shall not unreasonably withhold acceptance of such service, repair or replacement.

_____
_____
_____
_____
_____
_____
_____
_____
_____
_____
_____
_____
_____
_____
_____
_____
_____
_____
_____

36 **2. WAIVER OF FURTHER INSPECTIONS AND REMOVAL OF INSPECTION CONTINGENCY.** BUYER has made an inspection of the
37 property or has had the property inspected by inspector(s) chosen by the BUYER. BUYER hereby confirms and asserts that such
38 inspection(s) was/were performed in a diligent, prudent, thorough and competent manner and that such inspector(s) was/were qualified to
39 inspect the property. Further, BUYER hereby confirms and asserts that BUYER has completed all inspections, investigations, tests,
40 surveys and has reviewed all applicable documents and disclosures. **Excepting only those items specifically set forth in Paragraph 1**
41 **above, BUYER hereby elects to proceed with the transaction and hereby waives the right to further inspection of the property**
42 *(except for any final walk through inspection provision set forth in the Purchase and Sale Agreement)* **and removes the BUYER'S**
43 **inspection contingency.**

45 To the extent the terms of this ADDENDUM modify or conflict with any provisions of the Purchase and Sale Agreement including all prior
46 Addendums, these terms shall control. All other terms of the Purchase and Sale Agreement including all prior Addendums, or Counter
47 Offers not modified by this ADDENDUM shall remain the same.

49 The herein agreement, upon execution by both parties, is made an integral part of the aforementioned Agreement.

52 **BUYER:** _____  **Date:** _____

54 **BUYER:** _____  **Date:** _____

57 **SELLER:** _____  **Date:** _____

59 **SELLER:** _____  **Date:** _____

Reprint with permission from IAR

## Figure 4 – Counter Offer

**RE-13 COUNTER OFFER #**_____ (1,2,3 etc.)

**THIS COUNTER OFFER SUPERSEDES ALL PRIOR COUNTER OFFERS**

THIS IS A LEGALLY BINDING CONTRACT, READ THE ENTIRE DOCUMENT, INCLUDING ANY ATTACHMENTS.
IF YOU HAVE ANY QUESTIONS, **CONSULT YOUR ATTORNEY AND/OR ACCOUNTANT** BEFORE SIGNING.

1  This is a COUNTER OFFER to the Purchase and Sale Agreement Dated:_____

3  ADDRESS:_____ ID#:_____

5  BUYER:_____

7  SELLER:_____

9  The parties accept all of the terms and conditions in the above-designated Purchase and Sale Agreement with the following changes:
10  ☐**This is a SELLER counter offer**. The SELLER reserves the right to withdraw this offer or accept any other offers prior to the receipt of a
11  true copy of signed acceptance of this Counter Offer within the time frame specified herein.
12  ☐**This is a BUYER counter offer**. The undersigned BUYER reserves the right to withdraw this offer at any time prior to the receipt of a
13  true copy of signed acceptance of this Counter Offer within the time frame specified herein.

14 _____
15 _____
16 _____
17 _____
18 _____
19 _____
20 _____
21 _____
22 _____
23 _____
24 _____
25 _____
26 _____
27 _____
28 _____
29 _____
30 _____
31 _____
32 _____
33 _____
34 _____
35 _____
36 _____
37 _____

39  To the extent the terms of this Counter Offer modify or conflict with any provisions of the Purchase and Sale Agreement including all prior
40  Addendums, the terms in this Counter Offer shall control. All other terms of the Purchase and Sale Agreement including all prior
41  Addendums not modified by this Counter Offer shall remain the same. **Buyer and Seller acknowledge the down payment and/or loan**
42  **amount on Page 1 of Purchase & Sale Agreement may change if purchase price is changed as part of this Counter Offer.** Upon its
43  execution by both parties, this agreement is made an integral part of the aforementioned Agreement.

45  If a signed acceptance is not delivered on or before (date): _____ at _____ ☐A.M. ☐P.M.
46  this Counter Offer shall be deemed to have expired.

48  DELIVERY: Delivery shall be to the agent/broker working with the maker of the Counter Offer in person, by mail, facsimile or electronic
49  transmission of any signed original document, and retransmission of any signed original document. Retransmission of any signed facsimile
50  or electronic transmission shall be deemed to be the same as delivery of an original.

53  SELLER_____ Date_____ Time_____ ☐A.M. ☐P.M.

55  SELLER_____ Date_____ Time_____ ☐A.M. ☐P.M.

58  BUYER_____ Date_____ Time_____ ☐A.M. ☐P.M.

60  BUYER_____ Date_____ Time_____ ☐A.M. ☐P.M.

# Questions – Chapter 17

1. Unless there's an emergency bill, when do legislative law changes take place?

   A. January 1
   B. April 15
   C. July 1
   D. December 20

2. When earnest money is received, it should be delivered to:

   A. Selling agent
   B. Seller
   C. Title company
   D. Broker's office

3. If earnest money is returned before deposit where must a written and dated notation must be placed:

   A. Purchase and Sale Agreement
   B. Ledger card
   C. Both Purchase and Sale Agreement and ledger card.
   D. Trust account record

4. What's the penalty to the seller who requires the buyer to use a particular title insurance company against the buyers choice for a federally related mortgage?

   A. Total amount of the title insurance
   B. Buyer has no recourse
   C. 3 times all charges for title insurance
   D. No penalty to the seller

5. When is the Sellers Property Disclosure form required to be delivered to the buyer?

   A. Prior to writing a contract
   B. Within 1 day of execution of a contract
   C. Within 10 days of execution of a contract.
   D. Within 5 days of loan commitment

6. When must a disclosure statement be given to the homeowner by a general contractor making improvements exceeding $2,000?

   A. Prior to entering into a contract
   B. Prior to being paid for the job
   C. Within 10 days of completing a job
   D. The contractor is not required to give a disclosure statement

7. A business day is defined as:

   A. Monday thru Friday, midnight to midnight
   B. Monday thru Saturday, 8:00 am to midnight
   C. Monday thru Friday, 8 am to 5 pm
   D. Monday thru Saturday, 8 am to 5 pm

8. Once an offer has been completed and signed by the purchaser(s), the offer must be delivered to:

   A. Escrow
   B. Selling brokerage
   C. Seller
   D. Title insurance company

# Chapter 18

# Closing The Transaction

**Prior to Closing**

Prior to closing, both the buyer and seller should be in close contact and communication with their respective agent and be available to assist with inspections, access for appraisal, repairs, financing requirements, and any other issues that need attention.

**Walk Through**

Plan on the walk through enough ahead of the planned closing date to fix anything that needs to be repaired or replaced. Usually the walk through is scheduled 2-3 days prior to closing.

It's a good idea to have the buyer initiate the homeowner insurance application soon after acceptance of the Purchase and Sale Agreement so the insurance will be in place upon closing. In the event the property is located in a flood plain, the buyer needs to be advised of the additional cost for flood insurance coverage.

Cash, commercial, private financing, and non-federally related loans are not regulated by the Real Estate Settlement Practices Act.

**RESPA**

### RESPA - Real Estate Settlement Practices
But on January 1, 2010, the new Real Estate Settlement Practices Act (RESPA) went into effect for federally related residential loans.

**New Rules**

The new RESPA rules significantly change the way lenders handle settlement services for any federally related residential loan. Some of the highlights are:

> Lenders must provide borrowers with a standard origination charge for the loan which must include all points, appraisal, credit, and application fees, administrative, lender inspection, wire, and document preparation fees.

> Lenders have the option of providing borrowers with a list of approved service providers such as closing attorneys and title insurance companies.

A tolerance range has been specified for various categories of loan/closing costs to prevent unnecessary escalation of promised vs. actual charges.

- Fees quoted for lender origination charge cannot change.

- Fees for title and closing costs where the lender selects the provider or where the borrower selects the provider from the lender's approved list cannot change by more than 10%.

- Fees that borrowers can shop for themselves can increase (or decrease) by any amount.

The final page of the GFE (Good Faith Estimate) contains worksheet like charges to compare different loans and terms that the borrower can use to shop pricing.

Controversial lender payments to mortgage brokers, known as yield-spread premiums, must be disclosed in a standard manner.

The charges quoted on the GFE are then carried over to the HUD-1 Settlement Statement to ensure that the prescribed tolerances are met.

**Review 1 Day Before Closing**

RESPA allows the buyer to review HUD 1 settlement statement 24 hours prior to closing. Coordinate with the lender and escrow to have everything ready for both the buyer or agent(s) at least 1 day or 24 hours prior to closing.

By having the escrow/closing officer and real estate agent(s) review the closing documents before the actual closing, errors may be detected and corrected before the actual closing takes place. Most errors can be corrected prior to closing and both the buyer and seller will have a more pleasant experience during closing with error free closing statements.

Figure 1

Figure 2

Figure 3

Generally speaking, there may be two different closing statement formats; one with debits (minus) and credits (plus) supplemented with a HUD 1 statement. Both show the same exact numbers but are presented with two totally different formats.

A real estate licensee should become familiar with each format so whatever form the escrow officer uses to explain the closing statement to the buyer or seller, it will be fully understood.

## Planning For Closing and Signing Documents

**Planning for Closing and Signing**

The escrow/closing officer will usually plan the day and hour to conduct the closing for both the buyer and seller. Usually one party signs in the morning and the other in the afternoon. A little known tip is to have the buyer sign first. Why? Because if any errors are found in the closing statement they are most often with the buyer. If the error can be easily corrected, there will only have to be one signing by each party.

If the seller signs first and an error is found with the buyer's settlement statement, the seller will have to sign again with a 'new' closing statement to acknowledge the error. The less the buyer and seller have to deal with errors, the better. That's why it is such a good idea to have the agent and escrow review the closing statements before the buyer and seller are brought to closing.

## Responsible Broker

**Responsible Broker**
**IC 54-2048 (1)**

The 'responsible broker' shall be responsible for the transaction, transaction records, funds and closing. The responsible broker shall ensure the correctness and delivery of detailed closing statements which accurately reflect all receipts and disbursements for the respective accounts to both the buyer and seller in a transaction.

Even if the closing is completed by a real estate escrow closing agent, title company or other authorized 3$^{rd}$ party, the responsible broker is still responsible for the accuracy and delivery of the closing statement.

**Potential Errors**

Some areas where errors can occur include:
- Closing date pro-rations
- Tax pro-rations
- Mortgage pro-rations
- HOA pro-rations
- Rent pro-rations
- Missing items that should have been included
- Items that should have been excluded

Many errors are not the escrow/closing officer's fault. Sometimes addendums or changes are made during the transaction process in which the escrow officer did not receive the appropriate documentation. If everyone works together, team work can accomplish and solve most issues without delaying or slowing down the closing process.

**Agent Responsibilities**

## Agent Responsibilities

If possible, the agent should attend all closings; if for no other reason, to be a 'security blanket' for the buyer and/or seller. Closing can be a very intimidating experience for buyers and sellers. The closing is perhaps the first time they have met a escrow/closing officer. Having a 'friendly face', like their agent, helps bridge the anxiety that is normal.

The agent is primarily a bystander; just sit back and observe. Let the escrow/closing officer do their job. However, the agent might be able to assist and answer questions the escrow/closing officer may ask to clarify different issues.

Remember, statistically speaking, buyers and sellers will be involved in buying or selling homes around 5-7 homes in their whole lifetime. Each event is somewhat traumatic. The closing is where the agent can really build rapport for future business.

## Figure 1 – Buyer Closing Statement - page 1 of 2

### Pioneer Title Company of Ada County (208) 377-2700
**Buyer's Closing Statement**

Buyer(s)

Seller(s)

Lender

Property

| Closing date | 4/9/2010 | | Proration date | 4/9/2010 |
|---|---|---|---|---|
| Bank | 15 - ▮▮▮ Bank | | | |
| Escrow Unit | 5 - Meridian | | | |
| Escrow Officer | Alana Pierce | | | |

| | Debit | Credit |
|---|---|---|
| **Contract Sales Price** | 197,000.00 | |
| **New Loan:** | | |
| Principal amount of new loan(s) from . | | 193,431.00 |
| **Deposits:** | | |
| Deposit or earnest money | | 1,000.00 |
| **Prorations:** | | |
| City of Boise Acct Initiation Fee to City of Boise | 11.27 | |
| County taxes | | |
| From 1/1/2010 to 4/9/2010 @ $8.32060/day | | 815.42 |
| **Other Adjustments:** | | |
| Seller Paid Appraisal Fee | | 400.00 |
| Seller Paid Closing Cost | | 4,500.00 |
| Seller Paid Owners Title Insurance | | 896.00 |
| **New Loan Charges:** | | |
| Our origination charge to . | 2,351.05 | |
| Appraisal fee to | 400.00 | |
| **Interest Charges:** | | |
| Daily interest charges to | | |
| From 4/9/2010 to 5/1/2010 @ $27.82000/day | 612.04 | |
| **Premiums:** | | |
| Mortgage insurance premium to | | |
| for 0 months | 3,326.84 | |
| Homeowner's insurance to ▮▮▮ Insurance | | |
| for 1 year | 439.34 | |
| **Impounds/Reserves:** | | |
| Homeowner's insurance to . | 109.83 | |
| County property taxes to | 1,144.36 | |
| Aggregate Adjustment to . | | 73.22 |
| **Title Charges:** | | |
| Settlement or closing fee to ▮▮▮ Title Company of Ada County | 318.00 | |
| Owner's title insurance to ▮▮▮ Title Company of Ada County | | |
| Liability amount $197,000.00 | 896.00 | |
| Lender's title insurance to ▮▮▮ Title Company of Ada County | | |
| Liability amount $193,431.00 | 441.10 | |
| Doc Retrieval Fee to ▮▮▮ Title Company of Ada County | 6.91 | |
| **Recording Fees/Transfer Charges:** | | |
| Deed/Mortgage/Release to ▮▮▮ Title Company of Ada County | 51.00 | |
| **Additional Charges:** | | |
| Amount due to City of Boise | 8.09 | |
| Subtotal: | 207,115.83 | 201,115.64 |
| Balance due from Buyer: | | 6,000.19 |

Page 1

Figure 1 – Buyer Closing Statement - page 2 of 2

| | Totals: | 207,115.83 | 207,115.83 |
|---|---|---|---|

THE UNDERSIGNED, by the execution hereof, hereby (i) acknowledge that they have read the above and foregoing Closing Statement, (ii) acknowledge that the same is true and correct, and (iii) authorize and direct the Closing Agent to receive all amounts and disburse all amounts pursuant to the foregoing Closing Statement.

It is mutually understood and agreed the taxes are estimated and in case of adjustment same will be made between the parties hereto. The Closing Agent is relieved of any responsibility with the adjustment of said taxes.

# Figure 1 – Seller Closing Statement

## Pioneer Title Company of Ada County (208) 377-2700
### Seller's Closing Statement

Seller(s)

Buyer(s)

Lender

Property

| | | | | |
|---|---|---|---|---|
| Closing date | 4/9/2010 | | Proration date | 4/9/2010 |
| Bank | 15 - ▮▮▮ Bank | | | |
| Escrow Unit | 5 - Meridian | | | |
| Escrow Officer | | | | |

| | Debit | Credit |
|---|---|---|
| **Contract Sales Price** ........................................................................................... | | 197,000.00 |
| **Prorations:** | | |
| County taxes to | | |
| From 1/1/2010 to 4/9/2010 @ $8.32060/day........................................... | 815.42 | |
| 2nd half 2009 taxes to Ada County......................................................... | 980.88 | |
| **Other Adjustments:** | | |
| Deposit or earnest money I ........................................................ | 1,000.00 | |
| Seller Paid Appraisal Fee ....................................................................... | 400.00 | |
| Seller Paid Closing Cost to ..................................................................... | 4,500.00 | |
| Seller Paid Owners Title Insurance to .................................................... | 896.00 | |
| **Payoffs:** | | |
| Payoff of first mortgage loan/▮▮▮ to ▮▮▮ ......................................... | 39,440.18 | |
| **Commissions:** | | |
| 2% based on $197,000 Less $140 to ▮▮▮............................................. | 3,800.00 | |
| 3% based on $197,000 to ▮▮▮................................................................ | 4,910.00 | |
| **New Loan Charges:** | | |
| Tax service to . ices........................................................................... | 75.00 | |
| Inspection Fee to , ................................................................................. | 75.00 | |
| **Title Charges:** | | |
| Settlement or closing fee to ▮▮▮ Title Company of Ada County............ | 318.00 | |
| **Additional Charges:** | | |
| Window to ▮▮▮ Glass.............................................................................. | 530.00 | |
| Home Warranty to Home ▮▮▮................................................................. | 355.00 | |
| Amount due to City of Boise................................................................... | 25.00 | |
| Subtotal: | 58,120.48 | 197,000.00 |
| Balance due to Seller: | 138,879.52 | |
| Totals: | 197,000.00 | 197,000.00 |

THE UNDERSIGNED, by the execution hereof, hereby (i) acknowledge that they have read the above and foregoing Closing Statement, (ii) acknowledge that the same is true and correct, and (iii) authorize and direct the Closing Agent to receive all amounts and disburse all amounts pursuant to the foregoing Closing Statement.

Figure 3 – HUD 1 - page 1 of 3

| 4/26/10 7:18 PM | | OMB No. 2502-0265 |
|---|---|---|

| A. U.S. Department of Housing and Urban Development | B. Type of Loan | |
|---|---|---|
| | 1. [X] FHA  2. [ ] RHS  3. [ ] Conv. Unins. | |
| | 4. [ ] VA  5. [ ] Conv. Ins. | |
| | 6. File Number ▮▮▮ | 7. Loan Number ▮▮▮ |
| **Settlement Statement** | 8. Mortgage Ins. Case No. ▮▮▮ | |

**C. Note:** This form is furnished to give you a statement of actual settlement costs. Amounts paid to and by the settlement agent are shown. Items marked ("POC") were paid outside the closing; they are shown here for information purposes and are not included in the totals. POC(B) represents paid outside of closing by borrower, POC(S) represents paid outside of closing by the seller, POC(L) represents paid outside of closing by lender, and POC(M) represents paid outside of closing by mortgage broker.

**D. Name of Borrower:**

**E. Name of Seller:**

**F. Name of Lender:**

**G. Property Location:** L

**H. Settlement Agent:** ▮▮▮ Company of Ada County (208) 377-2700
**Place of Settlement:** 1872 S Eagle Road, Meridian, ID 83642

**I. Settlement Date:** 4/9/2010          **Proration Date:** 4/9/2010

| J. Summary of Borrower's Transaction | | K. Summary of Seller's Transaction | |
|---|---|---|---|
| **100. Gross Amount Due from Borrower** | | **400. Gross Amount Due to Seller** | |
| 101. Contract sales price | 197,000.00 | 401. Contract sales price | 197,000.00 |
| 102. Personal property | | 402. Personal property | |
| 103. Settlement charges to borrower (line 1400) | 10,031.34 | 403. | |
| 104. | | 404. | |
| 105. | | 405. | |
| *Adjustments for items paid by seller in advance* | | *Adjustments for items paid by seller in advance* | |
| 106. City/town taxes | | 406. City/town taxes | |
| 107. County taxes | | 407. County taxes | |
| 108. Assessments | | 408. Assessments | |
| 109. | | 409. | |
| 110. | | 410. | |
| 111. | | 411. | |
| 112. City of Boise Acct Initiation Fee | 11.27 | 412. | |
| **120. Gross Amount Due from Borrower:** | 207,042.61 | **420. Gross Amount Due to Seller** | 197,000.00 |
| **200. Amounts Paid by or in Behalf of Borrower** | | **500. Reduction in Amount Due to Seller** | |
| 201. Deposit or earnest money | 1,000.00 | 501. Excess deposit (see instructions) | |
| 202. Principal amount of new loan(s) | 193,431.00 | 502. Settlement charges to seller (line 1400) | 10,088.00 |
| 203. Existing loan(s) taken subject to | | 503. Existing loan(s) taken subject to | |
| 204. | | 504. Payoff of first mortgage loan Wells Fargo | 39,440.18 |
| 205. | | 505. Payoff of second mortgage loan | |
| 206. | | 506. Deposit or earnest money | 1,000.00 |
| 207. Seller Paid Appraisal Fee | 400.00 | 507. Seller Paid Appraisal Fee | 400.00 |
| 208. Seller Paid Closing Cost | 4,500.00 | 508. Seller Paid Closing Cost | 4,500.00 |
| 209. Seller Paid Owners Title Insurance | 896.00 | 509. Seller Paid Owners Title Insurance | 896.00 |
| *Adjustments for items unpaid by seller* | | *Adjustments for items unpaid by seller* | |
| 210. City/town taxes | | 510. City/town taxes | |
| 211. County taxes  1/1/2010  to 4/9/2010 | 815.42 | 511. County taxes  1/1/2010  to 4/9/2010 | 815.42 |
| 212. Assessments | | 512. Assessments | |
| 213. | | 513. | |
| 214. | | 514. | |
| 215. | | 515. | |
| 216. | | 516. 2nd half 2009 taxes | 980.88 |
| 217. | | 517. | |
| 218. | | 518. | |
| 219. | | 519. | |
| **220. Total Paid by/for Borrower** | 201,042.42 | **520. Total Reduction Amount Due Seller:** | 58,120.48 |
| **300. Cash at Settlement from/to Borrower** | | **600. Cash at Settlement to/from Seller** | |
| 301. Gross amount due from borrower (line 120) | 207,042.61 | 601. Gross amount due to seller (line 420) | 197,000.00 |
| 302. Less amount paid by/for borrower (line 220) | 201,042.42 | 602. Less total reduction in amount due seller(line 520) | 58,120.48 |
| **303. CASH (X)FROM ()TO BORROWER** | 6,000.19 | **603. CASH ()FROM (X)TO SELLER** | 138,879.52 |

The Public Reporting Burden for this collection of information is estimated at 35 minutes per response for collecting, reviewing, and reporting the data. This agency may not collect this information, and you are not required to complete this form, unless it displays a currently valid OMB control number. No confidentiality is assured; this disclosure is mandatory. This is designed to provide the parties to a RESPA covered transaction with information during the settlement process.

# Figure 3 – HUD 1 - page 2 of 3

| | L. Settlement Charges | 4/26/10 7:18 PM | | File Number: 314471 | |
|---|---|---|---|---|---|
| 700. | Total Real Estate Broker Fees | based on : $197,000.00= $8,710.00 | | Paid From | Paid From |
| | Division of commission (line 700) as follows: | | | Borrower's | Seller's |
| 701. | $3,940.00 + ($140.00) | to ▉▉▉▉ | | Funds at | Funds at |
| 702. | $5,910.00 + ($1,000.00) | to ▉▉▉▉ | | Settlement | Settlement |
| 703. | Commission paid at settlement $8,710.00 | | | 0.00 | 8,710.00 |
| 704. | | | | | |
| 705. | | | | | |
| **800.** | **Items Payable in Connection with Loan** | | | | |
| 801. | Our origination charge | (from GFE#1) $2,351.05 | | | |
| | to Academy Mortgage Corporation | | | | |
| 802. | Your credit or charge (points) for specific interest rate chosen | (from GFE#2) | | | |
| 803. | Your adjusted origination charges | (from GFE A) | | 2,351.05 | |
| 804. | Appraisal fee | to ▉▉▉▉ | (from GFE#3) | 400.00 | |
| 805. | Credit report | (from GFE#3) | | | |
| 806. | Tax service | to ▉▉▉▉ | (from GFE#3) | | 75.00 |
| 807. | Flood certification | (from GFE#3) | | | |
| 808. | Inspection Fee | to ▉▉▉▉ | | | 75.00 |
| 809. | | | | | |
| 810. | | | | | |
| 811. | | | | | |
| 812. | | | | | |
| **900.** | **Items Required by Lender to Be Paid in Advance** | | | | |
| 901. | Daily interest charges   04/09/10 to 05/01/10 | at $27.82000/day x 2: (from GFE#10) | | 612.04 | |
| 902. | Mortgage insurance premium | ▉▉▉▉ (from GFE#3) | | 3,326.84 | |
| 903. | Homeowner's insurance | 1 year   Three Rivers Insuranc (from GFE#11) | | 439.34 | |
| 904. | | | | | |
| 905. | | | | | |
| **1000.** | **Reserves Deposited with Lender** | | | | |
| 1001. | Initial deposit for your escrow account | (from GFE#9) | | 1,180.97 | |
| 1002. | Homeowner's insurance | 3 mo.@ $36.6100 per mo. | $109.83 | | |
| 1003. | Mortgage insurance | | | | |
| 1004. | City property taxes | | | | |
| 1005. | County property taxes | 7 mo.@ $163.4800 per mo. | $1,144.36 | | |
| 1006. | Annual Assessments (maint.) | | | | |
| 1007. | | | | | |
| 1008. | | | | | |
| 1009. | Aggregate Adjustment | ($73.22) | | | |
| **1100.** | **Title Charges** | | | | |
| 1101. | Title services and lender's title insurance | (from GFE#4) | | 766.01 | |
| 1102. | Settlement or closing fee | to ▉ Title C $318.00 | | | 318.00 |
| 1103. | Owner's title insurance | to ▉ Title Company of A | (from GFE#5) | 896.00 | |
| 1104. | Lender's title insurance | to ▉ Title Company of A $441.10 | | | |
| 1105. | Lender's title policy limit | $193,431.00 | | | |
| 1106. | Owner's title policy limit | $197,000.00 | | | |
| 1107. | Agent's portion of the total title insurance premium | $1,203.39 | | | |
| 1108. | Underwriter's portion of the total title insurance premium | $133.71 | | | |
| 1109. | Agent Name: Pioneer Title Company of Ada County | | | | |
| 1110. | Underwriter Name:Old Republic National Title Insurance Company | | | | |
| 1111. | Doc Retrieval Fee | to ▉ Title C $6.91 | | | |
| 1112. | | | | | |
| 1113. | | | | | |
| **1200.** | **Government Recording and Transfer Charges** | | | | |
| 1201. | Government recording charges | (from GFE#7) | | 51.00 | |
| 1202. | Deed/Mortgage/Release | Deed $6.00  Mortgage $45.00 | | | |
| 1203. | Transfer taxes | (from GFE#8) | | 0.00 | |
| 1204. | City/County tax/stamps | | | | |
| 1205. | State tax/stamps | | | | |
| 1206. | | | | | |
| **1300.** | **Additional Settlement Charges** | | | | |
| 1301. | Required services that you can shop for | (from GFE#6) | | 0.00 | |
| 1302. | Window | to  Fast Glass | | | 530.00 |
| 1303. | Home Warranty | to  Home Warran | | | 355.00 |
| 1304. | Amount due | to  City of Boise | | 8.09 | 25.00 |
| 1305. | | | | | |
| 1400. | Total settlement charges (entered on lines 103, section J and 502, section K) | | | 10,031.34 | 10,088.00 |

# Figure 3 – HUD 1 - page 3 of 3

| Comparison of Good Faith Estimate (GFE) and HUD-1 Charges | | | Good Faith Estimate | HUD-1 |
|---|---|---|---|---|
| **Charges That Cannot Increase** | | | | |
| Our origination charge $2,351.05 | # | 801 | $2,351.05 | $2,351.05 |
| Your credit or charge (points) for specific interest rate chosen | # | 802 | | $0.00 |
| Your adjusted origination charges | # | 803 | $2,351.05 | $2,351.05 |
| Transfer taxes | # | 1203 | | |

| Charges That in Total Cannot Increase More Than 10% | | | Good Faith Estimate | HUD-1 |
|---|---|---|---|---|
| Government recording charges | # | 1201 | $56.00 | $51.00 |
| Appraisal fee | # | 804 | $400.00 | $400.00 |
| Credit report | # | 805 | | $0.00 |
| Tax service | # | 806 | $50.00 | $0.00 |
| Flood certification | # | 807 | | $0.00 |
| Mortgage insurance premium | # | 902 | $3,326.84 | $3,326.84 |
| Title services and lender's title insurance | # | 1101 | $1,339.49 | $766.01 |
| Owner's title insurance | # | 1103 | $1,500.00 | $896.00 |
| | # | | | |
| | # | | | |
| | # | | | |
| | # | | | |
| | # | | | |
| | # | | | |
| **Total** | | | 6,672.33 | 5,439.85 |
| **Increase between GFE and HUD-1 Charges** | | | $ -1,232.48 or | -18.5% |

| Charges That Can Change | | | Good Faith Estimate | HUD-1 |
|---|---|---|---|---|
| Initial deposit for your escrow account | # | 1001 | $979.38 | $1,180.97 |
| Daily interest charges | # | 901 | $27.82000/day $612.04 | $612.04 |
| Homeowner's insurance | # | 903 | $360.00 | $439.34 |
| | # | | | |
| | # | | | |
| | # | | | |
| | # | | | |
| | # | | | |
| | # | | | |
| | # | | | |
| | # | | | |
| | # | | | |

## Loan Terms

| | |
|---|---|
| Your initial loan amount is | $193,431.00 |
| Your loan term is | 30.00 years |
| Your initial interest rate is | 5.250 % |
| Your initial monthly amount owed for principal, interest, and any mortgage insurance is | $1,154.70 includes<br>[X] Principal<br>[X] Interest<br>[X] Mortgage Insurance |
| Can your interest rate rise? | [X] No  [ ] Yes, it can rise to a maximum of _____%.  The first change will be on _____ and can change every _____ after _____.  Every change date, your interest rate can increase or decrease by _____ %.  Over the life of the loan, your interest rate is guaranteed to never be lower than _____% or higher than _____%. |
| Even if you make payments on time, can your loan balance rise? | [X] No.  [ ] Yes, it can rise to a maximum of $_____. |
| Even if you make payments on time, can your monthly amount owed for principal, interest, and mortgage insurance rise? | [X] No.  [ ] Yes, the first increase can be on _____ and the monthly amount owed can rise to $_____.<br>The maximum it can ever rise to is to $_____. |
| Does your loan have a prepayment penalty? | [X] No.  [ ]Yes, your maximum prepayment penalty is $ _____. |
| Does your loan have a balloon payment? | [X] No.  [ ] Yes, you have a balloon payment of $ _____. due in _____ years on _____. |
| Total monthly amount owed including escrow account payments | [ ] You do not have a monthly escrow payment for items, such as property taxes and homeowner's insurance.  You must pay these items directly yourself.<br>[X]  You have an additional monthly escrow payment of $200.09 that results in a total initial monthly amount owed of $1,354.79. This includes principal, interest, any mortgage insurance, and any items checked below:<br>[X] Property taxes  [X] Homeowner's insurance<br>[ ] Flood insurance  [ ] _____<br>[ ] _____  [ ] _____ |

**Note: If you have any questions about the Settlement Charges and Loan Terms listed on this form, please contact your lender.**

Previous editions are obsolete        Page 3 of 3        HUD-1

# Questions – Chapter 18

1  RESPA allows the buyer to review the closing statement within what period of time before closing?

    A. 6 hours prior to closing
    B. 12 hours prior to closing
    C. 24 hours prior to closing
    D. 36 hours prior to closing

2.  Why should a walk through prior to closing be scheduled 2-3 days before closing?

    A. To make sure the property is substantially the same condition as when the offer was accepted
    B. So the buyer can request changes they didn't see when they made their offer
    C. Get any information from the seller necessary to take possession
    D. Make arrangements to get keys to move in

3.  What type of financing is not regulated by the Real Estate Settlement Practices Act?

    A. Loans with VA program
    B. Any federal related loan program
    C. Loans with FHA program
    D. Commercial loans

# Chapter 19

# Critical Thinking and Ethical Application

If used properly and practiced regularly, critical thinking and ethical application will be translated to adopting professionalism in the business world and the real estate industry. It's really nothing more than - 'doing it right'.

However, the need of consistent improvement with application modification takes effort. Constant understanding of changes in society expectations, legislated regulations, constant increased education and economic changes; requires constant monitoring. Everyone dealing with real estate activities need to coordinate with each other with a common goal to arrive at a successful conclusion.

Ethics dealing with real estate can be interpreted as taking moral character and applying fairness connected to good business applications; positive experiences will occur for all participants to a real estate related activity. The process of fair dealing takes careful thought and critical thinking.

There are many resources available to assist with ethical applications including but certainly not limited to:

- Idaho Real Estate License Law and Rules handbook
- National Association of REALTORS® - Code Of Ethics
- Federal Fair Housing Act
- *Doing The Right Thing*, 3rd Edition, Deborah Long
- *Real Estate Ethics*, 3rd Edition, William Pivar and Donald Harlan
- Daily interaction with other colleagues

## Idaho Real Estate License Law and Rules handbook

The handbook is the 'bible' of real estate law application to licensed real estate agents. There are references throughout the handbook that regulate activities of a real estate licensee including:

- Broker responsibilities
- Agency disclosure
- Advertising
- Licensees dealing with their own property
- Grounds for disciplinary action
- Penalty for acting without a license
- License revocation, suspension or other disciplinary action

The Idaho Real Estate Commission is the regulatory agency that oversees licensed and unlicensed activities. Their Education Department and Education Council constantly keeps the real estate industry updated on various laws affecting real estate licensees.

## National Association of REALTORS® - Code Of Ethics

The National Association of REALTORS® has an excellent resource for ethical behavior and critical thinking with their Code Of Ethics. By creating standards of conduct to promote ethical practices by all real estate licensees, not just those who join the trade organization, the Code Of Ethics serves as the foundation of ethical real estate practice. The Code Of Ethics is made up of Articles followed up with Standards of Practice that are reviewed and addressed annually.

- Articles  1 thru  9 - Duty to clients and customers
- Articles 10 thru 14 - Duty to the public
- Articles 15 thru 17 - Duties to REALTORS®

Members of the National Association of REALTORS® are required to take a mandatory ethics course at least once every four years to maintain their membership in the organization.

## Federal Fair Housing Act

The federal Fair Housing Act was created to make discrimination an illegal act based on a series of protected classes. In addition, the federal Fair Housing Act addresses activities associated with discrimination by using 'testers' to assist in the verification of violations that carry criminal penalties.

## *Doing The Right Thing*

Author, Deborah Long, has specialized in ethics training of real estate practitioners for may years for both real estate regulatory agencies as well as the real estate industry at large. Her book, *Doing The Right Thing*, is an excellent practitioners guide that addresses:

- Ethics and the practice of real estate
- Values, principles, and ethics
- The evolution of moral reasoning
- Ethical systems
- Models for ethical decision making
- Professional perspectives
- Applying ethics: agency
- Applying ethics: fair housing
- Applying ethics: environmental hazards
- Applying ethics: working with colleagues and employers
- Applying ethics: community and public concerns

*Doing The Right Thing* is designed to allow individual and group discussions alike with case studies and exercises. The lively book is designed to guide the reader to making clear and ethical decisions not only in a professional setting but in a personal life as well.

## Real Estate Ethics

Both authors, William Pivar and Donald Harlan, have been in the real estate industry for many years and have authored numerous books relating to real estate. The book specifically addresses a real estate practitioners day to day activities categorically divided into 8 areas of practice:

- Understanding ethics
- Responsibilities to your principal
- Responsibilities to the buyer
- Responsibilities to the general public
- Responsibilities to other licensees
- Responsibilities to other licensees within your office
- Broker trust funds
- Advertising and ethics

With *Real Estate Ethics*, the reader will learn how to address the daily issues of 'what if' scenarios and 'how to' issues.

## Interaction with other colleagues

Nothing helps bridge ethical issues better than just good communication between anyone and everyone involved with real estate. If one isn't sure about how to handle a questionable situation, seek outside assistance from others. Get a '2nd opinion' and research.

Remember the law doesn't always agree or abide with ethical behavior. When in doubt, follow the golden rule and treat others as you would like to be treated. Don't compromise ethical behavior for personal gain or avoiding personal responsibility. You'll sleep better at night.

# Answer Key

## Chapter 1      Real Estate Business and Idaho Law

1.   B    The National Association of REALTORS® is one of the largest **trade organizations** in America and was founded in 1908

2.   C    In the first quarter of 2010, the Idaho Real Estate Commission reported over **7,500** active licensees.

3.   C    All licensees, active and inactive, fund the Idaho Real Estate Commission with **licensing fees**. The IREC receives no money from the State of Idaho.

4.   B    The Idaho Real Estate Commission consists of **4 commissioners**; one from each area of Idaho so the whole state is fairly represented. IC 54-2005

5.   D    A total of **6 members** comprise the Idaho Real Estate Education Council; 4 appointed members plus 1 commissioner and the Executive Director IC 54-2008

6.   A    The Real Estate Commission meets **monthly**.

7.   B    Although many complaints are from phone calls, they must be **submitted in writing** for the Investigation Department to initiate an investigation.

8.   D    Although the Investigation Department send results of an investigation to the Executive Director, the **Commissioners** invoke the penalties for disciplinary action. IC 54-2059

9.   B    The licensee shall within **20 days** of such conviction, declaration or judgment, forward to the Commission a copy of the legal document evidencing the same. IC 54-2061 (3)


## Chapter 2      Preparing for Real Estate Practice

1.   B    Any person, who, directly or indirectly, while acting for another, for compensation, or promise of or expectation of compensation will be required to have an **active** real estate license. IC 54-2004

2.   D    Property management **does not convey** an interest in real property. IC 54-2003

3.   B    An individual must be **18 years of age** or older. IC 54-2012 (1) (b)

4.  A  The minimum hours for license renewal are **16 electives plus the Core** which can be no more than 4 hours (the Core could be less than 4 hours) IC 54-2023 (b)

5.  A  Each new license shall be for a period of **1 year plus the months up to and including the next birth date** of the licensee, not exceed a period of 2 years and shall expire on the last day of the month of the birth date of the licensee.

6.  C  Each new license shall be for a period of **1 year plus the months up to and including the next birth date** of the licensee, not exceed a period of 2 years and shall expire on the last day of the month of the birth date of the licensee.

7.  B  Fingerprint results are good for only **6 months**. Even if one has previously been fingerprinted, new fingerprints are required anyway. (Pearson-Vue Handbook)

8.  D  An inactive real estate licensee is not require to have any insurance. An **active** real estate licensee is required to have Errors and Omissions Insurance. IC 54-2013

9.  C  Tail coverage must be purchased within 90 days from cancellation. Rule 119 (01) (h)

10. D  A **high school diploma** or equivalency is required to secure a real estate license in Idaho. IC 54-2012

11. D  Guideline 17 allows performing **clerical duties** to the broker or broker associate. The unlicensed personal assistant cannot show a home, create and distribute information on their own, or negotiate at an open house.

12. A  The maximum fine for a natural person shall not exceed **$5,000**. IC 54-2065

13. C  An active real estate licensee must conduct the purchase or sale of their own property through **their own broker** regardless if the property is listed or not. IC 54-2055 (3)

14. D  A licensee shall give written notice no later than **3 business days** after the effective date of termination. IC 54-2056 (1)

15. D  A broker shall, within **10 business days** of termination, notify the Idaho Real Estate Commission, in writing, of the termination and give the facts leading to the termination. IC 54-2056 (3)

16. C  An **associate broker**, who is licensed and associated with the absent broker can be appointed to manage, supervise and oversee the regular office operations. IC 54-2039

17. B  Records must be kept by a broker for **3 calendar years after the year** the event occurred, the transaction closed, all funds were disbursed, or written extension expired. IC 54-2049

18.  B   In no event shall the balance of broker or firm funds in the account exceed **$300**.
IC 54-2042 (7)

19.  A   Maintenance funds shall not be disbursed for any purpose other than **to cover bank charges** charged directly to the trust account by the bank.  IC 54-2042 (7)

20.  B   Each trust account must be established and maintained under the licensed **business name** of the broker.  IC 54-2042 (3)

21.  C   The **Idaho Real Estate Commission** must be notified of opening a trust account with a Commission-approved form.  IC 54-2042 (6)

22.  B   No deposits to the trust account shall be made of funds that belong to the broker or real estate firm **except for the purpose of maintaining** the trust account not to exceed $300.  IC 54-2042 (7)

23.  A   The designated broker is required to reconcile the trust account **at least once each month**.  IC 54-2044

24.  D   All consideration received by a sales associate in connection with a real estate transaction shall be **immediately** delivered to the broker or broker's office.
IC 54-2045 (4)

25.  C   Trust account checks must be imprinted with the words **"real estate trust account"**
IC 54-2044 (5) (b)

26.  B   Moneys received by a broker for another in a real estate transaction are to be deposited on or before the **banking day immediately following the receipt** of such funds.  IC 54-2045 (1)

27.  C   Discretionary disbursement by the broker based on reasonable review of the known facts **is not a violation** of license law, but may subject the broker to civil liability.
IC 54-2047 (2)

28.  C   In the case of a cooperative sale, the **broker who holds entrusted funds** shall be deemed the broker responsible for the transaction.  IC 54-2048

29.  D   The **responsible broker** shall ensure the correctness and delivery of detailed closing statements which accurately reflect receipts and disbursements.  IC 54-2048 (1)

30.  D   All offers presented to the seller and not accepted by that seller shall be clearly **marked and dated** as rejected.  IC 54-2048 (3) (d)

31. A  No sales associate shall accept any fees from any person except the **real estate broker** with whom the sales associate is licensed. IC 54-2054 (9)

32 B  Setting prices between competitors is an example of **price fixing** which is an illegal act based on the Sherman Anti Trust Act.

## Chapter 3    Agency

1. C  The most practiced form of agency is that of a **special** agent where the principal authorizes the agent to do a particular act over a specific period of time.

2. D  The Idaho Representation Act was created to clearly identify what duties and obligations exist between the consumer and the **real estate brokerage**. IC54-2082

3. D  There can be as many as **four** types of brokerage relationships. IC 54-2084

4. A  Signing the Agency Disclosure Brochure **does not** create any contractual relationship with a licensee. It only acknowledges the buyer or seller received it. IC 54-2085 (1)

5. B  Confirmation and acknowledgment will be contained in the **Purchase and Sale Agreement** with mandatory language. IC 54-2085 (4)

6. C  The agent must maintain **confidentiality** with a client whereas confidentiality is not required for customer relationships. IC 54-2087 (6)

7. B  A client relationship is with the **brokerage** and its licensees. IC 54-2087

8. A  A brokerage acting as a limited dual agent may, at the option of the brokerage and with the express **written consent** of all clients offer assigned agency IC 54-2088

9. C  **Each brokerage** shall keep a signed and dated record of a buyer's or seller's receipt of the agency disclosure brochure. IC 54- 2085 (1)

10. D  Each party understands that he is a "**Customer**" and is not represented by a brokerage unless there is a signed written agreement for agency representation. IC 54-2085 (4)

11. C  A nonagent means a brokerage and its licensees working with or assisting a buyer or seller as a **customer**. 54-2083 (13)

12. B  If a brokerage is acting as a limited dual agent and assigns separate sales associates to act on behalf of the separate clients, the **designated broker** continues to act as a limited dual agent. IC 54-2088 (5) (a)

13. B With a written contract for representation, the buyer becomes a client of the brokerage. There is no representation with another company so the agent remains a '**single**' agent as far as representation is concerned. IC 54-2087

14. A In Idaho, representation is not fiduciary in nature. Agency is legislated and requires certain duties to be fulfilled which is based on **statute**. IC 54-2095

15. D Automatic renewal clauses in an exclusive representation agreement are **prohibited**. IC 54-2050 (3)

16. C Confidentiality duty extends beyond termination of representation as long as information **does not become generally known** in the marketing community. IC 54-2087 (6) (a)

## Chapter 4      Different Perspectives Of The Real Estate Market

1. B In 2010, surveys indicate Idaho has a total population of around **1,500,000.**

2. C There are **44** counties in Idaho

3. C The state income tax rate in Idaho approximates **7-8%**

4. A The total land area in public ownership is 63%, leaving **37% in private ownership.**

## Chapter 5      Real Property and The Law

1. D 'Chattel' is movable, mobile, and **not permanently attached**.

2. B Personal property is transferred with a **Bill of Sale**. Real property is transferred with a deed, and an automobile is transferred with a Certificate of Title

3. B The **State of Idaho** owns the water in Idaho and the Department of Water Resources issues permits to use. IC 42-101

4. D No more than ½ acre can be irrigated with domestic water unless a permit has been filed and approved to use more water. IC 42-111

5. D Total use of domestic water shall not exceed **13,000** gallons per day. IC 42-111

6. C Water needs to be put to beneficial use for a **5 continuous years** or the water will be lost and forfeited. IC 42-222 (2)

7.   D   Only a **licensed well driller** can officially abandon a water well.  IC 42-238

8.   A   Only the **Department of Water Resources** has the authority to appropriate ground water recharge.  IC 42-4201

9.   A   The transfer of ownership of a manufactured home (personal property) is with a **Certificate of Title** (like an automobile).  IC 63-304


# Chapter 6      Legal Descriptions

1.   C   Three types of legal descriptions can be used in Idaho: Government Rectangular Survey, Metes and Bounds, and Lot and Block (from recorded Plat)

2.   A   A Tax Parcel number **will not** meet legal description requirements.  It only identifies the parcel for tax purposes only.

3.   D   The 'initial point' is closest to **Kuna** and is located off the Swan Falls road on top of a knoll.  A large brass cap identifies the 'initial point'.

4.   C   Township **65** North meets the Canadian border.  All legal descriptions in Idaho initiate from the 'initial point' near Kuna, Idaho.

5.   C   Using R6W and R46E, the width would be **312 miles**; 6X6=36 miles and 6X46=276 miles.  The total is 312 miles.  Remember a township is 6 miles by 6 miles.

6.   B   A development of **5 or more lots** for sale need to meet the requirements of subdivision laws in Idaho.  However, local cities and counties may adopt more restrictive subdivision requirements.  IC 50-1301 (15)

7.   D   Recorded plats identify parcels by 'lot and block' and **will meet** the requirements for legal descriptions since each lot has been properly measured and recorded when the plat map was recorded.

8.   A   After a survey has been completed, a record of survey shall be filed within **90 days** after completing a survey.  IC 55-1901

9.   A   The minimum size of a survey marker will be **½ inch by 2 feet** long to make a permanent market that is magnetically detectable.  IC 54-1234

## Chapter 7      Real Estate Interests

1.    D    Homestead protection protects home against **unsecured creditors**. The owner can have only one homestead exemption at a time.

2.    C    The maximum net value for homestead protection **is $100,000.** IC 55-1003

3.    C    To maintain homestead protection, the home must be occupied at least **6 months** a year (this proves it is their primary home).

4.    D    The **owner must file** to abandon (to release current home) and file declaration of homestead for new property they are moving to. IC 55-1004

5.    D    A lease for more than one year **must be in writing** to be valid. The Statute of Frauds states an agreement is invalid unless the agreement is in writing. IC 9-905

6.    B    A written list of violations must be sent in person, **certified mail**, or with an employee at the landlord's usual place of business. IC 6-323

7.    B    The landlord has **3 days** to remedy violations. IC 6-323 (6) (d)

8.    B    Month-to-month notice of rental increase must be at least **15 days**. IC 55-307

9.    D    A landlord must give not less than **1 month** written notice to terminate. IC 55-208

10.   C    Security deposit refunds must be made within **30 days** after the surrender of the premises by the tenant. IC 6-321

11.   A    Manufactured home lot rents must be **in writing** to be valid. IC 55-205

12.   C    A minimum of **90 day notice** must be given a tenant in a mobile home park for any increase of services, utilities, or changes in rules. IC 55-2006

13.   A    If a landlord decides not to renew existing rental space, the landlord must give the tenant not less than **180 days** written notice. IC 55-2010

## Chapter 8      Forms of Ownership And How Ownership Is Held

1.    B    A partnership is a **single entity** and therefore 'sole' ownership.

2.    A    Application for limited liability company is filed with the **Secretary of State**. IC 30-6

3.    C    Failure to file the annual report with the Secretary of State can result in **administrative dissolution.** IC 30-6-705

4.　D　Property owned either by husband or wife **shall remain his or her sole property** unless co-mingled after marriage.  IC 32-903

5.　B　All property acquired after marriage, regardless if sole or separate, will be treated as **community property**.  IC 32-906

6.　D　The annual report of a LLC is to be filed annually by before the end of the **month the company was organized**.  IC 30-6-209

7.　A　'Community property with rights of survivorship' creates a simple **joint tenancy** and will avoid probate.  IC 15-6-401

8.　D　An LLC may be reinstated if filed within **10 years** from dissolution.  IC 30-6-705

## Chapter 9　　　　Transferring Title to Real Estate

1.　D　The only way to prove death is with a certified or **authenticated copy** of a death certificate.  IC 15-1-107

2.　A　**½ of the decedents property** passes to the surviving spouse.  IC 15-2-102

3.　C　**Death** is what triggers a will to take effect.  IC 15-3-101

4.　B　The high water mark is where the water impresses for a sufficient period of time to **deprive the soil of its vegetation**.  IC 58-104 (9)

5.　C　Adverse possession can be claimed if held for not less than **20 years**.  IC 5-210

6.　C　Easement by prescription must be held for not less than **20 years**.  IC 5-210

7.　A　A water right can be lost if not used for **5 consecutive years**.  IC 42-222

8.　B　Eminent domain is an involuntary 'taking' for **public** use.

## Chapter 10　　　　Conveyance Documents

1.　D　Transfer of real property must be signed and in writing to legally transfer.  IC 55-601

2.　C　The **Statute of Frauds** requires certain documents to be in writing including deeds.

3.　D　'Grant, bargain, and sell' only gives **implied ownership** without warranty.

4.   C     'Convey, release remiss, and forever quitclaim' is the least protection to the grantee. There are **no covenants or warranties** of any kind.

5.   D     When a document is recorded, the **date, time and hour, and minute** is stamped on the document and entered into the public records accordingly.  IC 31-2413

6.   D     There is **no transfer tax** in Idaho (along with 12 other states).

## Chapter 11     Limitations On Rights of Ownership & Encumbrances

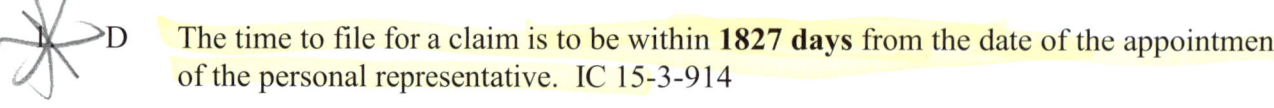

1.   D     The time to file for a claim is to be within **1827 days** from the date of the appointment of the personal representative.  IC 15-3-914

2.   D     Solar lot lines (shadow) are often referenced on the shadow cast on **December 21**.

3.   A     **Conservation easements** assist to protect wildlife, open space, views, farm land.

4.   C     'First in right, first in time' is based on prior appropriation.  **Senior water rights get priority** over junior rights.  Junior rights may not be able to get water.  IC 43-106

5.   C     Only a **licensed well driller** can drill a water well.  IC 43-106

6.   B     Before a water well can be drilled, a **drilling permit** is required.  IC 42-238

7.   B     Zoning regulations are examples of **Police Power** which is the authority of the government to adopt and enforce laws.

8.   A     At least **1 public hearing** must be conducted to change the comp plan.  IC 67-6502

9.   B     At last **15 days** advance public notice must be given before a meeting can be held.

10.   C     One of the primary purposes of zoning is to regulate **density**.

11.   D     A zoning **variance** is an individual accommodation for a change from existing zoning

12.   C     A **professional land surveyor** shall certify the correctness of the plat and place his seal, signature and date on the plat.  IC 50-1309

13.   B     The penalty for selling subdivision lots before plat approval **is $100**.  IC 50-1316

14.   C     **3 categories** allow cities to annex land outside their jurisdiction.  IC 50-222

15.   D     The Idaho Building Code Act adopted **International Building Code**.  IC 39-4105

16. A    Contractors doing extensive renovation to pre 1978 homes must be **Certified** if they disturb more than 6 s.f. interior or 20 s.f. exterior surface.  40 CFR 745.223

17. C    Bail bond isn't released until a verdict and **sentencing** has been given. IC 19-2922 (1)

18. B    A mechanic's lien **expires after 6 months**.  IC 45-501

19. D    **Laborers** get first priority for processed mechanic's lien claims.  IC 45-512

20. D    Although assessors value all property every year, they are only required to physically preview and value property once every **5 years**.  IC 63-314

21. A    All property is valued as **of January 1** every year.

22. A    Homeowner Exemption is for owner occupants of a **primary dwelling**. IC 63-602 (G)

23. B    Circuit Breaker is **reviewed annually** by the Idaho Legislature and appropriate adjustments are made based on cost of living index.  IC 63-701

24. C    If applying by age only, one needs to be at least **65 years old.** IC 63-701

25. C    Occupancy tax applies to newly constructed homes that have **never been occupied**. IC 63-317

26. D    Newly occupied new construction will receive **2 tax statements;** one for the land and the other pro-rated for the dwelling the first tax year.  Subsequent tax years will come with only 1 statement for both land and dwelling.

27. C    Tax statements are sent out no later than **4th Monday in November.** IC 63-903

28. D    If property taxes are paid in installments, the first installment is due no later than **December 20**; 2nd installment due June 20 of following year.  IC 63-903

29. C    If taxes are not paid and property redeemed within **3 years** the property will be sold at public auction.  IC 63-1005

## Chapter 12    Real Estate Contracts

1. C    Rule 303 clearly states - 'A real estate broker or sales associate **shall not discourage** any party to a real estate transaction from seeking the advice of an attorney.  Rule 303

2.  D   Leases extending beyond 1 year **must be in writing** to comply with the Statute of Frauds.  IC 9-505

3.  B   A person practicing law without a license can receive a fine up to **$500, or be imprisoned up to 6 months,** or both.  IC 3-420

4.  D   Representation Confirmation must be included with a Purchase and Sale Agreement, an attachment thereto, or other document drafted in connection with a regulated real estate transaction.  IC 54-2085 (4)

5.  B   A counter offer **terminates** the original offer and becomes a brand new offer from the person making the counter offer.

6.  D   All offers presented to and not accepted by the seller must be **marked and dated** as rejected.  IC 54-2048 (3) (d)

7.  C   The use of a 'double contract' is strictly **prohibited**.  IC 54-2054 (5)

8.  A   When earnest money is received, it shall be **immediately delivered** to the broker or the broker's office.  IC 54-2054 (4)

## Chapter 13     Recording of Title Information

1.  B   Although a deed has been signed and recorded, it isn't effective until the grantee (new owner) actually receives and **accepts** the deed.

2.  A   Any recording shall be in **English;** the official language of Idaho..  A document in another language shall be translated and certified into English.  IC 73-121 (3)

3.  C   **The Department of Insurance** regulates the title insurance industry.  IC 41-2704

4.  D   Title that is **free from objectionable** defects is marketable; it does not have to be 'free and clear'; must free from objectionable defects.

5.  D   The Uniform Commercial Code deals with **commercial transactions** and personal property that could have a secured interest.

6.  C   An owners extended policy protects the **borrower** (new owner) against items that may not yet be of record; i.e. mechanic's liens.  Extended lenders only protects the lender.

7.  D   Recordings give a ongoing or **perpetual history** of a parcel regardless of how many times the parcel may have been transferred.

# Chapter 14     Market Analysis

1.  A  The purpose of a market analysis and opinion of price of a property is to secure a **prospective listing or sale**. IC 54-4105 (2)

2.  D  A **broker or associate broker** can provide a price opinion for a fee. IC 54-4105 (3)

3.  C  One of the 8 requirements of a broker's price opinion is the **intended purpose**. IC 54-4105 (3) (a) (I)

4.  D  Cost approach uses the concept of - **cost minus depreciation plus land**.

5.  B  The **cost approach** is most accurate when fewer adjustments are made; thus, new construction would have little or no depreciation.

6.  C  The income approach is for **income producing properties** and is based more in income generated as opposed to cost factors.

7.  D  The equivalent of **2,000 training hours** are required before a residential appraisal license will be earned.

8.  A  **90 classroom hours** are required, in addition to 2,000 training hours, to secure a residential appraisal license

9.  B  The **Bureau of Occupational Licensing** will direct an inquiry to the Idaho Real Estate Appraiser Board.

# Chapter 15     Working with a Buyer as a Client or Customer

1.  D  The agency disclosure brochure must be given to a buyer or seller at first **substantial business contact**. The key word is 'business' contact. IC 54-2085 (1)

2.  C  Signing the agency disclosure brochure only verifies the consumer received the brochure and is a signed and dated **record of receipt**. IC 54-2085 (1) & Guideline #4

3.  C  There are several statutory duties including disclosing any **adverse material facts** the licensee should have reasonably have known. IC 54-2086 (1) (d)

4.  C  A properly executed Buyer Representation Agreement contains language that states it is a legally **binding contract**.

5.  A  Initially the high bidder will receive **a Certificate of Sale** and followed up with a Sheriffs Deed after the statutory redemption period has passed.

6.   C   The mortgage redemption for **more than 20 acres is 1 year**; 6 months for 20 acres or less.  IC 11-104

7.   A   If a deed of trust is not brought current or paid off prior to sale, the foreclosure sale is final with **no redemption period**.

8.   C   A debtor has **115 days** to bring past due payments current.  If they pay after 115 days but prior to 120 days or date of sale, they must pay off the total balance due.. IC 45-1506 (12)

9.   B   A '**trustees deed**' will be issued.

10.  D   A HUD Settlement booklet must be given to a borrower for a federally related loan **within 3 days of loan application**.

11.  D   The key is that the loan became a 'source' of funds that was not disclosed to the loan underwriter; thus, the use of a **double contract** occurred.  IC 54-2004 (20)

## Chapter 16        Working with a Seller as a Client or Customer

1.   A   The purpose of the first listing appointment is to **gather information** so you can use the information to put together an accurate CMA.

2.   B   **Sold** properties give absolute information regarding sales prices whereas on market properties do not reflect sold prices.  However, in a declining market, one may find 'on market' properties to sometimes be lower than comparable 'solds'.

3.   D   All property must include the **brokerage business name**.  IC 54-2053 (2)

4.   C   Ceiling height must be at least **7'** to be included as living space.  Be careful of counting basements that have 6' ceilings.  ANSI Z765-2003

5.   A   Often steep roofs provide interior living area that is less than 5'.  Anything **less than 5' cannot be counted** as living space.  A-frame mountain cabins are good examples.

6.   C   It's the **sellers duty** to complete the Sellers Property Disclosure form.  IC 55-2508

7.   A   Sellers of newly constructed residential property are required to address **annexation** as well as several other issues including availability of city services.  IC 55-2505

8    B   Covenants, Conditions, and Restrictions are **private restrictions** and any violations are handled with civil action as opposed to police power.

## Chapter 17     Writing and Presenting Purchase & Sale Agreements

1. C    All legislated laws become effective on **July 1** unless they are emergency bills.

2. D    Earnest money shall be immediately delivered to the **broker's office**   IC 54-2045 (4)

3. C    **Both** the Purchase and Sale Agreement and ledger card must have a written notation of the earnest money being returned before it was deposited.

4. C    If the seller requires a particular title insurance company be used as a condition of a transaction and without the purchasers approval, the penalty and liability to the buyer shall be equal to **3 times all charges** made for the insurance 12-27-2608 USC

5. C    The Sellers Property Disclosure form is required to be delivered to the buyer or the buyer's agent **within 10 days of execution** of the agreement.   IC 54-2501

6. A    A general contractor making improvements **exceeding $2,000** must give a disclosure statement to the homeowner prior to entering into a contract.   IC 45-525

7. C    A business day is defined to be **Monday through Friday between 8:00 am and 5:00 pm**   IC 73-108

8. C    A broker or sales associate shall, as **promptly as practicable**, tender to the seller every written offer to purchase obtained on the real estate involved, up until time of closing.   IC 54-2051 (1)

## Chapter 18     Closing The Sale

1. C    RESPA allows the buyer to have **24 hours prior to closing** to review the HUD 1 Settlement Statement

2. A.    The purpose of a walk through is to make sure the property is **substantially the same condition** as when the offer was accepted and if any repairs were required, that they were completed in a satisfactory manner.

3. D    **Cash, commercial and non federally related** loans are not regulated by the Real Estate Settlement Practices Act.

## Chapter 19     Critical Thinking and Ethical Application

No questions are attached to this chapter.

# Index

**Page 247**